A. E. STODDART.

A. F. Harding.
(London Welsh.)
Photo. by A. & G. Tay'

A. E. Hind.
(Leicester.)
Photo. by Russell & Sons, London.

A. L. NOVIS

CHURCHMAN'S C.

D. A. KENDREW

WILLS'S CIGARETTES.

C. D. AARVOLD

WILLS'S CIGARETTES.

G. R. BEAMISH

CHURCHMAN'S CIGARETTES

B. H. BLACK

ALL BLACKS

v LIONS

ALL BLACKS

v LIONS

Ron Palenski

Hodder Moa Beckett

National Library of New Zealand Cataloguing-in-Publication Data

Palenski, Ron.
All Blacks v Lions / Ron Palenski. 1st ed.
Includes bibliographical references.
ISBN 1-86971-004-5
1. All Blacks (Rugby team)—History. 2. Lions (Rugby team)—History. 3. Rugby Union football—
New Zealand—History. 4. Rugby Union football—Great Britain—History. I. Title.
796.33365—dc 22

First published in 2005 by Hodder Moa Beckett Publishers Ltd
[a member of the Hodder Headline Group]
4 Whetu Place, Mairangi Bay, Auckland, New Zealand

Designed and produced by Hodder Moa Beckett Publishers Ltd
Cover design by Newman Design
Printed by Tien Wah Press Ltd, Singapore

Contents

Acknowledgements

The publisher and author acknowledge and gratefully thank the photographers whose works illustrate this book. The thanks are extended to the team at Fotopress, Peter Bush, the ever-helpful Bob Luxford at the New Zealand Rugby Museum, Fairfax Sunday Newspapers, Getty Images, Colorsport, Ray Saunders, Dave McLaren and Charl Visser.

Photographic credits

Ron Palenski Collection: 19, 20, 22, 30, 32, 36 (top), 45, 46 (top), 50 (top), 52, 65, 66–67, 74, 77, 78, 80, 83, 94, 97, 100, 101, 103, 109, 110, 120, 127, 133 (top), 142, 146 (inset), 177

Fotopress: 70, 76, 131, 133 (bottom), 136–137, 141, 146, 150, 152, 153, 154, 155, 156, 157, 158, 159, 160, 160 (inset), 162, 164, 166, 167, 168, 169, 170, 171, 172, 173, 174–175, 178 (top and bottom), 179, 180 (top and bottom), 181, 182

New Zealand Rugby Museum: 21, 24–25, 26, 27, 28–29, 31, 33 (bottom), 34–35, 36 (bottom), 40, 41, 42, 44, 46 (bottom), 47, 48, 50 (bottom), 53, 54–55, 56, 58, 59, 61 (inset), 62, 63, 64, 67 (inset), 68, 69, 71, 72, 73, 88–89, 107

Fairfax Sunday Newspapers: 60, 79, 82, 84, 85, 86, 87, 91, 92, 96, 98–99, 102, 104–105, 106, 116, 117, 118, 119, 125, 130, 132, 134, 143, 145, 148

Peter Bush: 115, 123, 124, 126, 128, 163

Ray Saunders Collection: 18, 23, 33 (top), 37

Colorsport: 2–3 (Bryan Williams on attack for the All Blacks in the fourth test of the 1977 series, at Eden Park, Auckland.), 112, 114, 139

Charl Visser Collection: 121

Getty Images: 61

Front endpapers: Ray Saunders Collection

Back endpapers: New Zealand Rugby Museum and Colorsport

Preface

A friend of mine is keen on his rugby but he is not, he shouldn't mind me saying, one of those who stores rugby facts and minutiae in his active brain. His recollections are impressions of times well spent and chances well taken rather than a catalogue of what happened when and where and to whom. It took me by surprise therefore when he asked me one night what the given names of the Welsh and Lions loose forward, Alun Pask, were. When I gave him a querulous look that he interpreted as a woeful lack in my knowledge, he immediately plugged the gap: Alun Edward Islwyn Pask, he said with a great deal of sanctimonious glee.

This is what the Lions had done to him: reduced him to being a repository of facts — well, one fact anyway, useful only in a pub quiz or on similar occasions when bidding is brisk for bragging rights. Pask, who was in the 1966 British Isles team in New Zealand, had been adopted by my friend's school. When Lions teams toured, schools would nominate a player about whom they would collect every published mention and gather it all lovingly together in a scrapbook. Newspaper sales soared during Lions tours, such was the voracious demand by school pupils for any nugget on their nominated player. At some point toward the end of the tour, the scrapbook would either be sent to the player or, day of days, the player would visit the school, perhaps speak to the assembly, and be presented with the scrapbook, as reverently as if it was a crown being placed upon his head (which probably would have happened with Barry John anyway).

This was one player and one pupil and one Lions tour. Multiply that by thousands and it's possible to gain a reasonable impression of what the Lions have meant to generations of New Zealanders. The schoolboy of 1950 would carry with him for the rest of his days the warm regard he developed for the Lions who toured during his most impressionable and formative years; so it was for the schoolboy of 1959, of 1966, of 1971 . . . generations were marked by Lions tours.

This is not to suggest that my friend, or any other of the thousands who fell under the spell of the Lions, were being less than faithful to their own team, the All Blacks. Far from it. The enduring wish for the All Blacks to win has always been strong among those who see the team as their team, who see the players as their representatives on the paddock. The Lions brought with them the touch of the exotic; remember that for most of the history of the Lions, the separate British and Irish rugby countries didn't tour on their own. The only time British or Irish players were seen in New Zealand was when the Lions came to town. The Lions, more than the South Africans, the other great foes of all our yesterdays, were popular tourists. Perhaps part of it was because they represented a land from whence New Zealand's political structure and a lot of its people came; perhaps part of it was because New Zealanders loved the accents of the Irish, the Scots and the Welsh in particular; and perhaps part of it was because history and tradition said the Lions always had sparkling, gifted backs but were not so commanding in the forwards. Therefore, the Lions were good entertainment but the All Blacks should always beat them. And perhaps it was because they were such infrequent visitors.

And beat them mostly the All Blacks did, apart from 1971 when the Lions brought a whole constellation of stars, forwards and backs, and had with them a wizard of a Welsh coach, Carwyn James.

The length of the tours also aided the memories of New Zealanders. The Lions, until short tours became the financial norm, were in New Zealand for about three months, generally playing twice a week. Their players became as familiar to New Zealanders as did the

All Blacks; New Zealanders were as expert at picking the Lions test teams as the Lions selectors were (and sometimes better). But they weren't just on the field. In the glossy centre pages of the *Weekly News* and the *Free Lance*, the Lions would be eating oysters at Bluff, big game fishing in the Bay of Islands, playing golf at Wairakei, shaking political hands in Wellington, or cavorting about in the snow of Queenstown. In the age of long royal tours, the Lions made their own regal progress throughout New Zealand.

The rugby was hard and a succession of Lions managers said it was too hard. But that was the point. The tests aside, provincial sides would lie in wait for the Lions: it's one proud thing for a provincial team to win the Ranfurly Shield or, at the local level, to win the Seddon Shield or the Hanan Shield, it's quite another to knock over a touring team and if it's the Lions, so much the better. When provincial teams beat the South Africans, they'd get a springbok head to hang on their wall: when Lions were beaten, there was no need of trophies — the golden glow of enhanced reputation was enough. Some Lions revelled in the rugby atmosphere that was a tour of New Zealand; others found it strange and oppressive. Phil Bennett, the quiet, amiable captain of the 1977 team, talked of how rugby was too daunting in New Zealand, how it reached into the soul over all else. By contrast, Ian McLauchlan, the "Mighty Mouse" prop of 1971, loved the rugby that was all-pervading. He could walk down Princes Street in his native Edinburgh and not be recognised; he could walk down Princes Street in Dunedin and be offered advice, asked for his autograph and be told to go easy on the All Blacks.

Lions tours are not what they were and this is not a reference to Clive Woodward's *Ben Hur* cast or the need to take part in a ballot for tickets. Rugby's enormous changes enveloped the Lions as much as they did all other aspects of the game. Long tours, as enjoyable and enjoyed as they were, are no longer practical. But enough of the Lions' mystique has passed through the generations and has remained. They are rare visitors and their value lies in that rarity.

Managing director Kevin Chapman and editorial director Warren Adler of Hodder Moa Beckett, with their usual keen eyes on the market and their passion for rugby, came to me with the idea for a Lions book. It was an opportunity of a lifetime. Books about Lions tours have been published before and there have been general histories of the Lions, but they've been British-based: this is the first that relates the story of the Lions in New Zealand.

My thanks are due the authors of those other books and each is acknowledged separately in the Bibliography. I've drawn also on the extensive newspaper library I've acquired over the years. Some players were interviewed specifically for this book and others were interviewed over the years. Especially, I acknowledge the kindnesses of Phil Bennett, Gareth Edwards, Ian McLauchlan, Andy Irvine, Gavin Hastings and Will Carling. In New Zealand, Tane Norton was a fund of knowledge.

I'm particularly grateful to Steve Orsbourn, who made available to me transcripts of interviews he has taped for a TVNZ documentary on the Lions. I acknowledge also the wise counsel of Peter Sinclair and I extend my gratitude to Caroline Kidston and John Spicer at the New Zealand Sports Hall of Fame who covered for me when I wasn't there.

My main thanks, as always, are to my family.

Ron Palenski
Dunedin

Foreword

by Jock Hobbs, Chairman, NZRU

Generations of New Zealanders have grown up with their earliest and most enduring rugby memories being of the British and Irish Lions. Some people may remember being taken as a youngster to matches in the 1950s and 1960s and others may have learnt of the Lions through school visits undertaken by the players. The Lions have always been extremely popular in New Zealand, both on and off the field.

Whatever the circumstances, the Lions always left an impression. The names of the great players have been handed down through the years, men whose deeds signposted the years of their tours: Jack Kyle and Jack Matthews of 1950, Tony O'Reilly and Peter Jackson of 1959 . . . any number of the great team of 1971 that became the first to beat the All Blacks in a series.

For the British and Irish players, the fulfilment of their rugby aspirations was being named in a Lions team: being named to play for one's country is the ultimate achievement for any player anywhere; for the British and Irish they have the even higher level of playing for the Lions — a team unique in world rugby.

For a New Zealand player, tests against the Lions represented a challenge beyond the norm, a challenge not just because the team represented the best of British and Irish rugby but also because they were infrequent visitors. There have been many great All Blacks who have not played against a Lions team.

I was fortunate to make my test debut against the Lions and the series in 1983 remains indelibly in my mind. To my mind, it was like all the series that preceded it and the one in 1993 that followed: enormous public interest and test matches fought hard but played in the best competitive spirit.

As Ron Palenski relates in the following pages, the first combined British rugby team came to New Zealand in 1888. They weren't known as the Lions — a nickname they acquired in South Africa in 1924 — but they began the tradition that has endured.

For all the enormous changes in rugby, some things are of enduring value and Lions tours are one of them. Some people argued, when rugby went professional in 1995, that the Lions might have outlived their usefulness — that they had served their purpose in their time. Every genuine rugby lover would be delighted that has not come to pass. The Lions are one of the most precious gems in the rugby crown; in an age of change, the Lions are a shining constant.

Foreword
by Herbert Hainer, CEO & Chairman, adidas

It is my pleasure to be invited to write a Foreword for this marvellous book. We are excited to be part of a publication that brings together two of the most important adidas assets in the world of rugby, the British and Irish Lions and the New Zealand All Blacks.

This book celebrates the history of Lions tours to New Zealand. The wonderful selection of pictures shows that adidas always had a close association with both sides. Many stars of past tours used adidas rugby footwear. For the 2005 series we are proud to be the Official Outfitter of the New Zealand All Blacks. This wonderful partnership started back in 1999 and was recently extended into the next decade. Our partnership with the British and Irish Lions goes back to 1997 when adidas became the Official Kit supplier for their 1997 tour to South Africa. On top of that, the entire All Blacks team and numerous Lions players will endorse adidas rugby footwear on the field of play.

adidas has a clear mission: to be the leading sports brand in the world. And we have a clear vision: passion. There is no better platform to demonstrate how serious we are about achieving this mission than in one of the most exciting sports events in 2005: the Lions tour of New Zealand. That is where the best meets the best and for us this is a natural place to be. With this book you can relive the best moments of the historical matches between the British and Irish Lions and the New Zealand All Blacks. I am sure these memories will help you to get excited about the 2005 tour. I certainly am already and can't wait to get the game started.

Introduction

Why the Lions?

The British rugby team in South Africa in 1924 had a lion motif on the players' ties and newspapers there took to referring to the team as the Lions. It took a while for the name to catch on elsewhere, however, and it wasn't used during the 1930 tour of New Zealand. By the 1950 tour, the Lions had arrived. The name first appeared in print in New Zealand on 11 May 1950, when the *Nelson Evening Mail* headed a story the day after the team's first game: Singing Lions leave Nelson.

The All Blacks in Britain in 1924–25 took with them silver fern lapel badges to distribute and the British followed suit for their New Zealand tour in 1930, choosing a "Lion of England" badge adapted from the collar badge of The King's Own Royal Regiment (Lancaster), which now forms part of The King's Own Royal Border Regiment. In heraldic terms, the lion is "passant guardant", walking with head turned toward the viewer. The handing out of Lions badges became a feature of all subsequent tours.

"Unique" is one of those words that should not be qualified. Grammarians might argue it cannot be qualified but plenty of people unversed in the mysteries of the language try to anyway. But it should not be. "Unique" means something that is one of a kind, a stand-alone, having properties that nothing else does. "Unique" is a good adjective for the Lions or, to give them their 21st century politically and pedantically correct title, the British and Irish Lions.

Of course, every rugby team, especially the national team, is unique. The All Blacks are unique because of their playing record, because of their storied history and because they are the only team that represents New Zealand at the highest level of rugby. The Lions take the concept of a national team to an altogether higher and different plane. It's been written often enough that they are, to borrow a television phrase, the "best of British". But they're more than that, as the Irish would be quick to protest.

The Lions are the only truly multinational team in world sport. Such a status qualifies them admirably for the description of unique.

In their earlier days, the Lions used to be known as the British Isles Rugby Union Team, and when the initials for that grand title were printed on the team's baggage, they gave rise to the occasional use of the ugly acronym, BIRUT. The Biruts did not have quite the right ring about it; it sounded more like a Lebanese sevens team. The name was discarded but it more correctly reflected the origins of the players who make up the Lions. "British" can still be the adjective, but it's the British Isles rather than any sovereign political entity that the team represents, that is, Great Britain, Northern Ireland and the Republic of Ireland itself. It's a peculiarly rugby institution. Illogical even. It hints, as much in old rugby used to, of nationalistic compromise and of ploughing along with an idea regardless of political change.

The Lions, therefore, gathering their players from England, Scotland, Wales and Ireland, bridge political and geographical divides. There's nothing as unique in rugby as that.

For players anywhere in the rugby world, the achievement of playing for their country is the ultimate.

An Irishman, whether Catholic from the Republic or Protestant from the North, has a burning desire to don the emerald green of a united Ireland, uniquely united for purely rugby purposes. A Welshman, whether from Newport in the east or Swansea in the west, yearns to wear the scarlet of Wales. A Scotsman, Lowlander or Highlander, aspires to the blue with the white thistle. And Englishmen, from Cornwall to the Scottish border, covet the white jersey with the red rose. Their nationalistic ambitions are no less than those of New Zealanders who aspire to be All Blacks or Australians who want to be Wallabies.

The British (and Irish) players have, uniquely, an even higher step up the rugby ladder to aspire to.

As a Welsh and Lions player, Clem Thomas, once put it like this: "Playing for your country is a master's degree; playing for the Lions is a doctorate."

Other players put it differently, but each but each has the same message:

Willie-John McBride: "There's nothing better than playing for your country and your first cap and you will always remember wearing the jersey of your own country. But we're unique in this part of the world with the Lions. To be one of the best 30 players in the four countries, that's special, that's the cream of rugby football."

Phil Bennett: "It's absolutely incredible, it's unique. It's not playing for your small village or for your town or for your country — it's for the whole of Great Britain and the United Kingdom and Ireland and it's very special and we're all so very proud."

Gavin Hastings: "For a British or Irish rugby player, it's the ultimate in your achievement. Being selected for the Lions is an endorsement of everything you've tried to achieve on the rugby field."

Brian Moore: "Because you're picked from four countries and essentially the best in the northern hemisphere, apart from France obviously, it means quite a lot more to you because you've got a bigger pool of players. You appreciate the achievement perhaps more than you do with your first cap. It's just sheer excitement."

Jeremy Guscott: "The Lions is the biggest thing you can do as a player."

Gerald Davies: "The honour is a pinnacle of achievement. Becoming a Lion is a last act of fulfilment."

It's stating the painfully obvious to say that the Lions have changed enormously since a couple of cricketing entrepreneurs cobbled together the first combined British team in 1888 and contrived to play a variety of games in a variety of ways in New Zealand and Australia. The object of their tour was to show the colonial natives how rugby was played and to make a bit of money (for the promoters) on the side.

The missionary aspect of the early tours was paramount: the goal was to spread the values of the Empire through its games and to give the well-heeled amateurs who played the game a jolly good time in the process. The third tour of New Zealand in 1908 had another purpose in mind. Its aim was to bolster the amateur game at a time it was coming under threat from the new game of rugby league. This was in an era of Empire and Mother Country and of "Mother knows best".

The tours of South Africa in 1924 and of New Zealand in 1930 were the first in the familiar recognisable pattern. The earlier tours had had a melange of selection methods — some players were handpicked on the basis of whether they could afford to go, including the provision of their own dinner suit; working-class players were regarded as suspect; and in 1908 in particular, neither Ireland nor Scotland wanted a bar of touring New Zealand because of a perceived casual attitude toward professionalism by New Zealanders. It was only after British rugby was able to reorganise itself after the appalling losses of World War I that some order was brought into the structure of combined sides. But even then the Lions were not the ultimate that players later saw them as. For the 1930 tour of New Zealand, for example, the selection panel, comprising one representative from each of the countries, approached nearly 100 players before they could find 30 who had the time, and the money, to tour.

Amateurism, until relatively recent years, was held as the great strength of rugby, its single most distinguishing feature. That might be debatable, because it was also its greatest weakness. "Amateur", in the British sense, was an ideal rather than the simple concept of not being paid for playing. Rugby amateurs, therefore, were largely middle to upper middle class, many of them were of independent means (that is, they didn't have to work for a living). Picture the champagne-quaffing hurdler, Lord Burghley, from the classic Olympic film, *Chariots of Fire*. He was the epitome of all that was right and pure in amateurism. In the real world, however, most adult men had to work for a living and could not afford to take time off to gallivant around the world for three months playing rugby. It meant some of the Lions teams revered in mellow memory were without players who could have made a difference.

But it was the efforts and the style of the earlier teams that created the traditions and the heritage upon which later teams built. The uniqueness of the Lions comes into play again. "For a Welshman playing for Wales," as Bennett explained, "it's about your village, your town, your country. It's about the people you went to school with, grew up with or played club rugby with." It was playing for family, friends and country. It was pride in the nationalistic symbol on the jersey, it was goosebump pride in the pre-game ritual of the national anthem. The Irish, Scots and English no less than the Welsh played for the land of their fathers.

The Lions have no flag. They have no anthem (well, 75 per cent of them have God Save the Queen). They have to subjugate their nationalism in the narrow sense of England, Scotland and Wales being separate countries for the supranationalism of the Lions. Each national team playing in the Six Nations or going on tour already has a unity of purpose and a ready identity. The Lions have to find theirs every time they play — and when they do, they can be spectacularly successful, as the results in New Zealand in 1971 and South Africa in 1974 showed. When they don't, they can be spectacularly unsuccessful.

This is what makes the Lions so different. A national team's collective personality, its persona, is there all the time. It's been built up over years and the frequency of players coming and going doesn't change it. Welshman, day in and day out, tries to beat Englishman, and vice versa, and the same applies to the Scots and Irish. The three Celts separately love beating England more than they love beating anyone else. But every so often, the best of them are chosen for a Lions tour and have to put aside the primeval differences and unite for the common good. They can draw on the traditions of the Lions, they can take satisfaction from past results (or ignore them as one team tried to do), but essentially each Lions team has to start anew. "In the broad sense," one of the great Lions, Gerald Davies, once said, "a tour asks for a more pure form of commitment. Nothing can be built on what has gone before. Inspiration comes from within."

If this is so, and given Davies' experience and acuity it has to be assumed it is, Lions of the past should have been able to draw on every morsel of information from previous tours, they should have avoided the mistakes of the past and perpetuated what went right. But some didn't, some started anew, doomed to repeat earlier mistakes.

Coaches and captains have been troublesome appointments for the Lions. Egged on by Wales and, of all places, Ireland, Britain's Four Home Unions Committee eventually and belatedly agreed to the use of coaches (hitherto held to be not in the amateur spirit). Never mind that the All Blacks took a coach to Britain on their first tour in 1905. Good things take time. Their first coach was a Welshman, John Robins, appointed to the Lions tour of New Zealand in 1966. But he wasn't named as coach — he was officially assistant manager, a subterfuge also used by New Zealand until the 1980s. But Robins never actually coached. He became more a fitness trainer because the captain, Mike Campbell-Lamerton, assumed the role of coaching just as every previous Lions captain had. No one told him there was anything different so Robins was reduced to a sideshow role. It was only with the much more astute personality of Carwyn James in 1971 that the Lions adopted coaching in the sense it's understood now.

The Lions also had difficulty with captains. The traditional New Zealand way of picking the best players for a team, for touring or for tests, then picking a captain from those already chosen, was not always the Lions' way.

The Lions selection committees seemed to choose their leaders first for their ability to lead rather than because they were necessarily the best players in their positions. Sometimes they were, sometimes they weren't. Lions captains such as Doug Prentice (1930), Karl Mullen (1950), Mike Campbell-Lamerton (1966) were all left out of tests — or left themselves out of tests — in New Zealand. The 1983 captain, Ciaran Fitzgerald, played in each of the tests but in the face of constant criticism that he was not a better hooker than the other one on tour, Colin Deans, and that he wasn't even as good as one left at home, Peter Wheeler.

Selectors seldom say why they make decisions — or if they do there's a great deal of obfuscation about their comments — but undoubtedly, the cumbersome committees that chose the Lions selected their captains because they had to double as coaches and also play, to the full, the ambassadorial role that touring demanded. An ability to play was not the only prerequisite.

The mood of Lions tours until perhaps 1971 was that the object was to play enjoyable rugby, have a good time on and off the field and if matches were won, so much the better. If not, well, it's only a game. This was not just an impression. This was a decree. The manager of the hapless 1966 Lions in New Zealand was told in no uncertain manner by a member of the committee that appointed him: "Your top priority is not to win the tests in New Zealand, it is bringing the tradition of Lions play to Australia and New Zealand."

If the public popularity of the Lions was the ultimate aim, success was achieved. The Lions in New Zealand, South Africa and Australia — and probably also on secondary tours to Canada and Argentina — were generally the most popular of touring teams. Crowds flocked to see them, people enjoyed the free-flowing nature of their play but even more, they enjoyed watching the All Blacks beat them. The Lions of 1950 and 1959, generally held to have been the most appreciated teams, would not have been as popular if they'd beaten the All Blacks. When the 1959 Lions scored four tries in the first test in Dunedin and Don Clarke kicked six penalty goals to beat them, the record

crowd chanted "Red! Red! Red!" But that surely would have been more the plaintive cry for the underdog than any treasonable call. When Bob Stuart led his All Blacks to Britain in 1953, he said at a welcoming press conference at Heathrow that if his team was anywhere near as popular in Britain as the Lions had been in New Zealand in 1950, he would consider the tour a success.

For New Zealanders, the Lions were — are — a rarely-sighted rugby beast and valued all the more because of their rarity. They brought not the familiarity of the Australians — and Australians who, for most of the history of Anzac tests, had not been considered opponents of the first rank — not the exotic novelty of the Fijians and not the grim beat-them-at-all-costs crusades of the South Africans.

Lions tours were All Black tours of Britain in reverse. It wasn't until the 1960s that the British countries individually ventured far from their native homes: England first came to New Zealand in 1963, Wales in 1969, Scotland in 1975 and Ireland in 1976. For the greater part of New Zealand rugby history, the only time British players were seen was on the infrequent Lions tours. Aside from the early missionary tours as the "oval empire" took shape, it was 20 years from the Lions tour of 1930 until the next (admittedly with a war in between), nine years until the next, seven years until the next, then a gap of five years, then two gaps of six years, then 10 years and now 11 years. Some great All Blacks have never played against a Lions team; a generation of spectators has grown up without seeing one.

Part of the popularity of the Lions was their rarely-seen status; the once-in-a-lifetime chance to see great players who otherwise would have just been, in those days, read about in newspapers and books. However much players win praise from home-based critics, New Zealanders being the astute and sometimes harsh judges of rugby that they are, want to see for themselves and make their own minds up. So it was that New Zealanders with long memories who saw Jack Kyle, the gifted Irish first five-eighth, recalled him as one of the greatest if not the greatest to come to New Zealand. They recalled the contrasting wings of the 1959 tour, the ebullient Tony

O'Reilly and the poker-faced Peter Jackson, then the constellation of stars of the 1971 team, Barry John and Gareth Edwards pre-eminent among them. It's no coincidence those Lions were all backs; a common theme of Lions teams was that they had gifted backs who liked to attack but that their forwards were no match for the behemoths of New Zealand. Like all generalities, it's not entirely accurate but it suffices as an impression. No New Zealander, however, would sneeze at the achievements of a Willie-John McBride or a Gordon Brown or a Graham Price or Ian McLauchlan.

Another unique aspect of the Lions is the fusing together of the different nationalities for the common good. Although England, Scotland and Wales are all part of the United Kingdom and thus one country in the accepted sense, anyone familiar with Britain knows that each of the three have different nationalistic traits and see themselves first as Scots, or English, or Welsh, and second as British. Then add in the complicating factor of the Irish — the one British and the other decidedly not. It requires careful man management and astute captaincy to draw all the strands together for the common good. It's not just the fusing of the nationalities. There's always been also the fusing of the two halves of a rugby touring team, the Saturday players and the midweekers.

In New Zealand, the attitude within All Black teams in such situations has generally been that the midweekers are there to keep the Saturday players honest; to push them for their plum spots and to support them when playing sides are chosen. There have been All Black tours on which the midweekers have clubbed together and built their own team spirit, harnessing an energy for their own good and for the good of the whole touring party.

Such has not always been the case with the Lions. The 1930 team, so it was recorded, had more or less settled on its test lineup on the ship on the way to New Zealand and the "them and us" became so pronounced that the midweekers formed their own club that they called the Rank and File Society, not entirely in jest. This is not something just from the dim past. In the most recent Lions team to tour New Zealand, in 1993,

there was a distinct rift between the Saturday and the midweek players to the point that some of the test players castigated their supposed teammates for being on tour only for a good time. There were similar accusations after the most recent Lions tour, in Australia in 2001. Such rifts can have serious implications for the overall good of the tour. A team with internal dissension will seldom play with complete unity on the field.

The Lions are not just rare; they were also endangered to the point of becoming extinct. When rugby embraced professionalism and when each country of the rugby fraternity went its separate way in learning how to grapple with a range of complex new issues, the British and Irish adopted the well-established soccer method. Players were contracted to clubs and released for specific international matches. Since it is the clubs that pay the players and rely on those players to click over the turnstiles at their club games and to capture television viewers in the bewildering array of domestic competitions, it is the clubs that have the say. It is the clubs too, it should not be forgotten, which are almost entirely responsible for the spotting of young talent and for nurturing and developing players. The neatly pointed rugby pyramid started to change shape in 1995. No longer was international rugby automatically and rightly at the top. The base started to dictate to the apex. For the first time in 120 years of British rugby, the tail started to wag the dog.

Even before the precipitate dash for cash by the International Rugby Board, the Lions' days were counted as numbered. The World Cup was the catalyst for all the cataclysmic change in world rugby and the Lions were not immune. Arguing in 1993 that the cup meant the end of the Lions, journalist John Mason in the London *Daily Telegraph* said it was time for the Lions to go into eternity. Mason was no fly-by-night reporter with an opinion one minute and gone the next. He'd been around, he'd been with the Lions on tour in New Zealand, he knew British administrators intimately and he knew British players as well as any journalist can know them. For the Lions, he wrote, the courtesies and the rites must be observed: "Grateful thanks for an ambassadorial job soundly done. Their hour upon the stage is over."

The gist of his argument was that with a cup every four years, it was no longer realistic or practical to expect British and Irish players to subjugate their national good for the cause of the Lions. The focus, the only focus, would be on the cup. The Lions would just get in the way.

A few years later, after the Lions had toured South Africa in 1997, a former England prop, Jeff Probyn, a member of the English union, also argued for an end to a rugby institution. The Lions, he said, were the ultimate in "old fartism", a regurgitation of Will Carling's description in 1995 of the English union committee as being 57 old farts. The essence of Probyn's argument, as with Mason's, was that there was no room any longer for the Lions. The Lions, he said, took up one (northern) summer in four when England's time would be better spent touring separately preparing for the cup.

Probyn's argument went nowhere but the issue didn't entirely disappear. The place of the Lions in the international calendar was disputed again in 2004 when the New Zealand union was trying to put together the Lions itinerary for 2005. Leading the charge on this occasion was Premier Rugby, the body that represents the top English clubs. "I am a very strong supporter of Lions rugby," Premier Rugby's chief executive Howard Thomas said, "but I'm a bigger supporter of professional rugby. The Lions tradition is based in the amateur era . . . when Lions tours are shown to be significantly disruptive, it is entirely understandable that the premiership clubs should look at their priorities."

In the event, the Lions and the English clubs eventually reached agreement on the length of the itinerary and therefore on players missing key games at the end of the domestic season. Thomas said that the Lions were a nightmare issue and it's one that, although solved for the moment, won't go away. National unions, including New Zealand, want more games to earn more money; clubs are loath to release players more than they do already.

Another complicating factor could enter the equation. Rugby has for some time cast covetous eyes on the Olympic Games and it is now one of the sports in contention for a place at the Games in 2012. It wouldn't be real rugby, that is 15-a-side, because an international, tournament would be unmanageable in the timetable of the Games. It would be a sevens tournament but one of the planks of the Olympic platform is that sports admitted to the Games must involve their best players. At issue will be whether the sevens players on the regular circuit will be deemed to be the best players or whether clubs and national teams will be raided for the best. Rugby in the Olympics would then be an added pressure on an already crowded calendar. This also gives rise to another issue, one that is dear to the Lions because they solved it years ago. Under the Olympic format, the United Kingdom competes as Great Britain and Northern Ireland, that is, England, Wales, Scotland and Northern Ireland all together as a happy band of brothers and sisters. Ireland competes, of course, as Ireland. But what to do with Irish rugby players? Would those from Ulster, who were good enough, compete in the combined British team, leaving their southern Irish teammates to play on their own? Since competing teams at a Games are also supposed to have approved national bodies, any Northern Ireland players would have only half a national body. A solution to that little conundrum could have ramifications for the future of a united rugby Ireland and also for the Lions.

But that is an issue for the future. Rugby doesn't dwell in its past because no sport can afford to, but it's the past that provides the richness for the present and, properly managed, for the future. The Lions' past has richness in abundance. The future of the Lions was questioned seriously 10 years ago and has since been raised from time to time. It may yet be again. But in the meantime, the great strength of the Lions is their pulling power in New Zealand or wherever they may be and, more importantly, an ability to unite the disparate nationalities of the British Isles in a way that no other sport, and few other institutions, can. They are unique and like all who carry such a distinction, treasured all the more for it.

Dawn of the Oval Empire

The early British rugby teams, no matter what name they went by, were sent to New Zealand with all the same zeal that missionaries were dispatched with their Bibles to the colonies and other heathen lands.

Whatever may have been in the minds of the players, and it's reasonable to assume they were after a good time and some enjoyable rugby every bit as much as their successors, the rugby establishment was on a crusade. Whether by accident or design, the purpose of the tours was threefold: to aid the development of rugby; to continue to involve the whole Empire "family"; and to thwart even the merest hint of that most dastardly of curses, professionalism.

On some of the early tours these aims were implicit. On others, they were baldly stated. New Zealand — and South Africa and Australia and even Argentina — had to be protected from any imagined evils that ran counter to the Victorian-Edwardian upper-middle-class code and values which ruled rugby (and which ruled much else besides).

A British team first came to New Zealand in 1888 and others followed in 1904 and 1908. Each had "missionary" stamped all over them even though it was evident, even as early as 1888, that when it came to rugby, there wasn't much that Mother Britain could teach. The third tour, by an Anglo-Welsh team, wasn't so much missionary work as a police action to ensure that the new threat of rugby league was well and truly warded off. Not that New Zealand rugby administrators needed anyone from Britain to tell them what the threats were. They were as anxious to fight off the new threat of league as the British were and they were then, and would continue to be for another 80 years, as zealous as British officials in tracking down every transgression of the amateur regulations.

The difference between New Zealand and the English union, grandly styled The Rugby Football Union (RFU) with a disdain for country identification, was that New Zealand was more pragmatic. An amateur to New Zealanders was simply one who wasn't paid for playing. To the Corinthians of Britain, an amateur was a matter of class and style and breeding rather than one just of money. Under the British model, the amateurs were the players with wealth; the professionals were the workers. The different interpretation led to many squabbles, some minor and some not so minor, between the administrators of New Zealand and British rugby over the years. Britain took an elitist approach to rugby, and, it could be said, to its cost, while New Zealand took, or tried to take, a more egalitarian, all-embracing view.

The bedfellow of the British-style amateurism was hypocrisy and this was evident when the first British team came to New Zealand. It was a private team raised by two professional sports promoters, Alfred Shaw and Arthur Shrewsbury, whose main bent was cricket but who were keen to make money wherever it could be found. Cricket then was as hidebound about amateurism as indeed rugby was. Shaw and Shrewsbury, who both played for Nottinghamshire, managed an England cricket team in Australia at the time they decided to mount their rugby tour. Andrew Stoddart, who opened the batting for England and played on the wing for England, became a willing ally. Shrewsbury had been W.G. Grace's predecessor as England captain and Stoddart succeeded Grace. Grace, incidentally, was the most noted of 19th

Dual international Andrew Stoddart, who took over as captain of the 1888 team.

century amateurs and two years before the rugby tour had been given three testimonials which netted him £8835. As sports historian Brian Dobbs drily noted, "No one thought that made W.G. a professional any more than his acceptance of three pigs from an admiring farmer. Similar absurdities and anomalies made the concept of amateurism untenable even in those early times."

The distinction between professional and amateur was drawn much more boldly for one hapless rugby player who had signed for the New Zealand tour. J.P. Clowes was a Welshman who played for Halifax in the north of England and, like others playing in the area at the time, had been financially induced to move from Wales to the north. One of Halifax's rival clubs, Dewsbury, knew this, told tales to the RFU and Clowes was banned as a professional for the appalling moral lapse of accepting 15 quid. Clowes still came to New Zealand with the 1888 team, but didn't play a game — at least, not that was recorded. He could well have played without the denizens of the RFU finding out because it was one of rugby's more unusual tours. They played six games in New Zealand, losing to Taranaki and Auckland, then went to Australia where they played another 15 games, winning 13 and drawing two. They also played 19 matches of what was then called Victorian rules — what is now known as AFL — and, remarkably, won nine of them. Then they hotfooted it back to New Zealand for another 10 games of rugby and one game of cricket. By any standards, they were a remarkably versatile team on an arduous tour.

Dawn of the Oval Empire

On the basis of the Clowes case, the RFU had deep suspicions about other players in the team. Only three or four were what could be regarded as of the right social status to be true-blue amateurs. Eighteen played for northern clubs, would most likely have been categorised as working class and most probably had been, at some stage or another, like Clowes, induced to play. The RFU said it had formed "a very strong opinion" that Clowes was not the only transgressor and it therefore sought, on the return of the team, an affidavit from each player saying he had gained no financial benefit from the tour. Of course, they all swore blind they hadn't.

As to the rugby, the British team was supposed to show the colonials how the game ought to be played and there was much interest in New Zealand because rugby players here, aside from the few who had played in Britain, had no yardstick by which to gauge their progress, their tactics and style. There was no question that the British had players of genuine star quality — Stoddart first and foremost, but also the fullback, Tommy Haslam, who was regarded as the cleverest man to pull on rugby boots. Opinions in later years varied on what exactly the New Zealanders did learn. Otago, who met the British in their first two matches, learnt little, according to Sean O'Hagan, quoted in Otago's centennial book, *The Pride of Southern Rebels*. "It should hardly be surprising that all the tactics claimed to be introduced by the Englishmen were used in Otago and other parts of the

The 1888 British players, complete with winged collars, pinstripes, a top hat and their international caps, pose on board ship on their way to New Zealand.

The 1888 British team. Back row: J. Anderton, promoters Alfred Shaw and Arthur Shrewsbury, A. Lang, T. Banks, Dr D. Smith. Second row: R. Burnett, J. Clowes, C. Mathers, Dr Brooks, R. Seddon (captain), S. Williams, A. Paul, W. Thomas, H. Eagles. Third row: A. Stoddart, W. Bumby, J. Nolan, A. Stuart, W. Burnett, J. Haslam, A. Pinketh. In front (reclining): H. Speakman, T. Kent.

country before 1888," he wrote. "The laws of the RFU were everywhere, there were rugby enthusiasts arriving from 'the old country' at odd times bringing with them new ideas and most importantly, the rugby players at the time were not unimaginative drongos but men prepared to employ any extant move if it would help them win, and where none existed, to dream one up."

Rather than arrive bearing exotic and mysterious gifts, he said, what the British team did do was give a timely boost to the continuing development of rugby in New Zealand.

Dave Gallaher and Billy Stead, captain and vice-captain of the Original All Blacks, wrote at the end of their own pioneering tour that the British team's most important lesson was one of teamwork, showing that combinations were superior to individual skills. "It was left to Stoddart's team to show Maoriland the fine points of the game and the vast possibilities of combination," they said. "The exhibitions of passing which they gave were most fascinating and impressive to the New Zealander, who was not slow to observe the advantages of these methods."

Tom Ellison, one of the seminal early figures in the game and the man who gave New Zealand rugby the black jersey with the silver fern, rather sniffily dismissed the Brits. "Beyond learning the minor though petty and effective trick of feign passing from Mr Haslam and learning to disregard the strict law on offside play as regards forwards in the scrum, I challenge anyone to tell me what else they taught us," he wrote.

The Auckland team that beat the 1888 British team. Back row: E. O'Hare (trainer), M. Keefe, O. Wells, J. Lecky, R. McKenzie, E. McCausland. Second row: J. Conway, C. Marshall, R. Lusk, R. Whiteside (captain first match), T. O'Connor (captain second match), C. Madigan, W. Elliot. Front row: W. Hobson, A. Braund, F. Twiname, T. Brown.

Ellison's mention of the scrum reflected a prevailing view in New Zealand at the time that forwards could not heel the ball back from a scrum because they felt that if they did, they would be in front of the ball and therefore offside.

It was not a universal view though and players in other parts of New Zealand, who didn't necessarily know then how the game was played elsewhere, had a different idea. Samuel Sleigh, another innovative 19th century rugby man and manager of the first New Zealand team in 1884, wrote this after a club match in 1877: "We now saw that we had a chance of scoring and the scrimmages became very warm. After working the ball a little nearer to the goal-line, the signal was given, and the forwards allowed the ball to come through to the halfbacks. Rose, who was on the alert, picked it up and was behind their line like a flash of lightning."

The rugby, the AFL and cricket aside, it was a tour marked by tragedy. The original captain, Bob Seddon, was drowned while sculling on the Hunter River in New South Wales during the second leg of the tour. His boat apparently flipped and he was unable to free his feet from the strappings. Stoddart took over for the rest of the Australian leg and the return to New Zealand. He committed suicide in 1915 and one of the promoters, Shrewsbury, also killed himself.

The next British tour was organised along more orthodox lines, though had the novelty of being invited by the New South Wales Rugby Union, and New Zealand, therefore, in the manner of cricket tours, was added on at the end of the main Australian segment. The British discovered on that tour where the real strength of antipodean rugby lay. Although not truly representative of rugby in the British Isles, the team in 1904 reflected the realities of the game as they were

Members of British Team.

D. R. BEDELL SIVRIGHT (Capt.), Scotland.
C. F. STANGER-LEATHES, England.
P. F. McEVEDY   ,,
J. L. FISHER   ,,
F. HULME   ,,
J. SHARLAND   ,,
S. McK. SAUNDERS   ,,
D. DOBSON   ,,
R. ROGERS   ,,
S. N. CROWTHER   ,,
D. H. TRAIL   ,,
B. MASSEY   ,,
B. I. SWANNELL   ,,
R. W. EDWARDS, Ireland
C. D. PATTERSON,   ,,
E. JOWETT, Wales
A. F. HARDING, Wales
T. H. VILE   ,,
W. LLEWELLYN   ,,
E. MORGAN   ,,
R. J. GABE   ,,
PERCY BUSH   ,,
T. S. BEVAN   ,,
A. B. O'BRIEN (Manager), England

New Zealand Rugby Union.

BRITISH TEAM
in NEW ZEALAND, 1904.

Management Committee:
G. H. DIXON   G. C. FACHE   N. GALBRAITH
A. LAURENSON   J. O'SHEA   R. M. ISAACS
          W. COFFEY   D. D. WEIR
                        A. C. NORRIS, Hon. Sec.

then. England had 13 players in the squad but this was less than a decade after the great split in English rugby that led to the formation of league in Yorkshire and Lancashire, the hitherto dominant rugby counties. It also included eight Welshmen at the time of a great era for Welsh rugby, and among them were the famed Welsh threequarter line of Rhys Gabe, Willie Llewellyn and Teddy Morgan (who gained even greater fame for his role in the test against the Original All Blacks in 1905). The Welshman about whom tongues buzzed though was the uncapped first five-eighth (or flyhalf as the Brits call the position), Percy Bush. He emerged as the most scintillating back of the tour and went on to great fame in Wales, captaining them in the 1905 test against New Zealand, and being acknowledged as the progenitor of the long line of classy No. 10s to come out of Wales.

Two New Zealanders became British for the purposes of the tour — Pat McEvedy and Arthur O'Brien — both medical students studying in London at Guy's Hospital, which was also something of a rugby nursery.

The party also included two Irishmen and one Scot and it was the latter, David Bedell-Sivright, otherwise known as "Darkie" to all and sundry, who was the captain. He was, it seems, a commanding figure on and off the field and was described as an amazing dribbler and one of the roughest forwards of his day ("dribbler" in the sense of forward rushes with the ball controlled at the feet, which was a Scottish specialty of the day). This was an age, too, when "muscular Christianity" (healthy minds and healthy bodies and all that) was all the rage and Bedell-Sivright's particular brand of the desired muscular Christianity was described as being more Old Testament than New. For all his bulk and wild ways,

Top: The lion meets the fern . . . the New Zealand union's fixtures card for the 1904 tour.

Left: The first Scot to captain a combined British team, "Darkie" Bedell-Sivright.

Bedell-Sivright had the appropriate upbringing and education for a leader of men at the time (Fettes College, Cambridge and Edinburgh Universities) and he spoke, as one Australian report put it, like a toff. During one of the games in Australia, the referee went to send off one of the British players, Denys Dobson, for obscene language. Bedell-Sivright intervened, said Dobson hadn't used the offending words and remarked icily, "Mr Dobson is an Oxford man and a gentleman," as if that should be the end of the matter. It cut no ice with the referee so Bedell-Sivright took the whole team off for 20 minutes or, as one Australian newspaper put it, "His huff arrived so he departed in it." And another: "Mr Sivright picked up his valuable hyphen and marched his team off the field."

The British won each of their games in Australia but the rude awakening came in New Zealand. They won their first two games, against a combined Canterbury-South Canterbury-West Coast and against a combined Otago-Southland, but lost two and drew one of the remaining three. One of their losses was a significant one — their match against New Zealand at Athletic Park in Wellington on 13 August 1904, was the first test match to be played in New Zealand.

The New Zealanders (they weren't All Blacks then) were captained by the Southland first five-eighth, Billy Stead, a man whose true worth to rugby in New Zealand has not often been fully acknowledged. They included the Originals captain, Dave Gallaher, and other enduring luminaries such as Billy Wallace, George Nicholson and

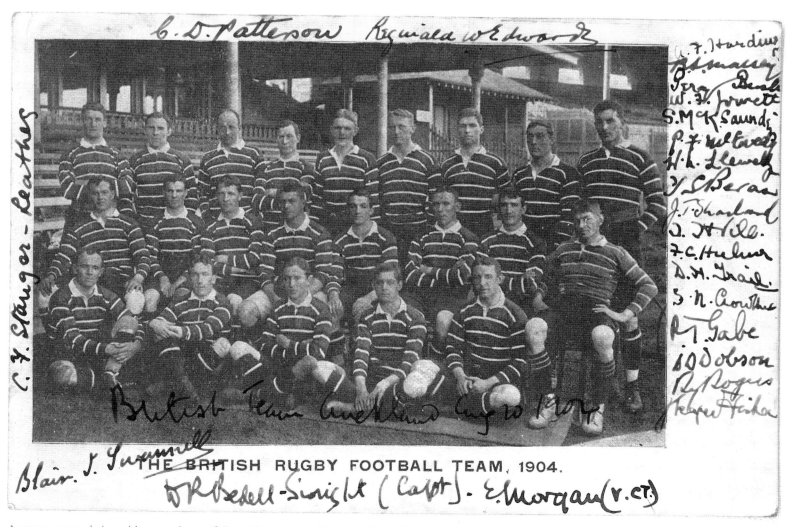

A rare postcard signed by members of the 1904 team, which was formally if little known as the Anglo-Australian rugby football team.

PRESENTED BY
BRITAIN V NEW ZEALAND
TRIES 0 TRIES 0
GOALS 0 GOALS 0
POINTS 0 POINTS 0
0 LAST SCORER 0 LAST SCORER
SOLE
N.Z.
AGENTS
"DADE"
LOOSE
LEAF

Bronco Seeling. Unlike the Brits, whose idea of training was to run the length of a rugby ground a couple of times a week, the New Zealanders had a training camp of a few days at Days Bay on Wellington Harbour where they were put through a range of physical tests by one of the foremost athletics coaches of the day, Dorrie Leslie.

Wallace and Arthur ("Boxer") Harding, a Welshman who later emigrated to New Zealand (and a distant forebear of 2002 All Black Sam Harding), each kicked a penalty in the first half but the New Zealanders, playing into the wind in the second, stole away with two tries to wing Duncan McGregor.

"The excitement was intense," Wallace later wrote. "Hats, caps and umbrellas flying into the air and I don't think that any of their owners regretted if they did not see their headgear again."

Bedell-Sivright, who broke a leg in the first game in New Zealand, thought the New Zealanders were a proficient team that might beat some of the English counties on the 1905 tour. He also had some harsh words to say about Gallaher's role as a wing forward (as Brits did for the next 25-or-so years), which was held to be obstructionist at best, cheating at worst. Yet Bedell-Sivright was given credit for developing the forward position the Scots and Welsh called "the rover" before he'd clapped eyes on Gallaher, and what was the rover but another name for the wing forward?

Left: The elaborate old scoreboard at Athletic Park for the first test match in New Zealand.

Above: The programme for the first test.

The All Blacks who played the first test in New Zealand, a 9–3 win against the 1904 British team. Back row: Bill Glenn, Charlie Seeling, George Nicholson, Dave Gallaher, Bernie Fanning, "Paddy" McMinn. Second row: Eric Harper, Tom Cross, Morris Wood, Billy Stead (captain), George Tyler, Billy Wallace, W. Coffey (manager). Front row: Dick McGregor, Jim Gerrard (reserve), Peter Harvey, Duncan McGregor, Jimmy Hunter (reserve).

One of several "death" notices that appeared in newspapers after the British loss in 1904.

IN MEMORY
OF THE
BRITISH RUGBY FOOTBALL TEAM,
Who departed this life at the
ATHLETIC PARK, WELLINGTON, N.Z.,
On SATURDAY, AUGUST 13th, 1904.
After a short illness.
DEEPLY LAMENTED.
GONE BUT NOT FORGOTTEN.

The Brits were, by all accounts, a little surprised at the manner and rapidity with which New Zealand rugby had developed — and a little put out by the seriousness with which New Zealanders approached games — but seemed to subscribe to Bedell-Sivright's view that the tour of Britain in 1905 would establish the true worth of New Zealand rugby. Well it did, but perhaps not in the manner he anticipated. As historian Brian Dobbs noted, "The Edwardians had their virtues, but awareness that there were others in the world beside themselves was not one of them."

British class distinction was a pronounced feature of especially the early tours on which "form" and etiquette were as important as playing rugby. Team unity was, it seems, subordinate to mixing with one's own kind and when the 1904 team was in Wellington, several of the players

A cartoonist's view of New Zealand's win in the 1904 test. Premier Dick Seddon congratulates the lion cub for beating its distraught mother.

stayed at Government House with the Governor, Lord Plunket, leaving the others to the "common" hotel.

The 1908 tour came as a direct result of the formation of league in New Zealand and Australia, but rather than being called Great Britain, as the earlier teams had been, it was called Anglo-Welsh because the Scots and the Irish didn't want a bar of it. It's been written in various Lions and general rugby histories that 1908 was a reciprocal tour for the Originals' odyssey in Britain, Ireland and France in 1905–06, but that is to gloss over the real reasons. The tour was organised, primarily by the English union, as an antidote to what was perceived in southern England as the rising threat of professionalism in the wake of the All Blacks' tour and the formation in New Zealand and Australia of league or, as it was known at the time, "the northern game". Some of the All Blacks in 1905 in the north of England had seen league matches and, once back home, the versatile wing George Smith was one of the principals in getting the game started in New Zealand. He was joined by some of his All Black teammates and organiser and esrtwhile rugby player Albert Baskerville. Together they formed what were originally known as "the professional All Blacks" for a tour of Britain. On their way, they stopped off in Sydney and picked up one of the leading Australian rugby players of the day, Dally Messenger, to join their team that subsequently

.. **Menu** ..

OF

DINNER

GIVEN BY THE

Canterbury Rugby Union

TO

The British
Rugby Football Team.

AT

WARNER'S HOTEL,
CHRISTCHURCH, N.Z.
6TH AUGUST, 1904.

Above: Early British tours were as much social affairs as they were serious rugby encounters.

Overleaf: Snow had to be cleared from Lancaster Park in Christchurch before the 1904 British team played a combined Canterbury-South Canterbury-West Coast team.

Above: The Anglo-Welsh, decked out in their winter finery, pose on board their ship, the *Athenic*, soon after arriving in Wellington.

Left: The New Zealand union's 1908 tour guide.

became known as the "All Golds". Their visit to Sydney was the catalyst for the beginnings of league in Australia. They toured Britain from August 1907 until February 1908, then played another 11 games in Australia (some under rugby rules and some under league rules) from April to June.

This was more than the English union could bear (and the New Zealand and Australian unions were none too happy either). The 1908 tour was a direct response to league's beginnings. The manager of the Anglo-Welsh team, and one of its main organisers, George Harnett, said, "If New Zealand is not to be abandoned to professionalism, the visit of the British team is a necessity."

Price War

A few ground members of provincial unions around the country had a bit of a grumble when the arrangements for the Lions tour in 2005 were first announced. Such was the unprecedented demand for tickets from Lions supporters in Britain, some ground members were told they may not be able to sit at their normal seats.

The fuss was nothing compared with the furore in 1908 when the New Zealand union announced that for matches against the Anglo-Welsh team, the admission charge would be two shillings — double the normal cost.

The Otago Rugby Football Union, less removed from its Scottish origins then than it is now, was outraged. At first, Otago sent a letter to Wellington saying the exorbitant charge would be ignored. New Zealand conceded on the cost of admission for the game against Otago, but remained adamant that it would be two bob for the test match. Like it or lump it, the suits in Wellington replied — "Arrangements will be made to play elsewhere."

Fearing an empty sporran, not to mention an empty Carisbrook, Otago fired back this missive: "While still of the opinion that the charges imposed by the New Zealand union are unnecessarily high, the committee agrees, in view of the fact that the preliminary arrangements have been made, to take control of the first test match in Dunedin."

So the union may have agreed, but the public was incensed.

Rumours flew around Dunedin that there was a break in the fence on the southern side of the Carisbrook perimeter — where the main stand now is. The story was denied by the Otago union, but a spectator at the match recalled in a letter years later:

"When we arrived at the ground, there were at least two, probably more, express vans backed against the fence on the southern side of the ground. Also, men with ladders and all were offering lifts over the fence for a few pence per person. Needless to say, the money collected did not find its way to the union."

While some spectators got in free by that method, that wasn't the end of the gatecrashing.

"A policeman patrolled up and down the ground between us and the touchline," the spectator continued, "very pointedly ignoring the noise of hammers and jemmy bars coming from the western fence behind the grandstand [on the western side of the ground]. However, when a metallic screech and a crash, accompanied by cheers, was too loud to be ignored, he decided that duty required his presence but as far as I know, he did not succeed in effecting any arrests."

Union officials evidently turned a Nelsonian eye to the non-paying intruders, but they may have been less tolerant in the following week when they realised they had to foot the bill to repair the fence.

Paid up or otherwise, 25,000 saw the All Blacks beat the Anglo-Welsh 32–5. Strange as it may seem, that was a New Zealand test record attendance until 40,000 went to Eden Park in 1921 to see the All Blacks play South Africa.

Halfback Fred Roberts kicks the first penalty goal for the All Blacks in the first test in 1908. The sunhatted referee is Jimmy Duncan, the first New Zealand test captain and coach of the 1905 All Blacks.

"Jumbo" Missing

The Anglo-Welsh team of 1908 may not have been any great shakes on the rugby field, but they had a grand old time off it, it appears.

Many of the reports on the tour mentioned the players' lack of fitness and a careful read between the lines would attribute that not just to a lack of training.

One report spoke of "extravagance, taradiddles and a crawling unquietness" in the public mind about what the players got up to and that some players "were unwisely wooed to folly by the damsels of Dunedin".

The team's trainer, Wellingtonian Dorrie Leslie, would have known better than anyone how carousing may have affected the players' fitness. "Truth to tell," he wrote, "18 out of 29 players were teetotallers, the remainder being strictly moderate in their requirements. When the great hospitality extended to the British team is taken into consideration, and the fact that before and after every match enthusiasts throughout the tour, friends in general and in particular were vying with each other as to who would do the players the greatest honours, the wonder is not that any of them fell to the temptation, but that the whole of the team did not."

One who seems to have fallen was the England centre, 21-year-old Henry ("Jumbo") Vassall, who was nowhere to be found when the team left Auckland for Sydney on the good ship *Victoria*.

The team's last game was on 25 July and three days later, the treasurer of the New Zealand union, Neil Galbraith, sent a telegram to the union in Wellington: "Vassall missed *Victoria* arrives Wellington tomorrow night please arrange passage Friday to Sydney . . ."

A contrite Vassall later wrote an apology to Galbraith: "Will you kindly convey to the members of your committee my sincere apology for anything in my conduct while in N.Z. which appeared to them to be a breach of the courtesy due from a guest to his hosts, or made them think that I treated the tour lightly, such was far from my intention, and I greatly regret anything I may have said or done to give rise to such an impression."

Top left: Henry "Jumbo" Vassall.

Above: His letter of contrition to the New Zealand union.

32

The Anglo-Welsh team beaten in their second game by Wellington. They were captained by New Zealander Pat McEvedy (with ball).

The New Zealand team that thrashed the Anglo-Welsh 29–0 in the third test.

The Scots and the Irish presumably thought New Zealand was already a lost cause. Neither wanted a part of the tour because they believed the All Blacks in 1905 had been de facto professionals in any case, pocketing three shillings a day expenses. This highlighted the difference in attitude between some in Britain and New Zealand. The 1904 British team and the 1908 Anglo-Welsh, plus presumably the British teams which had also toured South Africa, were paid two or three shillings a day "wine money" so what was at issue was not so much the money paid, but the calibre of men to whom the money was being paid. The distinction was not whether money was being paid but between so-called gentlemen amateurs and men who had to work for a living. There was a further distinction. The diehard British view was that rugby, as a pure amateur game, was to be played for enjoyment of the players and not for entertainment and not, heaven forbid, to train for and to win. The British viewed the New Zealand attitude, which involved hard training and even harder playing, as being counter to the amateur spirit. One of the Anglo-Welsh players wrote home during the tour with a sense of wonder: "You will find them [New Zealanders] on the ground or in the training sheds, at it for all they are worth. Why, for the test matches the players would leave their work 10 days before and go into training . . ."

There is also a view, largely postulated in academic circles, that the 1908 tour was also mounted to shore up Empire unity and to ensure that the colonies remained true to all that was held dear in Mother England. A speech of welcome to the 1908 team by the mayor of Dunedin, James McDonald, has been taken to underline this argument. McDonald said matches against British teams reminded New Zealanders "they

Dawn of the Oval Empire

formed a part of one people, a part of that great country, England, which they revered and loved, and part of this great and glorious Empire". He carried on in like vein, saying such visits "would ensure that in the future our beloved Empire would remain a united, a warm . . . and a loving brotherhood".

Granted it was a time for such rhetoric because it was at a time when New Zealanders learnt first of British heroes and of British derring-do, of when the Empire's call and cause was echoed by Richard John Seddon and other politicians, when New Zealand donated a battleship to Britain and when British soldiers came to New Zealand to organise the New Zealand army. It had not been too many years before that New Zealanders had enthusiastically raced off to fight for Britain in the Boer War, and not too many years away when New Zealanders in their thousands would rush to sign up to do their bit in World War I.

It is doubtful though, in a purely rugby sense, if New Zealanders could have given a toss about imperial unity or even what the Brits thought of amateurism. The aim, then as now, was to win and this the New Zealanders set about achieving with a sense of determination and thoroughness.

The Anglo-Welsh was not a strong team; it had none of the backline flair that the 1904 team had possessed, though it still had 10 full internationals with seven others who played for their countries later, and it had Harding, the Welsh loose forward who had toured in 1904, as captain. There was a sense though, that the Anglo-Welsh concentrated as much, if not more, on the breeding and education of their players as on their rugby ability.

The All Blacks seem to have control of the ball in this passage of play from the third test, which they won 29–0. The match was at Potter's Park (now part of Alexandra Park) in Auckland.

Jackson Dispatched

Name the rugby player sent home from tour who never made it home. Easy question? Keith Murdoch yes, but he wasn't the first.

One of the members of the 1908 Anglo-Welsh team, Fred Jackson, was dispatched home from the tour on the eve of the second test because he'd been suspended, in absentia, by the English union for alleged professionalism.

The Anglo-Welsh manager, George Harnett, received a cable from the English union on the eve of the second test telling him to get rid of Jackson immediately.

Jackson had played for Leicester against the All Blacks in 1905 and was one of several Leicester players who were supposed to have been paid in those strictly amateur days. Another report said Jackson had signed as "John Jones" and played one league match for Swinton. Nothing was ever proven and Jackson never returned to Britain to face the charges anyway.

He left Wellington as he was ordered but neither he nor his teammates were happy about it. "General was the regret at the unforeseen happening," wrote R.A. Barr in his book on the tour, "and all the players expressed sympathy with the big Cornishman, who felt parting from his comrades just in the middle of the tour very deeply, and made no effort to hide it."

Most of his teammates went to the wharf to see him off. "One of the most affected members of the British team was [John] Jackett, who took quite an affectionate leave of the Cornish player," Barr wrote. "The incident was doubly regretted as, in addition to being a general favourite, Jackson was, next to Edgar Morgan, the best forward in the team and the most reliable placekick."

Jackson left toward the end of June but by September, he'd got no further than Sydney. The New Zealand union treasurer, Neil Galbraith, who had travelled with the team throughout New Zealand, received a letter from a rugby contact in Sydney. "Have seen Jackson and it appears he wants to return to New Zealand," the letter said. "He offered to hand over his ticket to London in consideration of a ticket to Wellington." A deal was struck, Jackson cancelled his homeward passage and boarded a ship for Wellington. The letter to Galbraith and Jackson arrived in Wellington on the same ship.

The unusual tale of Jackson didn't end there. His banishment from the tour cost him a silver medal at the Olympic Games. A month after he'd returned to Wellington, Australia beat Great Britain 32–3 in the final (and only match) of the Olympic rugby tournament at White City Stadium in London. The British team was the Cornish team that earlier that year had beaten Durham 17–3 to win the English county championship and Jackson had been a key figure in the Cornish team. It was decided shortly before the Olympics that Britain would be represented in the rugby by the champion Cornish team. Two of his Ango-Welsh teammates, Jackett and "Maffer" Davey, both became silver medallists.

And even that's not the end of the Jackson tale. Banned from rugby, he turned to league and played for New Zealand against England in 1910. He married in New Zealand and among the couple's children were Everard Jackson, who played six tests for the All Blacks between 1936 and 1938, Sidney Jackson, who played for Hawke's Bay and New Zealand Maori, and Tutu Wirepa, who played for East Coast and New Zealand Maori. Among his grandchildren were nationally known figures Moana Jackson and Syd Jackson.

Top left: Fred Jackson.

Above: *The Sketcher* magazine's souvenir of the 1908 tour. The captain, Arthur Harding, is pictured on the cover.

SKETCHES OF THREE MEMBERS OF THE ANGLO-WELSH TEAM

JACKETT'S SENSATIONAL POT AT GOAL

Capt. Harding's "Winning" Smile

PONTY JONES THE WELSH GREYHOUND

Newspaper photography was in its infancy in New Zealand in 1908 so sketches of leading players were common.

Harnett had said quite baldly that he wanted Rhodes scholars. He didn't get any of them but he did have 20 who had been educated at public schools, six at universities and four from Guy's Hospital. Among the latter was McEvedy, the New Zealander who had also been on the 1904 tour and who later returned to New Zealand to work and became president of the New Zealand union.

The moral cleansing aspects of the tour took a bit of a hit when the team was heading for Wellington for the second test and Harnett received a cable from the RFU in London telling him that one of his star forwards, Fred Jackson, had been suspended for professionalism and to send him straight home. "Forthwith" was the word used and forthwith he went. Jackson had played in six of the matches to that point, including the first test in which he'd converted the only Anglo-Welsh try.

With or without Jackson, a big Cornish forward of a build that would be described as rangy, the Anglo-Welsh were not of the first rank as rugby players. They lost to Wellington and Otago before the first test, to Canterbury before the second and to Taranaki and Auckland before the third. Along the way, they'd beaten Wairarapa-Bush (then a combined side for the purposes of just this match), Southland, South Canterbury, West Coast-Buller, Marlborough-Nelson, Hawke's Bay, Poverty Bay, Manawatu-Horowhenua and Wanganui.

The All Blacks, led by Stead, gave the Anglo-Welsh a good old-fashioned hiding in the first test in Dunedin, winning 32–5 and scoring seven tries to one. It was an experienced All Black pack backed up by Fred Roberts, Stead and Jimmy Hunter, the inside back combination that had played and dominated most of the main matches on the Originals' tour. Such was the confidence gained from this match the selectors made eight changes for the second test, producing almost a New Zealand B team for the game in Wellington, though they did bring back the redoubtable Billy Wallace at fullback for his last match. The second test, played in wind and rain and on a boggy surface, was drawn 3–3. Things reverted to normal for the third test played at Potter's Park (where Alexandra Park now is) in Auckland: back came the stars, including another Original, Frank Glasgow, and out went the Anglo-Welsh, 29–0.

The British determination to enjoy themselves could have cost them in the third test. They'd been in Rotorua for several days before the match where they apparently had a grand old time, including playing a hastily arranged match against a Maori team.

The Anglo-Welsh were patently not fit enough to play rugby against teams as dedicated and as committed as the All Blacks, or the provinces for that matter. This was acknowledged by Harding. "We could not help noticing the fine state of fitness in which every man appeared to take the field," Harding wrote of the New Zealanders. "Teams in New Zealand are in much better training than at Home [his capital] and . . . it is quite evident much more attention is given to preparation than in the Old Country, where a man practises twice a week only and such a thing as getting a side to live together for a week prior to a match — no matter of what importance — is

absolutely out of the question and unheard of, and would not be tolerated by the governing bodies."

Stead, who made it plain he did not get on with Harding ("My only misgiving was at the appointment of A.F. Harding as captain"), thought the Anglo-Welsh players individually were as good as the All Blacks, though they admitted to less keenness and "should also have admitted to less training".

"This was an outstanding feature of their tour which cannot be pardoned," Stead wrote, "and if conditions in the Old Country do not permit of so much time being devoted to this pastime as pertains in New Zealand, there is no reason while on tour they could not have been 'unorthodox' and made their physical fitness their first thought."

Then, as later, Harnett, Harding and others remarked on the state of the New Zealand game, especially criticising the wing forward even though the Anglo-Welsh adopted the rover position. They were also at first amused and then annoyed at the New Zealand habit of replacing injured players and leaving the field at halftime. Neither practice was sanctioned by the RFU and neither should be allowed to happen. Harnett also felt that New Zealand rugby had "a tendency to roughness".

Cry of '08

The English and Welsh players on board ship on their way to New Zealand in 1908 sat down one day and tried to work out how to play the New Zealanders at their own game.

They knew from experience of the Originals tour that the All Blacks rendered a haka before most, but not all matches. The Welsh reminded their English colleagues how when the All Blacks did the haka before the test in Cardiff, the Welsh team responded by singing their national song, "Land of My Fathers" — thereby beginning another rugby tradition.

So the Anglo-Welsh got to thinking and put pen to paper and came up with their own war cry and practised it assiduously on board ship, trying to make it as stirring as possible.

The words, at least, reflected the players' origins if not their aptitude for songwriting:

Rule, Britannia, Cymru am byth
Rule, Britannia, Cymru am byth
Rule, Britannia, Cymru am byth
Hip! Hip! Hip! Hoorah!
Hip! Hip! Hip! Hoorah!
Hip! Hip! Hip! Hoorah!

1930
Winging Forward

The Lions team of 1930 was the first of the "modern" tours, however misplaced that adjective may be more than 70 years after the event.

The British team was managed by a man who was to become infamously influential in New Zealand rugby, James Baxter, and was the first to New Zealand to be chosen by the combined British and Irish unions. It was also the first combined British team to make a long tour of New Zealand — 21 matches — and to play four tests against the All Blacks, the norm until touring patterns changed again in the 1990s. No one then or later seemed to question the playing of four tests, despite the potential for a squared series. The number was arrived at by the application of the sometimes peculiar British rugby logic. Each of the "home" countries and France played four tests each year in the Five Nations, which was styled officially and grandly as The International Rugby Championship, and since each country played four tests in that, then so it would be four on tours.

The 1930 team lost the series 3–1 to the All Blacks but the tour had a profound impact on New Zealand rugby which had, partly through geographic isolation and partly through innovative thinking, developed its own unique game. Central to this was the position of the wing forward, or rover, a sort of extra halfback who stood off the side of the 2-3-2 diamond-shaped scrum formation and did his best, and sometimes worst, to disrupt either their opponents' possession or their opponents' chances of harassing their own orthodox halfback. There was nothing new in this in 1930; quite the reverse. The wing forward had been castigated by various British rugby notables, and some critics less notable, ever since the position was first widely

The 1930 British team. Back row: A. Novis, T. Knowles, D. Kendrew, I. Jones, J. Reeve, G. Beamish, H. Jones. Second row: P. Murray, S. Martindale, C. Aarvold, W. Welsh, J. Hodgson, B. Black, M. Dunne, H. Wilkinson. Third row: H. O'Neill, H. Rew, W. Sobey, F. Prentice (captain), J. Baxter (manager), J. Farrell, H. Bowcott, D. Parker, R. Jennings. In front: T. Jones-Davies, G. Bonner, J. Morley, R. Spong, J. Bassett, H. Poole.

observed in Britain on the Originals' tour in 1905–06. Some British teams, especially in Wales, adopted the tried and true if-you-can't-beat-'em-join-'em principle and played wing forwards themselves under the name of rovers, but the criticism continued when the Invincible All Blacks laid low all before them in Britain, Ireland and France in 1924–25.

The wing forward and the five-eighths formation in the backs were distinctly New Zealand contributions to the game developed in the late 19th century by deep thinkers such as Tom Ellison, the first official New Zealand captain, Jimmy Duncan, the All Blacks' original coach, and others. The aim, to put it simply, was to overcome a forward clutter to ensure the ball moved quickly and cleanly to the backs so that more tries would be scored. These were not the only New Zealand departures from what was held to be the proper way of doing things in Britain. Laws at the time were framed by the English union and the International Rugby Board had been set up in 1886 largely as a final court of arbitration in the case of disputes about rulings or referees' interpretations.

British Rugby Football Tour
New Zealand.
1930.

Well Collared by
VAN HEUSEN

A pictorial souvenir of the All Blacks' 1930 series win. Though pictured in black, they wore white.

The English union, like the Royal and Ancient Club in golf and the MCC in cricket, had set itself up as the lawmaker, though by 1930 it had ceded that role to the IRB. New Zealand and New South Wales though applied some variations of their own making, again with the aim of making rugby a more pleasing spectacle to people who actually paid good money to watch it. This was anathema in Britain, where the game and players' enjoyment was thought to be uppermost and entertainment was far from their minds. Among the variations applied in New Zealand and New South Wales were that players were not allowed to kick the ball directly into touch from outside the 25-yard line, that throw-ins from touch must travel at least five yards, that injured players could be replaced and that a fair catch — a mark — could be claimed even

if the player's feet weren't firmly planted on mother earth. Each of these eminently sensible provisions of course are now enshrined in rugby's laws. But they weren't then and the British were not keen on them. New Zealand then — like Australia, South Africa and France — was not a member of the IRB but dearly wanted to be and had lobbied strongly for a seat at the international table during the Invincibles' tour, all to no avail. The New Zealand chairman at the time, Stan Dean, argued that if not membership of the IRB, at least there should be an "Imperial Advisory Board" on which New Zealand surely should be represented. The year before the British tour of 1930, the IRB passed a resolution that read: "As a condition precedent to the consideration of the creation of a consultative body under the supreme control of this board, all dominion unions should agree to adopt the laws of the game as framed by the international board." In other words, the price of having a say is agreeing with what we do.

A copy of this resolution found its way to New Zealand and in November 1929, six months before the British tour, the secretary of the New Zealand union, Alf Neilsen, copied it to all provincial unions with his added comments: "This is a matter of extreme importance and before replying to the [English] Rugby Union, I am instructed to ask your Union to give the resolution careful consideration, and to forward, as soon as possible, an opinion as to whether the New Zealand union should accept the conditions contained in the resolution, which course of action is recommended by the English union." Some provincial unions were clearly not happy about capitulating to their far-off masters and dropping the New Zealand variations to the laws because it became the hot topic at the New Zealand union's annual meeting in 1930. Dean moved "that in New Zealand all games in future be played under the rules of the international board" and this led to a debate that caused the meeting to carry on into the night. Eventually an amendment suggested by another member of the New Zealand union management committee, Edgar Wyllie, was agreed. It carried a proviso that having a say in framing the laws was a prerequisite, so the motion then read: "That in New Zealand all games in future be played under the rules of the international board if and when we are given satisfactory representation in the framing of such rules."

That was carried so the kick-into-touch law and other local variations were kicked into touch, for 1930 anyway. But that still left the vexed question of the wing forward because the august lawmakers in

England, despite protests for going-on 30 years, had done nothing about it. The laws said only that the game is played "by not more than fifteen players on each side" and New Zealand chose to interpret that as meaning it could arrange its players how it saw fit, providing there were only 15. There was an offside law which, as it affected the wing forward, said players not in a scrum had to be behind the ball.

Now enters the infamous James Baxter, or "Bim" to his friends, of whom he did not have a huge number in New Zealand. Baxter was an archetypal pillar of the English rugby establishment. He'd played for England in the forwards in 1900, he'd won a bronze medal in yachting at the Olympic Games in 1908, he'd refereed six tests, he was an England selector, he'd managed a British team in Argentina in 1927 and was president of the English union in 1926–27.

Journalist Gordon McLean, reviewing the tour for the Auckland *Sun*, said of him: "As a manager, Mr Baxter had a great number of good points, and several bad ones."

McLean didn't elaborate whether speaking his mind was one of Baxter's good or bad points.

The team's first game in New Zealand was against Wanganui which, as with most teams, fielded a wing forward. This was more than Baxter could bear. At the after-match function, an occasion when speeches are usually perfunctory platitudes, Baxter launched forth: "I watched this game today very carefully and I know some gentlemen sitting at this table are hoping for certain events to come to head. One of the best means of arriving at an understanding is to have one universal law, to play exactly the same game to the best of our ability. I am not going to criticise tonight, but there is one thing I dislike. That is your wing forward play. I am sure the gentleman who had the misfortune to play there, if he looked into his own heart, did not like it either. I won't say he is on the border line;

1930 British manager James Baxter.

Defying the Colour-code

To say the New Zealand union was miffed when its members realised the 1930 British team had dark-blue playing jerseys would be something of an understatement. The implication was clear: against New Zealand's black, someone would have to give way.

When the colour clash was discussed, New Zealand union officials were not happy. The union president, George Adams, said the All Blacks having to change would be a disaster.

One of the committeemen, Henry Leith, who'd managed the All Blacks in Australia in 1926 and who was also a first-class referee, said it would be a tragedy.

The British manager, James Baxter, was unmoved. When the team first arrived and it was pointed out to him that the dark blue of Britain would be barely distinguishable from the black of New Zealand, he replied the dark blue was Britain's traditional colour.

It was a disingenuous interpretation of tradition. The British team in South Africa in 1924 had worn dark blue, it is true, and so had a team in Argentina in 1927, but that was the extent of the tradition. The first two British teams in New Zealand, in 1888 and 1904, had worn red, white and blue stripes, and the 1908 team had worn broad red and white stripes.

New Zealand had twice toured Britain, in 1905–06 and 1924–25, and had gained their nickname of the "All Blacks" from the first tour, so no British rugby official should have been in any doubt about what the New Zealand colours were.

In the weeks leading up to the first test, the New Zealand union chairman, Stan Dean, and Baxter had several conversations about a number of contentious issues, including the jersey. Dean told him New Zealand wouldn't change and Baxter was equally adamant. Then both changed their minds. Dean said New Zealand reluctantly agreed to play in white but by this time Baxter had also offered to play in white.

Baxter trotted off to a meeting of the New Zealand union management committee and there showed them the blue jersey with its crest of three golden lions "passant guardant", heraldic-speak for walking.

After the meeting, Dean announced the union was grateful for Baxter's offer but that New Zealand had no option but to change its colours.

In each of the four tests, the All Blacks — labelled the "All Whites" in some reports — wore white jerseys with the silver fern on a black shield background, black shorts and the normal black socks with two white hoops.

They turned to white again 45 years later when Scotland first toured New Zealand in 1975, and have played in white on each of Scotland's subsequent tours, as well as matches against Scotland in the World Cups in 1987 and 1995.

Britain took the hint though and when they next toured New Zealand in 1950 they had the now-familiar scarlet jerseys.

The Irish members of the team in 1930 had their own problems with the British colours. The blue of the jersey represented Scotland, they felt, the red socks with white turnovers acknowledged Wales and the white shorts and the white of the socks were for England. So where, they wondered, was the green for Ireland. With big lock George Beamish leading the charge, they decided to add a green flash to the socks, similar to the type worn by Scots when in Highland dress. The theory was fine but it didn't work in practice because the pieces of green material tucked in under the tops of the socks didn't stay there long once action was under way in a game. The point was made though and thus was born the modern Lions sock with its green turnover.

he is over it and must be discouraged. He causes irritation to both sets of forwards. I am not speaking of the man playing in that position today, but of a man playing in that position. It is contrary to the spirit of rugby football."

Baxter went further after the next match, against Taranaki, and used the most inflammatory word in sport, "cheat".

Baxter's forthrightness seems not to have been matched by logic. It's not so much a position on the rugby field per se that can be accused of cheating, but the player who is in that position at any given time. If a wing forward — a position that was not outlawed — obeyed all other laws of the game, especially the offside rules, and if a referee did not penalise that player, was it logic or emotion that deemed him to be a cheat? Geoff Alley, an All Black in the late 1920s, who saw each of the 1930 games and who wrote a book about the tour, said Baxter's accusation was akin to saying, "This is a pig and it is brown — therefore all pigs are brown."

All Black captain Cliff Porter.

The controversy bubbled away for the rest of the tour, most notably in the Wellington game and the test in Wellington when the New Zealand captain, wing forward Cliff Porter, was vilified. It also brought counter-accusations of British cheating, most notably by one of the dominant figures of the New Zealand game at that time, Ted McKenzie, a New Zealand union management committee member and an All Black selector.

The end result was that back in Britain in 1931, the International Rugby Board — on which Baxter was one of the four England delegates — outlawed the New Zealand 2-3-2 scrum by decreeing that a front row must comprise three players and effectively that put paid to the wing forward. It meant that New Zealand rugby had to rethink its forward game and that took the best part of 20 years.

British captain Doug Prentice.

The wing forward wasn't all that got up Baxter's nose. At halftime in the Wanganui match, the local players trooped off as was their custom for a few minutes' rest, perhaps a cup of tea and a smoke, in their dressing room. The British players, resplendent in their white shorts the size of Bombay bloomers and with hands in pockets, stayed on the field, as was their custom during what they called "lemon time". Baxter felt compelled to point out that international laws required players to stay on the field and on this occasion, he had the majesty of the law on his side. Law 10 stated plainly: "No player should leave the ground at halftime without the permission of the referee."

Perversely, Baxter's fulminating ways probably did New Zealand rugby a favour. It was evident that for the international game to be taken seriously, one of its most proficient countries, New Zealand, needed to be on the international body and, equally, all countries, including New Zealand, needed to play to the same laws. The wing forward's days were probably numbered anyway because for all the success the position had brought New Zealand rugby, there were also New Zealand critics, most notably referees. The All Black dominance before World War I and also in the mid-1920s when the Invincibles met British rugby at a low ebb, was no longer as pronounced: they had struggled to draw the series with South Africa in 1928 and had been beaten by the re-emerged Australians in 1929. A rethink and a fresh approach was probably what New Zealand rugby needed. It is certainly what it got.

New Zealand rugby officials were conscious when the British team arrived that the state of the game was not in as healthy a position as they would have liked.

There were concerns that some of the leading All Blacks were getting on a bit and there were a few signs that players of such experience and brilliance as Bert Cooke, Mark Nicholls, George Nepia and Cliff Porter could be replaced with players of similar calibre. There were concerns too that the New Zealand 2-3-2 scrum formation might not be adequate against the British formation of 3-2-3, even though it was eight against seven.

The British had problems of their own. The organisers, the Four Home Unions Tours Committee, had sent letters to 90 players asking about their availability before finding 30 who could tour. The team that came to New Zealand in 1930 was without several players who had been regarded as automatic choices. Among them was an Irish wing of high repute, George Stephenson, who then had the world record for the most test matches, and the England captain of 1924, Wavell Wakefield, who had what was described as a deep-seated groin injury and stayed at home. Wakefield had been named as captain when the British squad was originally named in March of 1930. The tour may have developed along different lines had he toured and the British team — Baxter notwithstanding — may not have been as popular as it was. As Gordon McLean wrote in the *Sun*, "From remarks made by several members of the team during the tour, it is doubtful if the loss of Wakefield was a serious one. Not only was he said to be past his best playing days, but also he was considered to be something of a martinet, and a man who would not have been conspicuously tactful in his dealings either with the team or with New Zealanders."

Two other players, Ireland centre Morgan Crowe and England loose forward Peter Howard, had also been named in the original party but subsequently withdrew.

One player who surely was missed, but who was in New Zealand, was Wilf Sobey, the England halfback who had formed a canny and productive understanding with his first five-eighth, Roger Spong. The pair combined at school, for their club and for their country. But Sobey badly injured a knee in the opening game against Wanganui and never played in New Zealand again. Modern sports medicine specialists

RUGBY FOOTBALL UNION.

TWICKENHAM.

18 APR. 1929

Tour of a Rugby Union British Team to New Zealand and Australia in 1930.

Dear Sir

You have been provisionally selected to take part in the above Tour. The final selection will not, however, be made until two or three months before the Team sails.

The Team will leave England about the second week in April, 1930, and arrive back about the second week in October. Each player should be in possession of about £50 to £75 for incidental expenses.

We hope that the team eventually chosen will represent the full playing strength of the Home Unions, in order that we may give New Zealand and Australia a true idea of our standard of play, and we hope you will make every effort to take part in the Tour.

Will you please inform the Secretary of the Rugby Football Union, Twickenham, whether you would be able to take part in the Tour.

Yours faithfully

SF. Cooper

The letter every British player may have wanted — but some had to send their regrets.

would be horrified by the cavalier treatment originally given to Sobey. The British fullback, George Bonner, had left the field to have a cut under an eye attended to and, since there were no replacements and the British didn't want to be two short, poor Sobey had to hobble around in the backs until Bonner could regain the field, thus aggravating an already serious injury. It cost the British one of their most gifted players and, since they struggled at halfback for the rest of the tour, could conceivably have cost them more than that.

While the British played their opening matches, proving to be immensely popular both on and off the field, the New Zealand selection panel of six (three from each island) oversaw a series of trial matches upon which, some critics believed, they placed too great a reliance. Players who for whatever reason

Above: All Blacks Bert Cooke and George Nepia have their halftime oranges with referee Sam Hollander.

Below: Carisbrook during the first test. The wintry conditions may have been the reason for so few non-paying spectators on the railway line.

couldn't play in one of the trials were not considered for the final selection and any player whose previous high reputation was blemished in the trials was cast aside. The Canterbury halfback, Bill Dalley, evidently had one poor trial and that was the end of him, despite his previous claims to be among the best in New Zealand. "The problem of selecting 15 of the best of New Zealand's players is too tough a one to be solved by the somewhat hurried method of relying on three trial games," the 1928 All Black, Geoff Alley, remarked.

The British won their first four games easily, lost the next two to Wellington and Canterbury, but then won the last two before the first test, including a 33–9 spanking of Otago. This so alarmed the New Zealand selectors that they made it publicly known they hoped for wet weather in Dunedin for the first test in order to slow the British, especially their backs, down. They got their wish. It rained, sleeted and snowed in Dunedin on the morning of the match and after the Carisbrook gates opened, spectators endured what was described as one of the heaviest snowstorms experienced in Dunedin for some years. It was exactly the weather the New Zealand

selectors had wanted. But still the All Blacks lost — the first test victory by a British team in New Zealand. A glance at the final score, 6–3, and with knowledge of the weather, any reasonable reader would assume that one side kicked two penalties and the other, one, in a dour forward battle, and that the most the backs got up to was rubbing their hands together to keep warm. Such was not the case. The three scoring movements were all tries, tries moreover scored by wings using the speed which all wings are supposed to have. The first was set up by the brilliance of Spong, who kicked diagonally for his wing, Jim Reeve. Both he and the All Black wing, George Hart, went for the ball, but Reeve got it and ran round Hart for the try. Hart, who won the national 100 yards title in 1931, got his own back early in the second half when he scored from what was described as a sweeping threequarter move and the score stood at 3–3 until just minutes from the end. Then the British struck again. Their flanker Ivor Jones broke from a melee and took off upfield with wing Jack Morley in support and only George Nepia to beat. Nepia in 1924 was said to mesmerise his opponents and time and again he turned

opponents back. But Jones committed Nepia to the tackle and passed to Morley and the little Welsh wing hared for the corner with Cooke making up ground on him, but too little, too late. It was a remarkable win for the British in remarkable conditions and a sobering experience for the All Blacks.

The British captain, Doug Prentice, had watched proceedings from the stand. Not for the first time, and not for the last, the captain couldn't justify a place in a British test team. He'd been told shortly before the team left Southampton by ship for New Zealand that he was to lead the team, knowing that Wakefield would have been captain had he been available. On the ship, Baxter and senior players devised their tour selection method, which constituted a selection committee comprising Baxter, Prentice and one representative from each country, except Scotland who had only one player anyway, Bill Welsh from Hawick. Also on the ship, with form unseen, the teams for the main matches were pencilled in. The selection meetings bent toward high farce as the tour developed. "The truth was," Gordon McLean wrote, "that the test sides were, with one or

British fullback Jack Bassett attempts to evade All Black wing Don Oliver during the first test. At left is British wing Jim Reeve.

Odd Man Out

Spot the odd one out. Four tests between Britain and New Zealand in 1930 but five programmes. The third in the line-up, advertising the second test in Christchurch, was a pirate programme, sold outside the ground in competition with the official version, second from the left. Pirate programmes were common in the 1920s and 1930s and once forced the All Blacks to play with letters rather than numbers on their backs — the letters being printed in the official programme.

Beamish — Hero of Crete

It's tempting to believe that even in the supreme moments of danger during the withdrawal and evacuation of Allied troops from Crete in May 1941, some rugby might have been discussed.

The overall commander of Allied forces on the island was Bernard Freyberg, temporarily away from his prime role of general officer commanding the New Zealand division. By his side constantly was his aide-de-camp, Jack Griffiths, a 30-match All Black between 1934 and 1938.

And with the two of them during the final days on Crete, when the ill-equipped Allied troops fought rearguard actions and scanned the sea and skies for the transport that would pluck them away to safety, was a big, jovial Irishman, George Beamish, who also knew a thing or two about rugby.

Beamish had been one of the dominant players on the 1930 British tour. The biggest man in the forwards at more than 16 stone,

he had an extroverted personality to match his bulk. He was a key man on the field and a popular one off it. He was described as an enormous forward of fabulous might, whose party trick was to bend copper coins between thumb and index finger of one hand. When the midweek players felt disaffected and formed their Rank and File Society, it was Beamish who held the squad together and was rewarded with honorary membership of the society (his test-playing status otherwise disqualifying him).

Beamish, at the time of the tour, was a flight-lieutenant in the Royal Air Force and nine years later, at the start of World War II, he was a squadron leader in the role of senior operations officer at the RAF headquarters in Palestine. By 1940, with a promotion to wing commander, he was attached to the air staff headquarters in Cairo and in April 1941, he was made senior air officer on Crete. Beamish's role was to oversee the reception of squadrons after the withdrawal and evacuation from Greece. With the German airborne invasion of Crete in May 1941, Beamish found himself conducting the air defence of the island under the command of Freyberg.

Beamish also had another role, one that was to remain secret for another 50 years. He was the contact point on Crete

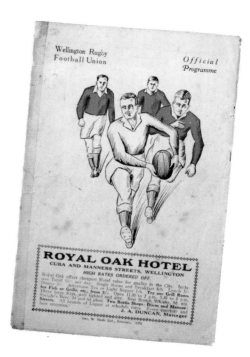

for information culled from intercepts and decoding of German signals. Originally named Boniface after an English missionary monk, the code-breaking later became better known as ULTRA. German wireless intercepts were transmitted to Bletchley Park in Buckinghamshire, the nerve-centre of British cypher intelligence, and the decoded messages were then sent on to Beamish on Crete. It was his role to tell Freyberg what the Germans were planning and in what strength, and Freyberg then had to devise countermeasures without the Germans realising their codes had been broken.

German air superiority was one of the main reasons for the fall of Crete and after the destruction of the majority of the Allied aircraft on the ground, Freyberg had to tell Beamish to send what aircraft were left to Egypt. According to Freyberg's son Paul, Freyberg told Beamish it would be too painful to see the last aircraft and their gallant young pilots shot down.

When the battle for Crete was lost, troops withdrew as best they could across mountainous passes to the southern side of the island from where an evacuation was planned. Among the last to make the hazardous journey was the Freyberg staff, which included Beamish. For four nights, British ships and flying boats took off thousands of Allied troops and while the evacuation proceeded, Freyberg and his staff sheltered for the final three days in a cave overlooking the embarkation point.

Freyberg intended to stay until the last but he received a direct order from the commander-in-chief of all Allied forces in the Middle East, Archibald Wavell: "You will return to Egypt first opportunity."

Freyberg and his staff, including Beamish, left by flying boat on the night of 30 May, arriving in Alexandria in Egypt at 3.30 in the morning.

A year later, Beamish was promoted to acting air commodore, the first officer to be trained by the RAF (that is, with no previous service in the army or navy) to attain air rank. His distinguished career continued until the mid-1950s and he retired with the rank of air marshal. He was knighted in 1955.

Beamish was one of three members of the 1930 British team to gain knighthoods. Carl Aarvold, who captained the British in three of the four tests against the All Blacks, was knighted in 1968 for his services to the judiciary and Douglas Kendrew, a prop, was a regular army officer who was knighted in 1963 and was governor of Western Australia.

two exceptions, predetermined either when the team left England or before it had long been on the boat." The cumbersome selection process was exacerbated when, as McLean reported, as many as half a dozen other players joined the meetings from time to time. It reflected poorly on Baxter, who was so assertive in other respects. "He was an autocrat who, despite the numbers present at committee meetings, usually dominated the scene," McLean wrote. "And even though he was perfectly unprejudiced in his judgments

and decisions, it was then the more unfortunate that a small coterie seemed consistently to enjoy the best things of the tour."

The "them and us" feeling thus created among the players, the midweekers and the Saturday players, was always a potential problem in the days of long tours. In 1930, those not in favour formed themselves, with some jocularity but with an underlying feeling of bitterness, into what they called the Rank and File Society. An England forward, Sam Martindale, was elected president and when the tour party was in Gisborne, they met and designed their own tie which had red raspberries, significantly enough, on a black background. Perhaps fortunately for the spirit of the tour, no tie manufacturer could produce them in the time left on the tour. The Rank and File's biggest official snub came after the first test at the time of games against Southland and South Canterbury. The whole British party had been invited for a couple of days to Mt Cook and Baxter decided there was no time for everyone to go, but that those players not required for the matches in Invercargill or Timaru could go on separate trips. As a result, eight didn't go at all because they played in both matches and they were the core of the Rank and File.

After the Australian test, which followed the New Zealand tour, one of the players wrote to a friend in Auckland: "Once again the R and F were absolutely ignored in favour of the select ones . . . unfortunately,

Left: The finely printed menu for the (doubtless) fine and formal test dinner in Christchurch.

Below: All Black prop "Beau" Cottrell, his sleeves rolled up, gets a kick away during the second test in Christchurch despite the pending attention of the British team's South African lock, Brian Black.

a very dissatisfied spirit has crept into the team, but we all see the reason for it. Personally, I think the sooner the tour is over now, the better it will be for all."

Prentice was chosen for the second test, which followed the Timaru match. It was probably just as well because it would have been even more of a blow to the team's morale if its overall captain had been welcomed into the Rank and File. Prentice replaced a loose forward, John Hodgson, who, in Dunedin, had achieved the unusual distinction of being capped for Britain before he had played for his country, England. The changes in the New Zealand team were born of desperation. A loss in Christchurch would have meant the series couldn't have been won and that would have been almost too much for New Zealanders to bear. Out went halfback Jimmy Mill and in came Merv Corner, one of the smallest to play for New Zealand (he stood just 1.65 m and weighed 60 kg); out also went five-eighth Herb Lilburne, who the year before had become New Zealand's youngest test captain, and in came the veteran Mark Nicholls. It was Nicholls who put New Zealand on the board first with a goal from a mark. In those days, marks could be claimed anywhere on the field and Nicholls had taken a fair catch of a clearing kick just outside the British twenty-five. Such things were gifts to Nicholls and the dropkicked ball soared between the uprights. (Marks were another source of contention between Baxter and New Zealand. He said marks could only be claimed if the player had both feet on the ground and if the player jabbed a heel into the ground at the same time as shouting "mark". The New Zealand view was that the ball had only to be caught — even if the player was in the air — and the cry uttered).

Carl Aarvold, who had captained Britain in the first test, scored two tries in the test, marking him out as one of the most outstanding threequarters to visit New Zealand. He gained distinction in other areas too, later becoming one of England's senior circuit judges, being knighted and serving for 19 years as president of the august Lawn Tennis Association. Prentice — the British had more goalkickers in the forwards than in the backs — converted both of Aarvold's tries. New Zealand also

A Social Lot

Rugby is often criticised for being over-regulated and having too many laws, but it also has its unwritten rules. One is that what happens on the field stays on the field. That's why the Lions prop Sandy Carmichael has never said, and will never say, who pummelled his face so badly in the Canterbury match in 1971 that his tour was brought to a painful end. Many people may think they know which Canterbury forward did the damage, but the name of the guilty has never passed Carmichael's lips.

Another of the unwritten rules is that what happens on tour stays on tour. That usually refers to the social side of touring, when a player's nocturnal habits may be common knowledge within a touring group but are never mentioned outside.

Such rules haven't been decided upon in team meetings or laid down by rugby unions. They've just evolved and apply to most touring teams.

The 1930 British team was a social lot. It was the way of the times. Upon selection, each player was required to stump up with £80 to pay for a dinner suit to be worn at all evening meals on board ship, and to pay for incidentals during the tour. The money was held in trust by the manager, "Bim" Baxter, who effectively acted as their banker. The players were also paid three shillings a day but in keeping with the rigid British view of amateurism, Baxter issued chits rather than money. The chits were for drinks or extra food and collected by the hotel, which would then present them to Baxter at the end of a stay and he would hand over the money. For some players, especially from Wales where rugby was less class-based, the provision of £80 was onerous and their clubs helped them find the money. Most players, however, were public school types and had private incomes, or parents on whom to call for that and a bit more besides.

"We were no better and no worse than the young men of today in our behaviour," one of the British team, Harry Bowcott, recalled. "We drank a bit and enjoyed female company but we tended to carouse only after matches. Wives would be chasing us and their husbands would be pleased if we looked after them. There was one woman who followed me all over both islands and I never abused it." There were doubtless husbands who wouldn't have agreed with that remark.

The Lion King

Was there anything the Welsh flanker on the 1930 tour, Ivor Jones, couldn't do? Jones acquired the nickname of "the King" during the tour — a title Barry John inherited in 1971 — and was regarded for years as the finest British player to be seen in New Zealand.

"Jones had in abundance the qualities of intelligence, anticipation and speed and developed into a master of the game's skills," British rugby historian John Griffiths wrote of Jones. "At his peak in New Zealand in 1930, his brilliant intuition created the openings which led to three of the seven British tries scored in the test series."

But it wasn't just his play as a forward that drew attention. The British team's first points in New Zealand came from Jones when he dropkicked a goal against Wanganui, but when halfback Paul Murray broke a collarbone in the second test, Jones played the rest of the game at halfback.

He said his proudest moment though was in the first test in Dunedin when he set up the winning try. With the score at 3–3 and the All Blacks on attack, Jones intercepted a pass from Jimmy Mill to Herb Lilburne and sprinted downfield. He committed George Nepia to the tackle and unloaded to wing Jack Morley, who scored to give the British a surprise, but merited, win.

As with several of the British forwards, Jones was an efficient goalkicker and on the Australian leg of the tour he kicked 10 conversions and two penalties.

He began his rugby life in west Wales as a fullback but when Llanelli signed him as a 20-year-old in 1922, he moved into the loose forwards. He made his debut for Wales in 1924 and though he played 16 times between then and 1930, he was not always top of the selectors' list. He was chosen for the British tour of South Africa in 1924 but had to withdraw and subsequently lost his position in the Welsh team, which cost him the game against the Invincible All Blacks.

Welsh selectors have been noted for their erratic ways and they were at their most erratic when they failed to choose him after 1930, despite the obvious form and class he showed in New

Ivor Jones

Zealand. Jones continued to play for Llanelli for five more years, which included a narrow loss to the All Blacks of 1935–36.

He later served on the International Rugby Board and was the Welsh president when Wales toured New Zealand for the first time in 1969.

His stint at halfback in the second test in New Zealand caused a sour note between the New Zealand union and the British manager, James Baxter. Wilf Sobey, Britain's No. 1 halfback, had been invalided out of the tour after the first game and Murray, who'd played in various back positions for Ireland and who was chosen for Britain as a centre, took over. This was bad luck for the other chosen halfback, Welshman Howard Poole, who nevertheless played in the third test while Murray recovered from his broken collarbone.

Baxter wanted to seek a replacement from either Britain or from India, where apparently there were a couple of suitable candidates working for the British Government. Chairman Stan Dean initially said the New Zealand union wouldn't pay, then changed his mind and said it would meet half the costs, then changed his mind again and said it would pay the lot. By that time, however, Baxter had decided against seeking a replacement, saying by the time he arrived by ship it would be too late. According to Gordon McLean in the *Sun*, "Baxter gave the British players his full authority to make it known that the New Zealand union's attitude was the only reason why another halfback was not coming."

The versatile Murray, incidentally, was a doctor, a handy person to have on tour in the days when no medical personnel accompanied teams. His ministering to his teammates, as well as to himself, prompted this limerick in the weekly magazine, *Free Lance*:

A doctor from Ulster is Murray
Who saved his team oceans of worry.
With splints and with pills
He first doctored their ills
And then patched himself up in a hurry.

1930 — Winging Forward

The Governor-General, Lord Bledisloe, is introduced to British fullback Jack Bassett by the non-playing captain, Doug Prentice. Scottish flanker Bill Welsh is next in line and players on Bassett's left are Harry Bowcott, Jim Farrell and Brian Black.

scored two tries, one to Hart and one to the other wing, Don Oliver, and Nicholls converted both of them. The difference in scoring, in the end, was Nicholls' goal from a mark but the significant difference of the match was that the New Zealand pack was better organised than the British, even given there were eight of them against seven New Zealanders. Geoff Alley in his tour book didn't think much of the British forwards: ". . . the British as a rule do not pay the same rigorous attention to scientific hooking as do New Zealand, South African and New South Wales sides. They often pile in and around the ball in a manner somewhat reminiscent of the days when a couple of hundred Rugby schoolboys partook of a game together as in *Tom Brown's Schooldays*."

A curiosity of test rugby as it used to be was a feature of the third test in Auckland. It was the habit of the touring side to provide one of the touch judges, and in the third test the nominated flag waver was none other than the British captain, Doug Prentice. The other touch judge was George Nicholson, one of the Original All Blacks and a test referee. But he was also a New Zealand selector. Any conflict of interest caused by this amalgam of roles would, it was determined, be overcome by honesty and integrity. Shortly after

halftime, Corner ran from the base of a scrum but was caught and engulfed by the British forwards and he was penalised by referee Sam Hollander for holding the ball. The British team's South African flanker, Brian Black — the leading scorer on the tour — kicked for goal. With thousands of pairs of eyes fixed to it, the ball sailed past an upright but whether inside or outside was decided by only two pair. Up went Prentice's flag to indicate it was a goal. But Nicholson's stayed firmly down. Black, a little nonplussed it has to be assumed, turned to Hollander. No goal, he said.

The test was won by New Zealand 15–10, with debutant loose forward Hugh McLean scoring two tries, no doubt to the delight of his two brothers in the Eden Park press box, Gordon, who covered the tour for the *Sun*, and youngster Terry, whose days in the reporting sun were still to come. The test was summed up rather neatly by Terry McLean's future employers, the *New Zealand Herald*: "There were four outstanding features in the match. These were the brilliance of Spong, who was the best back on the field, the magnificent defence of Cooke, which saved the All Blacks at least four tries, the great strategy of Nicholls, and the fine all-round game played by Porter, the New Zealand captain."

Going into the final test in Wellington, the New Zealand public was apprehensive. The All Blacks were a test up with one to play, it was true, but each of the matches had been tight. The New Zealand forwards had control for most of the first three tests and the All Black backs had done enough on defence against the quick and at times brilliant British backs. The concerns about New Zealand that preceded the tour, that the All Blacks were not as dominant as they once were, were still there and it was known that several of the players were retiring after Wellington. Porter, the captain and unofficial coach, took his players to Otaki on the Kapiti coast north of Wellington for some concentrated training (a practice frowned upon by Baxter, who held that international teams should assemble only a day or so before a match, conveniently overlooking that his team had been together for about three months).

Whatever it was that Porter did in Otaki, it worked. The All Blacks' 22–8 win in the final test was the most dominant of them all, with most reports talking about the overwhelming strength of the New Zealand pack and the staleness of the British team which, to the chagrin of the Rank and File, had pretty much played all of the important matches. New Zealand scored four tries to one, conclusive enough, but there was agreement that the try of the match was that scored by the British wing, Tony Novis, who also moonlighted as the team's trainer during the tour. The British forwards had made a dribbling rush but overran the ball so halfback Paul Murray had to quickly get it out to his backs. It found Novis and his speed took him down the touchline and past a despairing diving tackle from Nepia. The conversion by Black put the British within a point of the All Blacks but that was the last British sniff of the game.

Alley summed up both the test and the tour: "Once again the New Zealand forwards have saved the day, by reverting to the type of play so necessary to football salvation. The whirlwind beginning of the British side was in painful contrast to their somewhat lame finish in the final test in Wellington, where their forwards were beaten more decisively than in the other tests."

From halfway through May until halfway through August, the British played 21 matches for 15 wins and six losses — the losses outside of the tests being

Athletic Park in Wellington is packed for the fourth test.

to Wellington, Canterbury and Auckland. They scored 82 tries and in only one match did their backs fail to score, a reasonable indication of where their strength lay. While the better organisation and commitment of the New Zealand forwards, in tests and in provincial games, was one indication of the differences between the teams, there seemed also a contrast in attitude. This was reflected by Baxter in comments he made shortly before the team left for Sydney at the end of the tour. He asked New Zealanders to look after the game — another veiled reference to playing to the British-imposed laws? — and to play it with carefree enthusiasm for the game's sake . . . and not worry about the result which, after all, doesn't matter much. This attitude struck at the heart of the differences between British and New Zealand rugby. For the British, it was a game for the players and was a game to be enjoyed, a game to be played for its own sake. For New Zealanders, rugby was a game to win.

Right: Captains' farewell — Doug Prentice (left) and Cliff Porter say their goodbyes.

Below: Hugh McLean (in headgear) and Walter Batty (No. 9) in the thick of this find-the-ball action in the fourth test in 1930.

1950
A Pride is Born

When the four-engined BOAC Constellation carrying the New Zealand rugby team of 1953-54 taxied to a halt at what was then called London Airport to start the tour, a welcoming party stood waiting on the tarmac.

Among them were newsreel cameramen and radio reporters and no sooner had the team descended the gangway, than the speeches of welcome began. Manager Arthur Marslin and captain Bob Stuart both responded and both said much the same thing.

If their tour of Britain and Ireland, they said, could be regarded as half as successful and half as enjoyable as the tour of New Zealand in 1950 by the British team, they would be very satisfied indeed. It was a measure of the high regard in which the Lions team, managed by an English naval dentist, Ginger Osborne, and captained by an Irish doctor, Karl Mullen, had been held three years before. Most New Zealanders, it seems, would have agreed with the sentiments of Marslin and Stuart.

The Lions — and this was the first tour in which they were known as the Lions although the name wasn't used as frequently as it would be in later years — were an extremely popular side, both on the field and off it. There was none of the bitterness and rancour of the 1930 tour, caused mainly by the outspoken manager, James Baxter, and within the Lions none of the "them and us" divisions of previous or later tours.

Without getting too deeply philosophical or academic about it, the climate of the times unquestionably contributed to the good feelings the tour engendered. Britain and New Zealand, among other countries, had together recently come through a devastating war. Many of the players in 1950, on both sides, had served in the war and some of the New Zealanders had served with British forces. For all the New Zealanders who followed

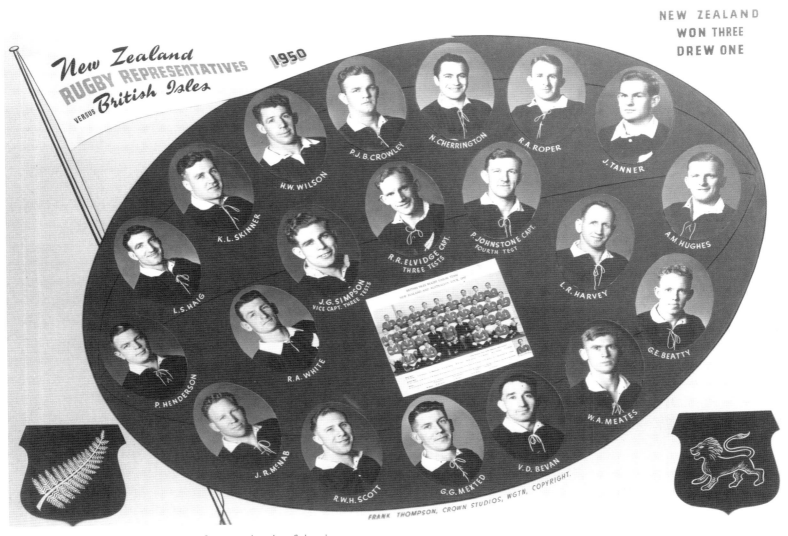

New Zealand
RUGBY REPRESENTATIVES
versus British Isles 1950

NEW ZEALAND
WON THREE
DREW ONE

H.W. WILSON
P.J.B. CROWLEY
N. CHERRINGTON
R.A. ROPER
J. TANNER
K.L. SKINNER
R.R. ELVIDGE CAPT. THREE TESTS
P. JOHNSTONE CAPT. FOURTH TEST
A.M. HUGHES
L.S. HAIG
J.G. SIMPSON VICE CAPT. THREE TESTS
L.R. HARVEY
P. HENDERSON
R.A. WHITE
G.E. BEATTY
W.A. MEATES
J.R. McNAB
R.W.H. SCOTT
G.G. MEXTED
V.D. BEVAN

FRANK THOMPSON, CROWN STUDIOS, WGTN, COPYRIGHT.

A souvenir of the 1950 tour in an often-used style of the times.

the tour, the war was a recent painful memory; in a sense, the tour was a coming together of friends. For the British, the effects of the war were still with them. Wartime rationing in Britain didn't end until 1954 so the Lions went from austerity to what they perceived as a land of plenty. British rugby looked fondly on New Zealand for providing in the northern winter of 1945–46 the army rugby team, the Kiwis, that did so much to reawaken rugby interests in Britain at the end of the war and they did it by playing exciting, entertaining rugby. It was a neat coincidence that the New Zealand governor-general at the time of the Lions tour, Bernard Freyberg, had been the commander of the 2nd New Zealand Expeditionary Force, and the motivating force behind the Kiwis' tour. He made sure he was at many of the Lions' games and

there were a couple of memorable parties at Government House, one a reunion of the Kiwis, during the tour at which the Lions were also present. It was no coincidence that the secretary of the Lions, the man who assisted the manager with the tour organisation, was Ted Savage, who had fulfilled the same role with the Kiwis.

The All Black fullback in 1950, Bob Scott, had been one of the Kiwis and later wrote: "The highest compliment I could pay the tour of New Zealand by the British Isles team of 1950 would be to say that it was the Kiwi tour in reverse . . . No finer pride of Lions has ever assembled. The players were cheerful, gregarious and extraordinarily popular."

The 1950s in New Zealand have been described as the innocent years, when New Zealand sat comfortably

1950 — A Pride is Born

The 1950 British team. Back row: G. Budge, R. MacDonald, J. McCarthy, M. Lane, D. Davies, V. Roberts, M. Thomas, T. Clifford. Second row: D. Smith, G. Norton, J. Nelson, D. Hayward, J. Stephens, E. John, R. Evans, J. McKay, N. Henderson, K. Jones. Sitting: W. Cleaver, P. Kininmonth, B. Williams (vice-captain), L. B. Osborne, K. Mullen (captain), K. Savage (secretary), I. Preece, C. Davies, J. Matthews. In front: A. Black, J. Kyle, W. Willis, G. Rimmer.

in its place as the South Pacific farm for Britain and when New Zealanders were still regarded as British citizens. There was a strong sense that the British and the New Zealanders were kindred spirits, a sense that was even more evident three years later when the Queen made her first tour of New Zealand. The Lions' tour was a football tour that celebrated the game and celebrated the togetherness of both sides playing it.

For all the fellowship, there was apprehension in New Zealand rugby. The British team for the first time comprised only established international players and, rarely, only two leading players, Welsh captain John Gwilliam, and England lock John Matthews, had been unavailable. For the first time, the three services gave their players paid leave for the duration of the tour, universities excused their students and other employers also entered into the spirit of things.

It meant that the party of 30 that arrived in Wellington by ship was almost fully representative of the strength of British rugby. It was representative, too, of recent results in the Five Nations: Ireland had won the championship in 1948 and 1949, the first time they'd won twice in succession, and Wales, shortly before the Lions left for New Zealand, had won the Grand Slam for the first time since 1911. Wales provided the bulk of the party with 13 players (and one more to arrive as a replacement), Ireland had nine, Scotland five and England just three. The Kiwis had seen some of the British team play and New Zealanders generally were well versed in the talent they would see over the next three months: foremost among them was the Irish first five-eighth, Jack Kyle, regarded still as one of the finest of his trade; the Welsh wing, Ken Jones, who had won a sprint silver medal at the Olympic Games in London two years before; the brilliant Welsh centre pairing of Bleddyn Williams and Jack Matthews, the Welsh utility back known as "Billy the Kick" . . . the list went on, though with the forwards, as so often with Lions tours, the more common adjective was "solid" rather than "flair". It was, however, a formidable British team and those New Zealanders who thought deeply as the tour unfolded — foremost among them the selectors, Arthur Marslin, Merv Corner and Tom Morrison — knew the tests were a critical time for New Zealand rugby. For all the success of the post-war Kiwis and for the unchallenged standing of rugby as New Zealand's main sport, the game was not in great heart. The changes made to the laws of the game after the 1930 tour, changes in large part brought about by Baxter, had forced a rethink in New Zealand's forward strategy; the wing forward was gone and so, too, was the old 2-3-2 scrum. The readjustments came during the 1930s when New Zealand tried the English-style 3-2-3 scrum and the South African method of 3-4-1, which later became the universal style. The war intervened to prolong the readjustment process, and in South Africa in 1949 the All Blacks adopted the embarrassing strategy of going to Danie Craven, who was then coaching the Springboks, for advice. The British tour unfolded against a background of the All Blacks losing six tests in a row — four in South Africa and another two by a third-string All Black team in Australia. It was not quite a crisis in New Zealand rugby, and seemed not to evoke the deep passions evident in 1956 after the All Blacks lost the second test to the Springboks, but it was a time for serious thought and preparation.

The promise of the Lions — and the apprehension in New Zealand — was reaffirmed after the first three matches when they scored 80 points and had just 15 scored against them. These were matches against the Seddon Shield sides, it is true, but it was the promise of what could be to come that sent shivers down New Zealand spines. But then the tour changed. The Lions' fourth match was in Dunedin against an Otago team in which every forward had played for New Zealand.

The All Blacks pose after training at Carisbrook before the first 1950 test. Back row: Merv Corner (selector), Hugh Harkness (reserve), Ron Elvidge (captain), B. Russell (reserve), Bob Scott, Roy Roper, "Tiny" White, Peter Johnstone, Lester Harvey, Hec Wilson, Johnny Simpson. Front row: Nau Cherrington, Vince Bevan, Bill Meates, George Beatty, Bill Dickson (reserve), Kevin Skinner, Arthur Hughes, Jack McNab, Tom Morrison (selector).

When Jackie Met Rocky

Even people with the most casual interest in boxing would know that Rocky Marciano retired as the undefeated heavyweight champion of the world. He had 49 professional fights and won 43 of them by knockouts.

Americans, especially, rightly hailed him as The Ultimate Champ. But few Americans would have known that Marciano — then Rocco Marchegiano — served with the American army in Wales for a time in 1943 and while there, he met his match in the ring.

Jack Matthews was then a young medical student and he climbed into the ring at an air-force base in south Wales against the then-unknown Italian-American. The contest went the scheduled three rounds and no winner was declared.

"That's the way it was, boxing just for the fun of it," Matthews recalled. "There were no knock-downs and I was still there at the end of three rounds." Matthews told journalist Peter Jackson: "I didn't know who I'd fought until years later, when it was confirmed that Marciano had been based at St Athan for a brief period. I'd been told before the fight that he was a useful boy who could punch a bit. He was a hard boy all right. I'd have been 14 stone then and he was a shade lighter, and that's about all I can remember."

Marciano presumably remained oblivious to the fact he'd gone three rounds with one of the great Welsh centres — and tacklers.

Rocky Marciano shows his ringcraft and inset, Jack Matthews.

Three of the backs had also, and another two would later. Otago had not been beaten at Carisbrook since 1946, they'd just completed their best Ranfurly Shield reign, and they were the undisputed masters of rucking. The Lions were beaten 23–9 and lost the next match as well, to Southland 11–0, again victims of rucking as it was practised in the south of the South Island.

The belief that the Lions had brilliant backs but average forwards was underlined. New Zealand confidence going into the first test therefore went up a notch. It possibly went up too many notches. The fullback, Bob Scott, one of the best to grace that position, recalled that before the first test some of the All Blacks openly talked to each other about a win by 30 points — such a margin in a test match was practically unheard of in those days. And such a margin wasn't heard of again after that first test either. The Lions and the All Blacks drew 9–9. It was a sobering experience for New Zealand. The British backs were as brilliant as it was expected they would be with Kyle and Jones scoring tries, but the British forwards and especially lock Roy John and flanker Bill McKay were much more competitive than anyone, including the All Blacks, had expected. New Zealand avoided defeat only by a try to their captain, Ron Elvidge, in the last couple of minutes. The warning note sounded in the

The try that gave the All Blacks a draw in the first test. Ron Elvidge levels the scores with minutes to go after evading Bill McKay (left) and Peter Kininmonth.

match itself was echoed in press reports. The *Evening Post* in Wellington was to the point: "New Zealanders by now should realise that the British model of rugby football is something with real substance and not merely an empty term. The 1905 and 1924 tours tended to create a delusion that this country had outstripped the Homeland in efficiently organised attractiveness. The year 1930 created some doubts which the present season has accentuated."

Kyle's try in Dunedin confirmed all that people had heard and read about him. One description of his try ran: "He showed off his talent for running in broken play, bringing the crowd to its feet after counter-attacking from a miskick, slicing through the All Blacks' rearguard, leaving the great Scott for dead with a high-speed swerve and then shrugging off a desperate high tackle to cross the line."

Kyle himself was more matter of fact: "Somebody kicked the ball into my arms. It wasn't from a set piece, it was done at a subconscious level as always. People say you scored this try and that try, but these things happened without you really knowing consciously what you were doing. You don't set off thinking, 'I'm going to beat this guy here then run round here', you just set off and hope something will work."

The "great Scott", All Black fullback Bob, was an ardent admirer of Kyle in a manner that is seldom now seen of current players about their opponents. Kyle had, Scott wrote, the ability to produce memorable rugby when it was most needed. "By ordinary standards, he was incalculable. He was an instinctive rather than a manufactured player and reacted to situations a flashing fraction of time ahead of anyone else . . . I think we treasured Kyle as an embodiment of all that was good in the Lions team. He was a man of the highest integrity, modest, religious, what I should call, however odd it may sound in rugby, a true Christian."

The All Black selectors could have panicked after Dunedin, but they didn't. They'd always intended to choose New Zealand's answer to Ken Jones, Peter Henderson, in the first test but he'd been injured and they brought him back for the second. "Sammy"

Henderson wasn't quite an Olympic sprinter in Jones's class, but he had speed, as his sprinting in the Empire Games in Auckland earlier in 1950 had proven, and he had rugby nous as his matches on the South African tour the year before had shown. The only other change to the All Blacks was the introduction at first five-eighth of Laurie Haig, whose brother Jimmy had played at halfback in 1946.

Top: Tour itineraries and scorecards were often produced by cigarette companies.

Above: The style of a champion — Jack Kyle.

Lions halfback Angus Black attacks in the first test. One of the All Blacks of the series, Pat Crowley, is at left. The other Lions are Roy John, Karl Mullen (obscured) and John Robins.

The forwards, whose confidence had been rocked in Dunedin, were not changed. The All Blacks in the second test in Christchurch were a much more determined and less cocky side than they had been in Dunedin. They gained an advantage, too, because the Lions, as they had in the equivalent test 20 years before, had to play most of the game a player short. Their livewire flanker, Bill McKay, was concussed and had his nose broken in a collision with an All Black and one of his own players and had to leave the field about halfway through the first half. There were some mutterings about All Black obstruction in lineouts but the ever-diplomatic Mullen had no complaints after the test was lost 8–0. He had no complaints about playing a man short either. His response was typical of the British attitude at the time:

"We feel that in playing football one of the main ideas is to foster team spirit," he said. "We go on the field with a team of 15 players and if we are unlucky enough to lose one, we believe that the remaining 14 members of the side should be able to reorganise themselves and make up for their loss."

The All Blacks' undoubted hero in the first two tests was an Auckland flanker whose name should perhaps be writ larger in New Zealand rugby history, Pat Crowley. Lions and All Blacks alike rated him the difference between the two sides. The Lions weren't too keen on rucking either, as Bleddyn Williams recalled: "The Otago-style rucking in the second test upset our forwards. In all the tests, the All Blacks rucked viciously in a manner we had never before experienced.

Pat Crowley proved to be a merciless and destructive scrumhalf killer . . . Crowley was killer No. 1 and the All Blacks owed more to him than to any other player for victory in the rubber."

The final two test matches, both won by New Zealand, remain notable in rugby recollections because of a try in each. In the third test in Wellington, it was a try by the injured All Black captain, Ron Elvidge, that was talked about long after the final whistle and in the fourth test in Auckland, it was a try by the Welsh wing, Jones, that stayed in the memories of all those who saw it.

A National Film Unit crew was given permission by the New Zealand union to film the third test in Wellington and for it to be later played at cinemas, but it was a still photograph that remained the enduring image of Elvidge's try. It first appeared in the Wellington morning newspaper, the *Dominion*, on the Monday morning after the test and was modestly headed: "Presenting the rugby picture of the year". It shows Elvidge diving across the line between Billy Cleaver and Bill McKay, who sported an ungainly-looking guard protecting the nose that he'd broken in the second test. Words were not necessary because surely by the Monday morning everyone in New Zealand knew the heroic tale of how Elvidge had been badly injured in a tackle by Jack Matthews and left the field, but how the All Black prop, "Iron Man" Johnny Simpson, had also left the field with a knee injury that abruptly ended his career. No replacements and two men down, Elvidge returned to the field, his head bandaged. The All Black No. 8, Peter Johnstone, had left the scrum to complement the backs because it was felt that as game as Elvidge was, he could play only in hope rather than expectation. The second half was only a few minutes old when the All

Black halfback, Vince Bevan, sensed a half-chance out to his left and the ball was spun through the backs with Elvidge on the outside of Johnstone. Blocked, Johnstone tossed it to Elvidge and the All Black captain dived into New Zealand rugby folklore.

Elvidge's courage somewhat overshadowed the magnificent effort of the remaining six All Black forwards and with Crowley again leading the way, they dominated the British pack. Syd Nicholls, the patriarch of the Nicholls rugby family from Petone, was back in New Zealand from his home in Sydney to write about the tour. The depleted pack in Wellington, he wrote, was the best he had seen in 20 years. "They were real All

Top left: The programme for the second test.

Above: The "Iron Man", Johnny Simpson, assisted from the field in the third test by captains Ron Elvidge and Bleddyn Williams.

Overleaf: Ron Elvidge, returning to play after being injured, scores his celebrated try in the third test. He dives between Lions defenders Billy Cleaver and Bill McKay (wearing a noseguard after having his nose broken in the second test). Inset: Elvidge, with chest and head injuries, is assisted from the field.

Cliff's Leg Up

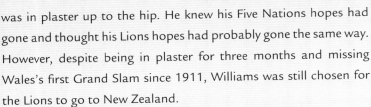

Chirpy Cliff Morgan, a future star for Wales and the Lions, was still only 19 when the 1950 team was chosen and hadn't made his international debut. Inexperienced, barely known and young, Morgan even then made his presence felt.

Lions centre Bleddyn Williams, seven years Morgan's senior, had reason to thank the chatty youngster for getting him on the tour.

Bleddyn Williams

Williams had badly injured a knee in a trial match in January of 1950 and was in plaster up to the hip. He knew his Five Nations hopes had gone and thought his Lions hopes had probably gone the same way. However, despite being in plaster for three months and missing Wales's first Grand Slam since 1911, Williams was still chosen for the Lions to go to New Zealand.

There was just the small matter of showing he was fit. "Coming out of plaster and then playing 10 days later, you can imagine what the muscles in my leg were like," he said.

The comeback match was an away game for Cardiff against Bath and inside Williams was Morgan.

Running onto the field, Morgan said to Williams, "The best way to show you're fit is to score a try in the last minute."

"So I went through the motions," Williams recalled. "I wasn't fit, not match-fit anyway. With about three or four minutes to go I saw Cliff sidle up to the referee and ask him how long to go."

Morgan then went over to Williams and said: "Are you ready?"

"I said, 'As ready as I'll ever be'. He got the ball from the scrum on the halfway line, waltzed past the flanker on the other side, beat the other flanker, came up to the fullback and I was able to get up outside him and I scored a try under the crossbar."

Next day the headlines read: "Williams fit". So, thanks to Morgan, Williams boarded the ship to New Zealand.

Ironically, another Lion, Scottish centre Doug Smith — who managed the 1971 Lions — arrived on tour with a broken arm and played only two games late in the tour.

Blacks . . . every man was a competent tradesman and it was this six who paved the way for their side's victory."

Thrilling tries that traverse the length of the field, involving most of a team or even just the one individual, are much more common today than they once were. All Blacks such as John Kirwan, Jeff Wilson, Christian Cullen and Joe Rokocoko could bring crowds to their feet with their speed and their skill; Jonah Lomu was able to score tries that defied description as much as they defied defenders. The special became commonplace. In 1950, such tries were a rarity and were appreciated all the more because of it. One such try was scored by the Welsh sprinter, Ken Jones, in the fourth test in Auckland. Bob Scott, one of the defenders, gazed in awe and called it the try of all our lives. It came, as such tries often do, from defence. The All Blacks were ahead 11–3 and attacking the British line. Jack Kyle got the ball away from a lineout and shot a hard, flat pass to Lewis Jones, the 19-year-old Welsh fullback who had joined the tour as a replacement. Such was the nature of the pass, and Jones's speed onto it, that it was reported then and later that the pass had been intended for Bleddyn Williams, but that Jones had intercepted it. Kyle disagrees: ". . . the try we scored was a move which we had practised and came from a throw over the top of the lineout. We gave the wing the nod, threw the ball over the lineout and I was looking for it. Lewis Jones was playing at fullback and as I got the ball he was bursting through the middle. So I gave it to him . . ." Jones, out in front of his posts, sidestepped through the All Black midfield and shot toward halfway. As he ran, he kept looking out to his right to make sure that the other Jones, Ken, was with him. He was. So too was the All Blacks' speedster, Noel Henderson, and the All Black centre, Roy Roper. In front of him was the All Black fullback, Bob Scott. Jones slowed as he reached Scott but with perfect timing, he looped a pass over to Ken Jones. It became a race between the two sprinters, Jones and Henderson, with Roper on their heels. As if with wings on his heels, Ken Jones raced from the 10-yard line, over halfway, down into an empty All Black half. On the twenty-five, he started to veer toward

1950 — A Pride is Born

Lions wing Noel Henderson and All Black No. 8 Peter Johnstone dispute possession in the third test.

Welsh speedster Ken Jones draws away from Roy Roper (diving) and Peter Henderson to score his spectacular try at Eden Park.

the posts and with the slight change in angle, Henderson was out of it but Roper dived. Despairingly, as it turned out. No matter that it was at Eden Park and 99.9 per cent of the 55,000 crowd was New Zealanders; no matter that a foe was going to score against the friend, no matter that it was a red jersey crossing the line. The crowd's noise was deafening; no one could have remained seated. A try at the same ground 44 years later, scored by France, was described as the try from the ends of the earth. If someone using the English language had been as eloquent in 1950 as the French captain was in 1994, something similar might have been said. The All Blacks won the fourth test 11–8, but it seemed a fitting finale to the tour that the most spectacular try had been scored by the Lions.

As journalist and Lion, Clem Thomas, later remarked, only Scott of New Zealand had any claim to rugby immortality, though he described Elvidge as magnificent. "While the Lions back division bristled with great names — some of the best in the world at the time — they failed to win a test match," he wrote. "This suggests that forwards win matches, especially in New Zealand, and that the Lions pack of 1950 simply failed to match them." Thomas, who rightly was regarded as one of the most knowledgeable men in rugby, thus confirmed the superficial impression New Zealanders formed of the 1950 Lions and of other British teams: great in the backs, ordinary in the forwards.

But there might have been more to it than that. In Britain, a coach is a bus. The British countries were

Lions fullback Lewis Jones is too late to stop All Black prop Hec Wilson scoring in the fourth test. The referee is George Sullivan of Taranaki, a brother of All Black and later administrator, Jack Sullivan.

latecomers to the concept of coaching in rugby, something which New Zealand adopted early on, discarded for a time, then took up again, although they shied away from calling their coaches what they were. Until relatively recent times, "assistant manager" was the New Zealand rugby euphemism for coach. The difference in approach to coaching between Britain and New Zealand was one of attitude. The British drew on the old amateur ethic of playing for the game's sake and playing for enjoyment; New Zealand played to win. Bleddyn Williams, the vice-captain of the 1930 team, was revealing. He made a statement — startling to New Zealand ears — during the tour that it was completely foreign to the British idea of things for a team to take the field with a preconceived plan. A team would simply play to its strengths, both individual and collective, and if either was found wanting, they'd try something different. But Williams said the lack of a plan or of a coach did not mean that winning was not the object. "If a man is not playing to win, then he is not a rugger man," he said. "But we attach great importance to the social side of the game, and we think that the main thing is to be able to feel afterwards that we have enjoyed a match."

Bob Scott warmed to this theme in the book he wrote with Terry McLean. Karl Mullen as captain of the Lions was responsible also for their coaching. Ginger Osborne's job as manager was the organisational role, to make speeches and to ensure the team did what it was supposed to do when it was supposed to do it.

Lewis Jones, who became one of the Lions' stars after joining the tour as a replacement, shows his kicking style in the fourth test.

Anything that happened on the field of play, or didn't happen, was Mullen's domain and, in the last two tests when he was injured and Williams was captain, the job fell to him. In language that seemed more McLean's than Scott's, Scott referred to the coach as "the man outside the game", the man upon whose shoulders the captain could lean, the man to whom the captain could turn for advice. Without a coach, Mullen had no one. For all his intelligence, his football skill and his likeable personality, Mullen could not also fulfil a role which in later years would be judged to be the most crucial to the success of any team. "The Lions proved that you could go a long way without coaching and they proved," Scott said, ". . . that public interest and support depended less upon a series of perfectly drilled manoeuvres than upon the gay spirit of adventure which the team put into most of its displays. But they also proved that, in the final analysis, a team wanting to prove itself in international matches needs, and in fact can be vitally dependent upon, the man outside the game."

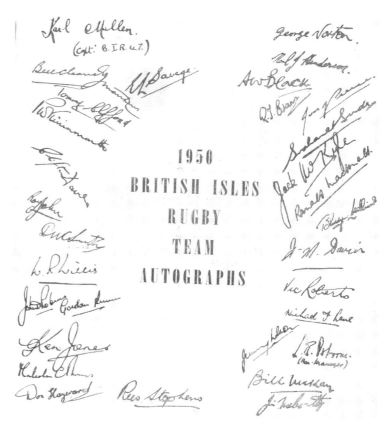

Sign here, please — the Lions oblige.

Matthews — Tackler Supreme

Few visiting international players to New Zealand have had such a deserved reputation as a deadly tackler than the Welsh and Lions centre in 1950, Jackie Matthews. His tackles were hard and venomous — when he tackled someone, they stayed down.

Matthews's tackling was something he had worked on in his youth. To earn some pocket money, he got a job helping forestry workers in his holidays. No chainsaws then, the young Matthews used an axe to cut down trees. And just to give a bit of edge to his fitness, he'd go running up and down the sandhills near his Bridgend home. And at his home, he rigged up a boxing-style punching bag and charged into it time and time again, imagining, no doubt, he was stopping a last-minute English try.

Matthews had a trial for Wales before World War II, but didn't make his international debut until after it, in 1947. By then, his skills were well honed and his reputation for tackling well established.

Wales won the triple crown in 1950 — and were on the way to winning their first Grand Slam since 1911 — when they beat Ireland in Belfast in March of 1950, just a couple of weeks before the Lions touring squad was named.

Far from Matthews's tackling being seen as an asset for the Lions, it appeared to be seen as a disadvantage.

"In Belfast just before the game I was in the toilets, spending a penny, and a chap came up to me and knocked me on the shoulder and said, 'If you tackle today as you did in the past, you won't be going on the Lions tour.' This was just two minutes before the game started!"

Matthews found out later this toilet loiterer was an Irish selector and, as such, had some influence with the Lions selectors.

"So I was intent on behaving myself — I always did anyway!"

Wales won 6-3, Matthews seemed to escape censure for any tackling, and he was chosen for the Lions.

The New Zealand selectors in 1950: Arthur Marslin, Merv Corner and Tom Morrison.

New Zealand did not have a designated coach for the 1950 series but the All Blacks had a manager for each of the four tests, Tom Morrison, as well as two selectors, Merv Corner and Arthur Marslin, who were at each training session, and if not named coaches, performed the roles now expected of coaches.

When the All Blacks were in South Africa in 1949, they agreed to seek, albeit reluctantly, the expertise of Danie Craven to overcome their scrum problems. No one in the British team in 1950 bothered to seek out the man acknowledged as the best coach in New Zealand at the time, Vic Cavanagh, whose rucking methods so worried the Lions in the tests and against Otago and Southland. It was a different story 21 years later. Not only did the 1971 Lions come to New Zealand with a well-respected coach, Carwyn James, but they won the series. And when the 1971 team was in Dunedin, who did James seek out for a couple of hours' conversation one afternoon? Cavanagh.

The Lions in 1950 could have won the first test, they should have won the third. They could therefore have won the series. A coach might have made all the difference.

As Clem Thomas observed, the 1950 tour was a success better measured by its friendship than in stark statistics. "They gave untold enjoyment to a generation of Kiwis and Aussies by the manner in which they played the game," he wrote. The manager, Ginger Osborne, was asked at the end of the tour what had impressed him most and he replied it was the toughness of the New Zealand footballer. "When they come on the field, they show a sustained and intense concentration," he said. "We will always recall the complete disregard for self with which a New Zealand forward charges for the line — almost as if there was no one to stand in his path."

1959
Age of the Don

A brief, clear word picture can be painted of the series in 1959 between the All Blacks and the Lions. The All Blacks won the series by three tests to one, a decisive enough margin you might think. But New Zealanders were not happy.

The Lions were decidedly unhappy. The Lions scored more tries than the All Blacks, nine to seven, but the Lions had 27 penalty goals kicked against them. The Lions manager, Alf Wilson, often diplomatic but sometimes bitter, had one of his bitter moments when he said his team was not beaten by the All Blacks, but by just one of them, Don Clarke. It was Clarke's prodigious kicking that gave the All Blacks their series win.

New Zealanders did not take pride in the win in the manner they had three years earlier when the South Africans had been beaten. According to reports at the time and later, there was a despondent mood in the country because the All Blacks won but did not win well. They had lost their scoring power. They were given wins because they had Clarke and because

referees saw infringements by Lions that the Lions themselves didn't see.

There was, toward the end of the first test in Dunedin, the extraordinary sound of the crowd of about 40,000 chanting "Red! Red! Red!" as the Lions forwards attacked the All Blacks' line in a vain attempt to score yet another try to overcome Clarke's six penalty goals. There could be no stronger indication of the crowd's feeling of injustice toward the Lions, their opponents, than that.

The result of the first test, headlined in the Dunedin *Star Sports* "Clarke 18, Lions 17", instantly became a part of rugby folklore, a result that stands out enduringly as being different from the norm. The results of the other tests have been less long-remembered and

A jacked-up picture of Don Clarke in All Black jersey and shorts and Waikato socks, but the sight of him preparing to kick was something the 1959 Lions dreaded.

Star Sports, Saturday, July 18, 1959.

Clarke 18, Lions 17

Sad Fate For Unlucky Lions' Four Tries

was a misfortune for the Lions that Hewitt should have foozled a comparatively easy kick.

The situation was uncertain for New Zealand when the ball went into play in the second half and the Lions promised great

RECORD CROWD

ball into touch, and Price, K. J. Scotland and finally Price completed a move of about 100 yards with a try which Risman beautifully converted.

With a lead of eight points, the Lions looked safe, even though the All Blacks by now were dominating the ground.

But still Mr Fleury needed to impose penalties and from 48 yards and then 45 yards D. B. Clarke placed two magnificent goals.

How the Saturday night paper, the *Star Sports* in Dunedin, headed the outcome of the first test.

it's worth pointing out that only the third, 22–8, was a decisive win for the All Blacks. The second was won 11–8 and the fourth was lost. The Lions, with some justification, felt they were only a referee's whistle blast away from winning the series, something a Lions team in New Zealand wouldn't do for another 12 years.

Inevitably, the Lions' focus fell on the standard of refereeing and there were complaints then, as now, of the different interpretation and application of the laws between the northern and southern hemispheres. One of the British journalists following the Lions was Welshman Bryn Thomas, better known by his byline, J.B.G. Thomas, but better known to some New Zealand journalists by the nickname bestowed upon him by Terry McLean, "Jaybejaysus". Thomas wrote for the *Western Mail* in Cardiff but also filed to papers in South Africa during the tour and among his musings was this little diatribe: "Rugby followers of New Zealand, get down on your knees and apologise to Danie Craven, Basie Viviers and the 1956 Springboks. They are a much maligned group. On Saturday, I saw them vindicated and it is right that the people of South Africa who were never quite satisfied why the Springboks lost the series should know why. The answer is simple — New Zealand referees. They are not biased, but they are not competent. That is the real trouble and why there will be differences of opinion this season and in the future."

He then went on to say that only when the standard of refereeing in New Zealand was better would tours be less of an embarrassment.

The quality of the refereeing or, rather, the correctness of some decisions, became the focal point of the tour, the cause of endless debate and, in the end, was held to be the reason the All Blacks won and the Lions lost. Blaming the referee is the first chapter in the well-thumbed book of excuses for rugby losses. Seldom is a referee thanked, not publicly anyway, for an incorrect decision that gives a side victory. But the hapless whistler always cops the blame first from an aggrieved side. The difficulty with Thomas's message to South Africans was that it implied, and near as dammit baldly stated, that the Lions in New Zealand in 1959 were unique victims. As McLean adroitly observed, "The difficulty was that Mr Thomas and the Lions as a whole quite lost their sense of proportion in making themselves believe that theirs was a unique experience. All major rugby tours are affected by a belief that the referees of the host country are not up to scratch." McLean wrote that in his book on the 1959 tour, *Kings of Rugby*, but it could equally have been written at any time about any tour between 1888, when the British first ventured beyond their shores, to 1979 when the principle of third-country referees (i.e. "neutral referees"

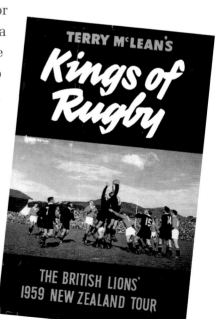

The Lions go through the pre-game ground inspection ritual at Carisbrook before the first test.

though the phrase is tautological) was universally accepted. All Blacks could moan long and hard about the standard of refereeing they encountered wherever they toured, as could South Africans, Australians and anyone else who felt maligned by a referee who owed allegiance to the same land as their opponents.

Implicit in the criticism of referees is the notion that but for an errant peep, the complaining team could have, probably would have, won. This in turn implies that the referee was the only reason for the loss, conveniently overlooking the possibility, or certain probability, of any number of other causes. There are 4800 seconds in a rugby match and in any one of them a game could be won or lost when the referee is but a silent observer. Dropped passes, missed tackles,

missed kicks, wrong options . . . rugby is replete with opportunities in which to lose, or win, matches. Most of them can be achieved without the strident musical note of the referee. Also implicit in the criticism of referees is that the accusers are demanding a standard of excellence, indeed perfection, from referees that the accusers themselves cannot attain because players, like referees, are also human and suffer all the human frailties and foibles. The Lions lost when they could possibly have won for more fundamental reasons than what referees did or didn't do.

As with most British tours until the most recent of years, the essential difference with New Zealand was one of attitude: toward the game itself and toward preparation for the game. The British view, rightly or

Halfback Roger Urbahn receives the ball from Wilson Whineray in the first test.

wrongly, (and in most New Zealand eyes it was just plain quaint) was the old, wider amateurism ethic of playing the game for its own sake and not allowing any of the various layers of professionalism to intrude. Coaching was a significant difference and may have been *the* significant difference. The Lions, as was their way, came to New Zealand with a manager, Alf Wilson, captain Ronnie Dawson of Ireland, and a secretary, Ossie Glasgow. There was no coach. The teams each week were chosen by Dawson and Wilson, and Dawson was solely responsible for trainings, for game plans and tactics. He was in effect the captain-coach, an intolerable and unworkable burden. The All Blacks, by contrast, had Jack Sullivan as their coach and at trainings the other two selectors, Dick Everest and Ron

King, were also present. New Zealand had a long but not unbroken history of having coaches with the All Blacks; to British teams, coaching was anathema. Even as late as 1975 when Scotland first toured New Zealand, they still couldn't bear to use the word "coach" and Bill Dickinson's official title was "advisor to the captain". New Zealand also prepared for the Lions in a unified manner, the New Zealand union encouraging and in some cases organising warm-up matches for provincial teams scheduled to play the Lions — or in the Maoris' case, organising a small tour. When the Lions assembled in Napier for the first game, the Hawke's Bay chairman and a man of many rugby parts, Norman McKenzie, summed up for the Lions the ethos of New Zealand rugby: "I'd like to give the visitors warning. You are in

O'Reilly — Ace of Wings

If the words "superstar" or "celebrity" were in vogue in 1959 when the Lions were in New Zealand, they would have been applied to just one man: Anthony Joseph Francis O'Reilly, a 23-year-old solicitor who had made his rugby name on the Lions' tour of South Africa four years before when he'd scored 17 tries.

He was known as the "glamour boy" and occasionally the "film star". O'Reilly, a far more studious man than his public reputation indicated, tried to eschew the glamour tag and hated the film star bit.

But there was a grain of truth in it, as he reluctantly conceded. Picture Charlton Heston in the 1959 epic, *Ben Hur*, then picture O'Reilly in the same role. To say it nearly happened would be drawing a long bow, but to say it could have happened is true.

While the Lions were in South Africa, an American film company began a worldwide search for an actor to play the key role. O'Reilly, who had acted in amateur dramatics at school and university in Ireland, was oblivious to this, but a friend submitted his name to the company.

Somehow a Dublin newspaper found out about it, a story appeared that O'Reilly was a contender for the part, someone in the film company in London saw it and tried to arrange for an audition. But that was when O'Reilly himself became involved and turned down the chance, especially when he found out that if successful, he would have had to have signed a seven-year contract. "I was in the middle of my law studies and they had to come first," he said when quizzed about it when he arrived in New Zealand.

The film star label stuck and O'Reilly was anxious to be rid of it. "Kill it, whatever else you do," he told the New Zealand reporter.

So O'Reilly the film star was always a remote possibility but given his effervescent personality and the success he's achieved in other spheres, he probably could have handled a Hollywood chariot every bit as adroitly as he's handled his multitude of business affairs.

O'Reilly was a hit on the field for his speed and enthusiasm,

The Great O'Gatsby, Tony O'Reilly.

even though there were occasional grumbles that he wasn't keen on the tackle and grizzles from the All Blacks that he was a clever obstructionist.

He was a hit off the field as well, teaming up with the Irish halfback, Andy Mulligan, who came to New Zealand as a replacement, in a running series of practical jokes and night-time exploits. Terry McLean, in his book on the 1959 tour, remarked that O'Reilly lived in a state of armed truce with the management. It's easy to imagine the manager, Alf Wilson, and secretary, Ossie Glasgow, having their senses of humour stretched by O'Reilly, while the captain, Ronnie Dawson, regarded his compatriot with a tolerant smile.

He and Mulligan liked to poke fun at players and especially officials, and once conducted a fictitious radio interview that purported to be with Wavell Wakefield, archdeacon of the English rugby hierarchy. It was so convincing that it was run on the New Zealand Broadcasting Service, as it was then.

That was but a minor transgression of tour protocol. A couple of nights before the final test, O'Reilly and Mulligan went out on the town in Auckland and ended up joining the band at a nightspot with the unlikely name of Hi-Diddle-Griddle. O'Reilly was on the piano and Mulligan on the guitar and doing, apparently, very nicely. But both were unaware that someone was taking photos and on the Thursday before the game, the *New Zealand Herald* ran a picture of the two Lions having the time of their lives while their teammates were seriously preparing for a test match.

"We had great dialogue with the management of the tour over whether this was the right way to prepare yourself for a test match," O'Reilly later remarked.

And in a typical O'Reilly line, he added: "Luckily, I now own the paper so I can suppress the facts."

Stories about, and by, O'Reilly are legion. When he was 34 and already managing director of Heinz Europe, he gained a surprise recall to the Irish team training to play England. He showed up at training on the Friday in an enormous, chauffeur-driven Rolls Royce. O'Reilly thought he would just be in the reserves but to his surprise, he was named in the team, which prompted his old mate Mulligan to send him a telegram: "Heinz beanz are haz beanz." O'Reilly played and retained his sense of humour in evaluating his performance: "At the last moment, I found myself reduced to bravery. A long English footrush was determined when, quite out of character, I dived at the feet of the English pack. As I was emerging from momentary unconsciousness, I heard a loud and (let me confess) Irish voice shouting from the terraces, 'And kick his bloody chauffeur while you're at it'."

There's a story that after a minor car accident in Dublin he was rushed to hospital and, while waiting treatment, was asked if he earned above the threshold that qualified him for state-subsidised treatment. "Do you earn more than £11,000?" he was asked. Wearily, O'Reilly looked up from his bed: "Some days I do, some days I don't."

That, it must be said, was before he became the chief executive of Heinz and before he diversified into a range of other businesses.

The entertainer of the 1959 tour never left O'Reilly. When he was 50, his parents put on a surprise birthday party for him at a sports centre near his lavish home in County Kildare. There were 500 guests and the Dublin Opera Society, together with orchestra, was hired for the night. Someone from the society took to the stage and announced sadly that the artist retained to sing excerpts from Gilbert and Sullivan's *Mikado* for the night had failed to appear. Cue staged groans and other expressions of disappointment. Then cue stage right: On strode O'Reilly, dressed in spontaneous Oriental splendour. The orchestra played the opening bars and O'Reilly's rich baritone rang out: "If you want to know who I am/I'm the emperor of Japan . . ."

O'Reilly apparently has turned down offers to stand for political office, something McLean in 1959 foresaw for him. McLean said O'Reilly the intelligent, passionate Irish patriot was a considerably more important and interesting figure than O'Reilly the footballer. "At a long-range guess, one felt reasonably sure that he would in time become president or premier of the republic."

There's still time.

a country which plays rugby fiercely, competitively." New Zealand wanted to win and made sure it was better equipped to do so.

Many teams at the start of tours have said boldly they planned to play open, running rugby but, once the reality sets in, they cut their cloth accordingly and play whatever style it takes to win. If it's attractive, so much the better, but winning comes first. Not so the 1959 Lions. Dawson and Wilson told anyone who would listen from the start of their tour they wanted to play what they called Barbarians-style rugby and this they largely tried to do, which went a long way to explaining their enormous popularity with New Zealanders. But such rugby can only be played effectively with the ball and the Lions did not have a forward pack good enough to ensure a consistent enough supply. They certainly had the backs, especially wings such as Tony O'Reilly and Peter Jackson — who scored 41 tries between them on the whole tour that also included Australia and Canada — and a fine, attacking fullback, Ken Scotland, but it was, in the end, the inability of the forwards to control the flow of possession that cost them matches. There was criticism, too, of their defence, which was regarded as individual rather than collective — in other words, it was up to each player to decide where to be on defence and who to tackle rather than to have a planned defensive pattern which was what the All Blacks had.

There were other differences, not telling in themselves, between the approach of the All Blacks and of New Zealand rugby generally, and that of British rugby. The International Rugby Board, which met in New Zealand for the first time during the tour, had decreed that test sides should not assemble more than 48 hours before a match. This was blithely ignored by New Zealand, as such conventions always had been. New Zealand test teams generally assembled on the Wednesday preceding the test so they could get two full training runs in, but they'd also had summer camps for a wider group of players and specialised camps for positions such as inside and outside backs. Another point of difference, which became something of a cause célèbre on the tour, was the New Zealand — and

Australian — penchant, especially among forwards, for wearing protective padding. This was deeply frowned upon by the IRB — and still is — which held that such padding could only be worn for genuine medical reasons and in each case the wearer had to have an authorising letter signed by a doctor. Alf Wilson, the Lions' manager, hit the roof in Timaru when 13 of the Hanan Shield team's players took the field wearing padding of one sort or another. "You'd think we were playing against a team of crocks," he remarked with some asperity. A harsher reaction was forthcoming in Christchurch before the third test when Wilson, and some members of the IRB, learnt that seven of the All Blacks would be wearing padding. Wilson demanded to accompany the referee, Cecil Gillies of Hamilton, into the All Blacks' dressing room to verify they had the necessary medical authorisation. Ossie Glasgow, the Lions' secretary, was quoted as saying, "I was so bloody wild I could scarcely read the names." On the Monday after the match, a newspaper photograph showed the All Black lock, Stan Hill, with his jersey off and leather protection exposed. According to McLean, an appalled chairman of the IRB, Sarsfield Hogan of Ireland, confronted the chairman of the New Zealand union, Cuth Hogg, with the photo and said: "How can you possibly justify this?" Hogg's response was not recorded but the New Zealand union later issued a statement saying each of the All Blacks who wore protection had permission and, still later, gleefully pointed out that some of the Lions, including captain Ronnie Dawson, also wore padding.

Tom Pearce, the former prop and outspoken Auckland administrator, was the manager of the All Blacks and he was told in Christchurch there were newspaper reports in South Africa emanating from New Zealand that the All Blacks had obtained false certificates to justify the padding. No one owned up to writing the story and Bryn Thomas was far from the only reporter on tour filing to South Africa. Pearce said the accusations were mischievous and libellous and Hogg referred to them as arrant lies. Players named as wearing some form of protection were Mark Irwin, Ron Hemi, Colin

Here, try this. The All Blacks' masseur, Charlie Buckley, offers Stan Hill some liniment during halftime in the second test.

Meads, Kel Tremain, Stan Hill, Roger Urbahn and Frank McMullen. "In every case," Pearce said, "there was a history of recent injury. Furthermore, all the pads were of soft material as stipulated by the laws of the game. Certificates from reputable practising physicians were produced in every instance to satisfy the referee that the wearing of the pads was warranted."

Such issues simmered along, occasionally rising to the surface, as the Lions made their progress through New Zealand between June and September. They'd played six games in Australia, losing only to New South Wales, and won the test by a decisive 24–3, then continued in New Zealand with a similarly impressive record, beating Hawke's Bay, East Coast-Poverty Bay, Auckland and New Zealand Universities and barely missing a beat. They came badly undone in Dunedin, however, when they were beaten 26–8 by Otago. This match more than any other showed the Lions what they could expect in the tests. It wasn't the greatest of Otago sides, certainly not of the calibre that had beaten the 1950 Lions, but they won through the forward cohesion on which the province's rugby pride had been founded. Thomas gave credit where it was due and after the Otago wing, Tup Diack, had kicked 14 points for Otago, was unusually prescient: "Good place-kicking may well win the tests."

How right he was because a fortnight later, after two more wins, the Lions were back at Carisbrook and lost the test to Clarke's mighty boot — or to the referee's whistle, depending on the point of view. Four times the Lions crossed the All Blacks' line for tries, two in each half — the first by O'Reilly, the second by the Welsh centre Malcom Price, the third by Jackson and then Price again. The All Black forwards dominated but it was Clarke's kicking from a tacky surface that kept them in the game. The All Blacks got out to 6–0 but the Lions led 9–6 at halftime. Then they went ahead 12–6, then 12–9 then 17–9 after Price's second try. Clarke had missed a couple of long-range attempts and while the Lions looked safe, and must have felt it, Clarke's boot continued as a nagging worry for the Lions. He got it back to 17–12, then 17–15 and finally, with two minutes to go, the kick that stabbed every Lion in the heart. One of Clarke's penalties especially stuck in the Lions' craw. Vivian Jenkins, who had been a Lion in South Africa in 1938 and later became a journalist and later still made New Zealand a second home, sat in the old stand at Carisbrook and swore — and continued to swear — that the ball slipped past on the outside of the left upright and that the Lion acting as touch judge, Mick English, waved it away. The other touch judge and referee Alan Fleury signalled it as good though.

The reaction to the result was long and lusty, so long that it was still being referred to when New Zealand belatedly accepted the principle of third-country referees in 1979. It also led to debate about the points value of a penalty and of a try, some arguing the penalty should be reduced to two points and some the try should be increased to four (which it was in 1972). Danie Craven had his say, as he usually did, and argued just two points for a penalty goal and he

Rail travel, especially in railcars, was a feature of Lions tours.

Ralph Caulton scores the first of his two tries in the third test. Frank McMullen is about to start a victory dance.

The Lions' mood hardly improved. They lost the following Saturday to Canterbury but joy at the wins against Wellington and Taranaki that followed was dampened by a growing injury list, which sidelined key players first five-eighth Bev Risman, outstanding centre Dave Hewitt (one of a family of Hewitts to play for Ireland), wing Peter Jackson and fullback Ken Scotland. Of necessity, the Lions had a rearranged team for the second test with Price, the double tryscorer from Dunedin, moved from centre to first-five. The All Blacks, for different reasons, also made changes. Though they had won in Dunedin, no New Zealander was fooled into believing it was convincing. Tup Diack, who had been chosen for the first test after his strong performances for Universities and Otago against the Lions, had had to withdraw because of an injured calf. He was given another chance in the second test, replacing his replacement, Bruce McPhail. On the other wing, Ralph Caulton took over from Pat Walsh and in an unusual change, one Taranaki inside back pair, Ross Brown and Roger Urbahn, was replaced by another, John McCullough and Kevin Briscoe. In the forwards, flankers Dick Conway and Kel Tremain were brought in for their first tests, Des Webb took Ron Hemi's place at hooker for his one test, and Colin Meads took over from Peter Jones for the first of his record number of tests against the Lions.

As in Dunedin, the Lions in the second test in Wellington again had cause to rue their nemesis, Clarke. This time though it wasn't Clarke's kicking that won the test for the All Blacks, it was a spectacular diving try and conversion in the last minute. Until then, the Lions had led 8–6 after a try from their new wing, sprint champion John Young, and a conversion and a penalty by fullback Terry Davies, who was in for the injured Scotland. All Black wing Ralph Caulton had scored two tries on debut, the All Blacks' sole scoring until McCullough ran the blind from a ruck not far out from the Lions' line. The Lions were a man down on defence and there was no one to oppose Clarke as he took the ball and dived — with a huge grin on his face — for the winning try.

had support from Jim Parker, the manager of the All Blacks in South Africa in 1949 when the All Blacks lost all four tests and Okey Geffin kicked 11 penalty goals. Parker mounted a compelling argument when he pointed out that the nature of the penalty had changed. In the old days, he said, the defending team stood on the mark and the kicker had to retreat, someone had to hold the ball for the kick and when it was placed on the ground, the defending team could charge. Penalty kicks in 1959 were easy by comparison, he argued. None of the Lions hierarchy suggested any law changes, Wilson diplomatically saying it was up to the IRB, but he praised Clarke for the magnificence of his kicking. The Lions hurt though and felt, in the classical boxing cliché, they had been robbed.

Tony O'Reilly surveys his options in Wellington. Those wondering what he's going to do are David Marques, Rhys Williams, Roddy Evans, Hugh McLeod, Colin Meads, Ronnie Dawson, Wilson Whineray and Des Webb.

Don Clarke shows he can score tries, too. This was his winning effort in the second test in Wellington. The Lions are Terry Davies, Dick Jeeps and John Young.

The Lions by then were realising just how much rugby gripped New Zealand and why winning mattered so much. "We all think that to some extent you people are quite mad," Wilson said in his speech at the formal post-match test dinner at the Hotel St George. "Though we may laugh and joke about it, we cannot fail to be impressed by the effect of a simple game like rugby upon a country like yours. Somehow we cannot express ourselves in the same way as you do, so we admire you for the enthusiasm you have for the game."

There was much talk as the tour progressed — especially after the second test as the Lions won against the unusual combination of King Country and Counties, then beat Waikato and Wairarapa-Bush — of the world crown, a championship of perception rather than one of reality. The theory went like this: before 1956, the Springboks had the world crown, then the All Blacks took it from them and so now the mythical title was being defended against the Lions. The Australians in those days didn't count. The crown, therefore, could be decided in the third test. And so it was, in the best of the All Blacks' wins. The Lions could have no complaints and didn't. The test in Christchurch was one in which the New Zealand forwards had all the dominance they needed and the Lions were outscored four tries to one. It was, said the Christchurch *Star Sports*, "New Zealand's most satisfying test victory for many a day" — well, since 1956 anyway. Vivian Jenkins, the Lion turned journalist, was open with his praise: "No complaints! The rope is round my neck and

Kevin Briscoe is securely held by his Lions opposite, Dick Jeeps, in the second test. Lion David Marques and new All Black Dick Conway have a wary eye on proceedings.

THIRD TEST

BRITISH ISLES

NEW ZEALAND

LANCASTER PARK, SATURDAY AUGUST 29, 1959
OFFICIAL PROGRAMME   ONE SHILLING

I am all ready for the last absolution, but there can be no arguing this time. At Dunedin the Lions had every right to think that they had been scurvily treated by Fortune, in the shape of Don Clarke's six penalty goals; at Wellington there was always the feeling that injuries had prevented the tourists from putting out anything like their best side. Today none of these things applied and the Lions were beaten fairly and squarely by a far better side."

The tour, as they said on long tours, was now on the downhill slope, heading for the fourth test and home or, in the Lions' case, two more games in Canada and then home. The danger in such thoughts was that the sights got set on the distant rather than the immediate and results could suffer. They didn't for the Lions though. After the loss in Christchurch, they didn't lose another game and that included a match against the Junior All Blacks, a rather bad-tempered encounter with New Zealand Maori, matches against a combined Bay of Plenty/Thames Valley and North Auckland and the last test.

How much influence the manager, Alf Wilson, had on the outcome of the test in Auckland is impossible to say. As a selector with Dawson and as the boss of the team, he had an overt influence anyway. But he may also have had more influence than he thought after some lengthy comments about his team that were published before the match. Wilson spoke to reporters, both British and New Zealand, at some length about the tour overall, with comments on New Zealand play and players and on his own team. Such a review of the tour was quite common. What was uncommon was that Wilson said his piece before the fourth test rather than after it and some of his players, reading his comments in the *New Zealand Herald* over breakfast at the Royal International Hotel, may not have been too impressed.

"I feel that our defeats were mostly of our own making," he said, "because in suffering them we neglected to carry out the policy of a free-running attack which we all endorsed at the beginning of the tour. Speed was always our strong point and our

principal hope for success against the All Blacks. When we neglected to use it by playing a defensive type of game, we were losing our main attacking weapon."

He accused the Lions forwards of lacking sternness, especially in the loose forwards, and poor handling in lineouts. Both faults contributed directly to defeats, he said.

"Alf the Manager", as he was known to all on the tour, had happily conceded at the start of the tour that he had hardly ever spoken publicly to journalists because no one had ever approached him and Scottish papers didn't pay much attention to rugby. He gradually warmed to the role, however, and in Auckland for the fourth test, he had been positively garrulous. Was he also cunning? Were the comments critical of his team carefully chosen to fire his side up ahead of the match? There's no way of knowing. Whatever he may have intended, or not, that was the effect they had. The Lions won the fourth test and won it well. It was, by common consent, the best Lions performance of the tour and their most emphatic win. Yet the scoreline was only 9–6 and, shades of Dunedin, Clarke could even have changed that had he succeeded with a long-range penalty goal attempt shortly before the finish. For all the closeness of the scores and for the chance the All Blacks had to draw, New Zealander and Briton alike were in agreement that the better team won. It also raised a question or two, especially as New Zealand minds were slowly turning toward the tour of South Africa the following year.

Fred Boshier in the *Evening Post* in Wellington put in print what was in a lot of New Zealand minds: "Today's result not only gave the Lions the consolation which everyone felt they richly deserved but made the result of the Christchurch test — caused by the complete superiority of the All Black forwards — more mystifying than ever. Today the British forwards not only held the All Black pack as they did in every test except the third but frequently played all over it." Of the All Black backs, Boshier wrote, there was only one man in it: Don Clarke.

Norman McKenzie, one of rugby's keenest brains,

knew precisely why the Lions won. The Lions team that played in Auckland, he said, was much better equipped than the one in Christchurch and, for New Zealand, the reverse was true. Irish and Lions flanker Noel Murphy, McKenzie said, was far more effective than Scotsman Ken Smith, who had been in the position in Christchurch, perhaps vindicating Wilson's remarks about a lack of sternness in the loose forwards. McKenzie was harshly dismissive of the All Blacks, calling the forwards "a mob of flatfoots" and saying that wings Caulton and McPhail probably realised after the game that wings can be like policemen in Gilbert and Sullivan operas. McKenzie also noted, unlike anyone else, that Ireland had six forwards in the pack for the first time, and ". . . did not

Ireland defeat France last April when all other of the home internationals had failed?"

Among the Irish was captain Ronnie Dawson, who became the first Lions captain in New Zealand to lead his team in every test. There were thoughts during the tour that the other hooker, Bryn Meredith of Wales, was a better all-round hooker than Dawson and was kept out of the tests only because of the need to play the captain. McKenzie thought that had England's Dick Jeeps, a possible substitute captain, been fit for the fourth test, Meredith might have replaced Dawson but he wasn't and he didn't and Meredith became the only fit Lion of 33 (including three replacements) not to play in a test match.

The Entertainers

Tony O'Reilly was regarded as the great entertainer of the 1959 Lions, but he had a close on-field rival, England wing Peter Jackson.

As O'Reilly once said of him, "Jackson the inimitable was such a crowd-pleaser that it was suggested to the Lions that he should be equipped with a one-wheeled bicycle and three juggling balls so he could keep the crowd entertained when play was not on his side of the field."

Jackson scored 19 tries on the tour of Australia and New Zealand.

Great All Black coach Fred Allen recalled Jackson in the opening tour match, in Napier. He remembered him scoring after wandering infield, beating man after man and then, ". . . seemingly on a private whim turn about again, beating man after man, possibly even the same men he had already beaten once to complete an uproarious, picturesque figure of eight."

Allen said Jackson wasn't fast compared with O'Reilly or another England wing, John Young, but scored tries by the trickery and deceptiveness of his running.

One of his tries for England, which earned victory against Australia in 1958, was described as being fit to rank with Alex Obolensky's two epics against the All Blacks of 1935.

When Jackson retired from rugby, the *Birmingham Post* rugby writer, John Solan, mourned the loss of those "mesmeric crossfield runs" and "excited conjecture".

Jackson was nicknamed "Nikolai" or the "Russian commissar" in New Zealand because of his pallor and expressionless countenance, but he wasn't as lacking in humour as was generally thought. He was tackled hard in the game in Greymouth and seemed to lie unconscious. His worried opponent approached him, Jackson sat up and shook hands, then immediately slumped to the ground again.

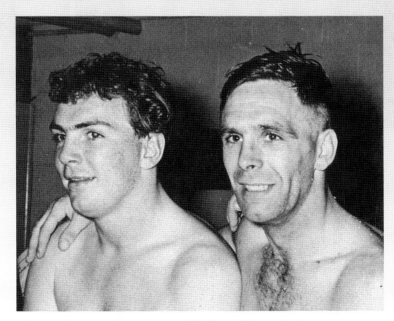

Wings and entertainers, Tony O'Reilly and Peter Jackson.

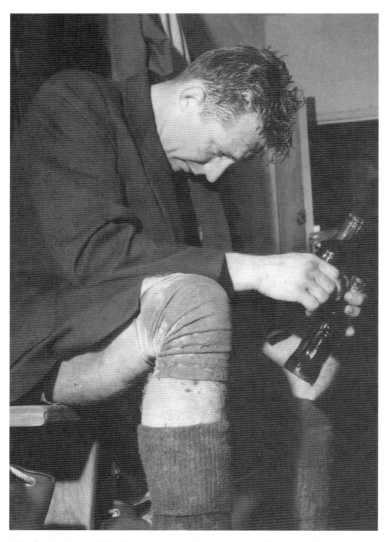

His day is done, his fight is over. Lions captain Ronnie Dawson reflects on the Lions' win in the fourth test.

Fullbacks unite: Don Clarke and Terry Davies after the fourth test.

One of the tries scored by the Lions in Auckland was by their much-publicised wing, Tony O'Reilly. It was his twenty-second try of the tour and broke the record set by Ken Jones in 1950. It was a statistical milestone barely remarked upon in New Zealand, but it was important to O'Reilly. He was conscious of the record and pursued it with the determination he took to his many later endeavours. "I'm by nature a Lions-type footballer and the two records I'm most proud of are the most tries scored by a Lion and the most tries scored by a Barbarian," he was quoted as saying.

For all the talk of the Lions' attacking back play, and for all the speed available to the Lions, the fourth test was not as riveting a spectacle as mellow memory may think. The scoreline of 9–6 may have been indication enough; even more indicative of the type of game was that there were 99 lineouts, 43 in the first half and 56 in the second. There were also 50 scrums and it was estimated that the ball was in play for just over 29 minutes. Still, none of the crowd of 60,000 seemed to mind — that was the way it was then.

New Zealanders wherever they lived didn't seem to mind the style of play. The total number of spectators for the tour was put at 798,750, a staggering number for a country of just over two million people. The 1956 Springbok tour was characterised as the national crusade, when people packed grounds wherever they were to see the South Africans. True enough, but 100,000 more saw the Lions than saw the Springboks.

1966
Doomed from Day One

When the Lions arrived in New Zealand in June of 1966, much was expected of them. They had come from eight matches unbeaten in Australia, including a 31–0 thumping of the Wallabies in the second test (they had won the first 11–8).

They were reported to have robust forwards and quick backs, a fairly standard line that applied to most British teams. They were said also to have finally adopted a "modern" management style and one newspaper headline went the whole hog, "Best managers ever with Lions".

The Lions arrived to a triumphal march. They left three months and 25 matches later to a dirge. Beaten in all four tests, the first British side anywhere to suffer such humiliation, they were beaten also in four provincial matches and drew two. To make matters worse, they lost to British Columbia on the way home.

So what went wrong? Any number of things, by all accounts. The tour was too long — five months including Australia and Canada; the itinerary especially in New Zealand was ill-planned (from a British perspective);

the conglomerate of British fishheads who chose both the management and the team got it wrong; there was confusion among the Lions about what game they ought to try to play; injuries as always had an influence; the captain, Mike Campbell-Lamerton, was a good bloke but not a good enough player.

Some of those reasons individually may have been valid; collectively and cumulatively they assigned the Lions to a forgettable place in rugby history. Complementing those particular reasons was the undeniable fact that British rugby in the 1960s was not at a high point — Lions sides played 12 tests in the 1960s and won none of them — but New Zealand rugby was at one of its peaks. An average Lions team was beaten by one of the great All Black teams.

In terms of the test matches in New Zealand alone, there were light years between the Lions and the All Blacks. The Lions had a coach for the first time, former Welsh and 1950 Lions prop John Robins, but as it transpired were ambivalent about what his role really was. They had players of genuine calibre, and none better than Mike Gibson and David Watkins in the backs and Willie-John McBride and Delme Thomas in the forwards. The issue was how best to use them and in this the Lions failed. The All Blacks, by massive contrast, were crystal clear in intentions and purpose. They had a coach, Fred Allen, who was unquestionably the boss and woe betide anyone who might have thought otherwise. They also had one of the best forward packs of any era, backs who were more than competent and they knew how they wanted to win matches.

Not for the first time, but perhaps for the last, there was a genuine difference in attitude between British and New Zealand rugby. The Lions manager, Des O'Brien, recalled years later an alarmingly revealing comment by a member of the Four Home Unions Committee that appointed him. O'Brien had told the committee in his interview that his top priority in New Zealand would be to win the four tests and to play Lions-style rugby. Your top priority is not to win the tests in New Zealand, he was told, ". . . it is bringing the tradition of Lions play to Australia and New Zealand". That comment, perhaps more than any other word or deed, explained why the Lions of 1966 performed so poorly. It was a throwback to the days of the missionary tours of the late 19th and early 20th centuries. The rugby world had moved on considerably since then, as it had to. Clearly, some

A Disneyesque souvenir tray from 1966.

British administrators had not. Another indication of the British attitude was that when the Lions assembled and were issued with their gear, O'Brien realised there were no trousers. Each player had two blazers and two ties, plus playing gear, but no trousers to wear with their blazers. They were expected to provide their own. O'Brien remonstrated with the committee and eventually trousers were issued. The Scottish union insisted that they be returned at the end of the tour.

Des O'Brien, an affable Irishman, however tautological that may be, had played 20 tests for Ireland as a flanker or No. 8 between 1948 and 1952 and must have gone desperately close to being included in the 1950 Lions. The captain of that team, Irish teammate Karl Mullen, certainly thought O'Brien should have come to New Zealand. In the curious way rugby sometimes works, O'Brien believed that his appointment as manager in 1966 was partly compensation for missing out as a player in 1950. O'Brien also had coaching credentials and had been the driving force behind organising the first coaching camps in Ireland in the late 1950s, to which young and promising players from England, Scotland and Wales were invited, as well as Irish. He obviously knew his rugby and he knew the players, but he had no say in the selection of the 1966 Lions. That job was entrusted to two members each from the four national unions involved. "I had no say in selection and I did object to that at the time," he recalled. "There were one or two players I wouldn't have taken because I didn't think they would give everything and I think I was probably right. I thought that, of the squad, there were talented and dedicated players who were going and would be magnificent, then there were dedicated players who would give everything and might make one test, and then there were talented players who just got on the Lions team and said, 'I've made it' and relaxed. And it turned out like that."

The judgment of O'Brien at the end of the tour was that he was too relaxed, too laid-back. He had expected the Lions to take responsibility for their own actions rather than be led. "I'm told I was a laid-back manager but I felt that because I would have given my right arm to have gone in 1950 — I still am disappointed really — they would give everything, too. They didn't." An indication of O'Brien's hands-off style was that he took a few days' break mid-tour and went off on holiday to Fiji, though he later said it was in an attempt to organise a game for the Lions on the way home.

For all their staid ways, the British administrators took the daring step for them of appointing a coach for the first time, though he did not carry the title of coach. He was designated "assistant manager", which was also the New Zealand euphemism for "coach" until the 1980s. The man they appointed, John Robins, had ideal qualifications. He'd played 11 tests as a prop for Wales and played in three of the tests on the 1950 Lions tour. He was a physical education expert at Loughborough College, that English sports nursery, and was said to have been well versed in the technicalities of rugby. He was well liked and respected by the players. But, and it may have been the biggest "but" of the tour, he was given little authority. His brief was that in all essential matters, the authority of the captain was paramount. The Lions therefore had a coach who coached only when the captain, Mike Campbell-Lamerton, let him. This was clearly not the fault of either man, but that of the Four Home Unions. It was as if the British administrators felt the appointment of a coach was so revolutionary they couldn't bring themselves to go the extra step and give him the authority a coach clearly needs.

Which leads to the captain. No Lions captain has been more maligned than Campbell-Lamerton. No one person has shouldered more of the blame for the poor performance on tour than him. Terry McLean wrote that Campbell-Lamerton had neither the background

nor the intellectual grasp of high-level captaincy. That was stinging criticism from McLean — McLean at his most waspish — and was surprising because McLean, as a former army officer, would have had a better understanding than any other journalist in 1966 of the training and attributes of a commissioned officer, which Campbell-Lamerton was.

Criticisms of Campbell-Lamerton during and after the tour were echoes of those which surrounded his appointment in February of 1966. He'd played for Scotland since 1961 and had captained them occasionally but not at all in the Five Nations of 1966. Scotland had two captains that year, neither of them Campbell-Lamerton, who was 32 when the Lions team was chosen. While there was surprise in Britain when he was named as leader, two prominent men in New Zealand rugby weren't surprised at all.

Wilson Whineray, whose international career had ended the year before, said he got to know Campbell-Lamerton on the All Blacks' British tour in 1963–64. "He is a very fine man, pleasant of manner, humorous, an excellent talker — in short, he has the qualities to keep his side happy and hard-working during the tour. I would say he could be an outstanding leader."

The other New Zealander was the Auckland fullback, Mike Cormack, who played in Britain for two years. "Campbell-Lamerton is a big strong man who in spite of his size doesn't carry an ounce of fat. He is very intelligent, a great talker about rugby and a great leader on the field."

Campbell-Lamerton himself felt that his selection as captain was probably a compromise. Leading contenders had been the Welsh captain, flanker Alun Pask, and the Irish prop, Ray McLoughlin, who had been dumped as Irish captain because he was never afraid to air his views, whatever they may have been. Mike Weston, who had captained England in New Zealand in 1963, was also regarded as a possibility. It is entirely possible that the two Welshmen on the selection committee wanted Pask, the two Englishmen wanted Weston, perhaps the two Irishmen wanted McLoughlin. Such a nationalistic impasse in rugby has historically been solved by compromise.

Lions on Ice

On the old long tours, the first test was always the most keenly anticipated. The lead-up provincial matches were but skirmishes before the set-piece battle to come. In 1966, there was more than usual anticipation. The All Blacks had a new captain, Brian Lochore, and three new faces. The Lions had not had a successful first section of their tour but judgment of their worth was suspended until after the test.

The All Blacks rolled into Dunedin on the Wednesday, much to the chagrin of the Lions manager, Des O'Brien, who adhered to the British view that teams shouldn't assemble more than 48 hours before a test and preferably about 24. He expressed a diplomatic surprise but the New Zealand union chairman, Tom Morrison, said there was no law — merely a convention that applied only in British rugby.

Above: Willie-John McBride.

Opposite page: The Lions on their unwanted jaunt to Queenstown. From left, Colin McFadyean, Frank Laidlaw, Allan Lewis, Willie-John McBride, Noel Murphy, David Watkins and Roger Young.

It was a minor little fuss as test day approached. While the All Blacks trained in their motley collection of provincial and club jerseys and socks on Dunedin club grounds, the Lions were nowhere to be seen.

The New Zealand union had arranged for the test players plus reserves — who couldn't take the field anyway – and O'Brien and hobbling coach, John Robins, to go to Queenstown.

While it may have been intended as a caring gesture by the New Zealand union to dispatch the Lions to the relaxing chocolate box scenery, it wasn't the ideal place for a team to prepare for a test match.

"Some of the ways we were stitched up were unbelievable," Irish lock Willie-John McBride recalled. "Now this is midwinter in New Zealand and they sent us to Queenstown to train . . . of course it was frozen solid, midwinter and we couldn't run, there was nowhere to train."

They had an unsatisfactory session in a school hall then when they discovered the ground on which they were supposed to train was frozen, they took off like tourists for Coronet Peak, trying out skiing and tobogganing, riding up and down in the chairlift, chucking snowballs at each other.

That night O'Brien looked for some of the players to go skating with him, but by 8.30 p.m. they were all in bed — exhausted from their afternoon in the snow.

Captain Mike Campbell-Lamerton, conscious that such frolicking was hardly conducive to a reputation-restoring performance in the test match, sought the advice of locals about where some training might be possible. He was told the airfield, so the airfield it was.

"We ended up at the airfield where there were grass runways and you could run on it reasonably well," McBride recalled. "And you know, we would be out there on the runway doing something and then somebody would shout, 'Aeroplane, aeroplane' and we'd all run like hell and hide in the hangar until after the aeroplane had come in. And then we would sneak out again, it was absolutely hilarious. We were completely stitched up by the New Zealand Rugby Union in sending us up there. It was amazing."

Ironically, the Lions left behind in Dunedin had far more rigorous and effective training runs under the guidance of Irish prop Ray McLoughlin.

The 1966 Lions captain, Mike Campbell-Lamerton, tells his troops what he wants during a training session.

The first test captains take the field, Brian Lochore and Mike Campbell-Lamerton.

Colin Meads seems to have secured possession in this lineout in the first test. Referee John Pring watches, from left, Ken Kennedy, Bruce McLeod, Ken Gray, Mike Campbell-Lamerton, Charlie Norris, Meads, Denzil Williams, Jack Hazlett, Brian Price, Stan Meads, Chris Laidlaw and Ron Lamont.

"One didn't ask to be captain," Campbell-Lamerton recalled in 2001. "There was strong feeling among the Welsh for Pask and maybe they were right. There was no one more surprised than myself when two press men phoned to inform me of my appointment. Although I'd captained Scotland, it had never entered into my head that I would captain the Lions and my first response was tentative. If you look at the wood for the trees, I was probably the compromise choice when the selectors couldn't agree on either Pask, Weston or McLoughlin."

Leadership was held at the end of the tour to have been the single most significant reason why the Lions had failed. That seems a fair assessment but it seems unfair to blame the men who were cast in the roles. As McLoughlin said, "On the tour there were no rows or politics but there was a lack of focus as far as leadership was concerned with each man not wanting to step on the other's toes. It would have been better if any one of

them had had total control and run it with an iron fist. But there was nothing the manager could do about it because he didn't have the mandate from home."

The fault, McLoughlin said, lay squarely with the system and organisation that had put the three men in their positions rather than with the men themselves. Each had clear instructions from the Four Home Unions as to what their roles were and each carried out their functions according to what they'd been told. The leadership faults were compounded in New Zealand when O'Brien went off on his holiday and when Robins snapped an Achilles tendon in a charity match and, after spending some time in hospital in Wellington, spent most of the rest of the tour on crutches. Campbell-Lamerton, loyal to a fault, has not criticised either man but has said: "I ended up doing a lot of administration because it was not in my nature, or in my training as a soldier, not to help out."

Courage in Korea

The word "hero" is bandied about to the point of total devaluation in sports writing. A last-minute tryscorer, the goalkicker who lands the winning goal from the touchline, the tackler who saves the game in the dying seconds . . . all carry the label of hero.

There have also been genuine heroes in rugby. One was the captain of the 1966 Lions, Mike Campbell-Lamerton, much maligned for both his team's and his own performances in New Zealand.

When the team was in New Zealand, it was written often enough that he was a serving army officer, that he had seen action in the Korean War 13 years before, and that he had badly mangled a foot when a parachute jump from a helicopter in Cyprus went horribly wrong.

What wasn't written, presumably because Campbell-Lamerton felt no need to tell anyone and his teammates probably didn't know enough to tell, was that he had played a critical role in one of the decisive battles toward the end of the Korean War in 1953.

As a second-lieutenant, he was a platoon commander in his regiment, the Duke of Wellington's. Another platoon commander just happened also to be a rugby player, David Gilbert-Smith, who had been on the side of the scrum for Scotland against England the year before. And to gild the rugby coincidence still further, the Duke's companies were a part of the 29th British Brigade, whose commander was Brigadier Douglas Kendrew. He had played 10 tests for England, including the Obolensky match against the All Blacks in 1936. Kendrew was later knighted and served a term as the governor of Western Australia.

In May of 1953, the 1st Battalion of the regiment, which included both the rugby-playing soldiers' platoons, was deployed along a conjunction of ridges known as The Hook, which dominated the Samichon River valley on the approaches to Seoul. Late in the month the Chinese bombarded the Duke's position for 12 hours before launching an infantry assault that led to ferocious close-quarter fighting. When the attack was beaten back, Campbell-Lamerton and Gilbert-Smith were given the job of regaining a position on top of The Hook that had been overrun by the Chinese.

The official history of the regiment said: "The initial plan proved unworkable as the whole of the top of the hill had literally changed shape, with rubble and tangled wire preventing any forward movement. The only way to make progress was up the line of the original trenches, a slow and laborious business."

The history laid out the terrain over which Campbell-Lamerton and Gilbert-Smith led their platoons: "Ten thousand Chinese shells had ploughed six foot furrows in the terrain, and trenches eight foot six inches deep, had been smashed in so that they were now scarcely more than knee high. Shredded sandbags and tangled bundles of barbed wire littered the area. Among the debris the grisly remains of Chinese soldiers testified to the effect of the counter artillery fire . . . the two young platoon leaders led their men across 400 yards of open ground under heavy shell and mortar fire. Although they took a significant number of casualties, by 3.30 a.m. on May 29 The Hook was back in the Duke's hands."

Both men were recommended for the Military Cross, the British army's third highest decoration for bravery in battle after the Victoria Cross and the Distinguished Service Order. It was decided only one could be awarded and it went to Gilbert-Smith or, as the history noted, "Mike drew the short straw".

Leader of men . . . Mike Campbell-Lamerton.

Mick Williment scores in the first test despite the tackle by Mike Gibson.

The foot soldiers in the Lions later acknowledged there was a leadership vacuum but none were critical of O'Brien, Robins or Campbell-Lamerton: all were critical of the system that put them in their unworkable positions.

What concerned the players more was their New Zealand itinerary, the hard competitiveness of New Zealand play and an injury list that restricted selections, although there seemed also to be disagreement about which players should be in the first-choice lineups and which shouldn't. Among a variety of selection oddities was the Welsh lock, Delme Thomas, being played at prop in the third test.

While the itinerary was undoubtedly draining, it has to be put in the context that 25 games in New Zealand did require a great deal more travelling than any British player in the 1960s was accustomed to. It wasn't as if the New Zealand union sandbagged the tour by having, for example, the Lions play one game in Whangarei then the next in Invercargill. It was arranged, as much as possible, to minimise travelling and matches were grouped in islands. The Lions didn't take kindly to having to play their first match in Invercargill and, as if to prove their point, they lost to Southland. Their complaint there was that they'd been in Brisbane for their last match in Australia and would have appreciated a more gradual acclimatisation. "Imagine the culture shock of swimming in the warm winters of sub-tropical Queensland one minute and being in Invercargill in the cold, wet and windy south of New Zealand the next," Welsh first five-eighth David Watkins said.

One Scottish Lion described Invercargill as being the Inverness of New Zealand, which brought to mind a rebuke by a 1971 Lion, Chris Rea, who was later a senior official with the International Rugby Board. Rea once accused a journalist: "You sit on every fence from Invercargill to Inverness."

Individually and collectively, the Lions were shocked by the opening fortnight of their tour and they never really recovered. Beaten by Southland in their first match, beaten by Otago in their third and by Wellington in their fifth, the skids were under the tour almost before it was fully under way. They struggled in their early games against sides which should have been put away with comfort such as the Hanan Shield combined unions and the combined Marlborough-Nelson-Golden Bay-Motueka. The Lions had, for reasons best known to themselves, decided they could win matches in the forwards, yet it quickly became clear that they couldn't and if they were to have any show at all, they needed to get what ball they could command out to their backs. It seemed pointless to ignore the talents they had such as Mike Gibson, David Watkins, Sandy Hinshelwood, Dewi Bebb, Stewart Wilson and Colin McFadyean. None of them, with the possible exceptions of Gibson and Watkins, were of the same stellar quality as a Jackie Kyle of 1950 or a Tony O'Reilly or a Peter Jackson of 1959, but all were more than useful players.

Deciding to subdue New Zealand forwards was the wrong way to go. It was a risk against provincial sides: it was madness in the tests. These were the days when provincial sides looked forward for months and perhaps years to their encounters with touring teams, when it was the aim of every provincial player to cut the visitors down to size. For many players, such matches were the highlights of their playing careers. Lions in 1966 and on other tours, just like South Africans or Australians, complained that provincial teams lay in wait to ambush the tourists. Of course they did.

This was the era of rugby when players sorted out their own disputes if the referees weren't quick enough or smart enough. Summary justice was dispensed and there were no intrusive television cameras to provide later retribution. One of the constant themes of the 1966 tour was the amount of fighting in games, each team accusing the other of starting it. It was also an era in which rucking was dominant and positively

One of the most graphic shots of Colin Meads on the burst.

Battleground. Lions David Watkins (left) and Ron Lamont lie injured after one of the flare-ups in the Lions' match against Canterbury.

encouraged and it was no coincidence that two of the Lions' early losses were to Southland and Otago, where rucking was an art form.

"In those days when rucking was key to the game," McLoughlin said, "a couple of guys locked on to each other to hit a ruck at the same time and if there was a guy there they just walked on him. As they saw it, it wasn't dirty, but there are different ways of walking and there was the odd kick. There are dirty players in every country but I never regarded them [New Zealanders] as dirty. I regarded them as hard and uncompromising and the sort who you didn't want to get in their way if you could avoid it, but never dirty. In fact, I think they were a joy to watch."

Manager O'Brien didn't agree. After the Lions lost to Canterbury, a match that was as hard and niggardly as any, he publicly climbed into the style of play in New Zealand. "Back home we play rugby as a game to enjoy. We love our rugby. Here we find obstruction, short-arm tackling and other illegal tactics. We're sick of it. We have enjoyed New Zealand's wonderful hospitality and great friendliness and it is often said that the least enjoyable part of the tour is the 90 minutes on the field. I add 10 minutes for the usual injuries. We went out

today to counter all this and this is the way we are going from now on."

Jim Telfer, the Scottish flanker who captained the Lions against Canterbury, warmed to O'Brien's theme: "I am not going to say today's game was dirty," he said, "because every game played in New Zealand has been dirty."

Harry Blazey, a Canterbury rugby man of note and older brother of administrator Ces, was president of the New Zealand union at the time. He slammed back at O'Brien: "It seems to me that before accusing his opponents of illegal play he should look at some of the illegalities the Lions are practising, such as consistently coming into rucks on the wrong side, failing to roll clear of the ball, and obstructing in the lineouts."

Blazey then accused Telfer of being peevish and ill-mannered. McLoughlin later remarked that the Canterbury match in 1966 had not been as violent as the equivalent game in 1971, which ended McLoughlin's tour after he broke a thumb when connecting with Alex Wyllie's head.

It wasn't just the Canterbury match. Others were said to have been spiteful games and the one against Auckland included a brawl involving most of the forwards from both teams. Tom Pearce, outspoken

Lions for Charity

It wasn't always the serious business of winning test matches that occupied the minds of the All Blacks and Lions in 1966. There was also some fun, although with a solemn purpose.

A third grade player for what was then the St Pat's club in Wellington had died in a club game a couple of weeks before the Lions played Wellington and a social match was arranged for the day after the game at Athletic Park to raise some money for the widow and her three children.

The Lions wholeheartedly entered into the spirit of things, although coach John Robins may have had second thoughts later.

A crowd of 6000 turned up at the park for the match — a crowd that some unions would have loved for a serious match, never mind a casual game that had only passing snatches of real rugby. The game was between an Onslow invitation team, led by the All Black captain, Brian Lochore, comprising Wellington players and a few past, present or future All Blacks, and a St Pat's invitation team led by the Lions manager, Des O'Brien, also with a mixture of players of varying ability and experience.

There was a story behind O'Brien's inclusion. A flanker or No. 8 for Ireland, he had been considered desperately unlucky not to have been chosen for the Lions tour of New Zealand in 1950. His "selection" for the charity game was compensation so he could finally say he'd played in New Zealand. He even scored a try, though not, it has to be admitted, in the most competitive of circumstances.

"I was playing No. 8," he recalled, "and at one stage we had a scrum on the opposition line. Brian Lochore, who was on my right, said we're going to heel this and go right. But the scrum screwed and I went left and I was saved by Colin Meads shouting, 'Go back, you silly bugger, go the other way.' So I sort of scuttled back round the scrum and a whole row opened up and I scored a try. It was a set-up to give the manager a try."

Don Clarke and a barefooted Bob Scott had a goalkicking duel from halfway at halftime and venerable Billy Wallace, then aged 87, had kicked off in the match. George Nepia was there as well to complete the quartet of famous fullbacks.

The touch judges were the Lions captain, Mike Campbell-Lamerton and the great Irish flanker, Noel Murphy, on his second tour of New Zealand. O'Brien's team was trailing toward the end of the game so the irrepressible Murphy tossed away his flag, ran onto the field, grabbed the ball and scored a try, then kicked the conversion for the scores to be suitably tied.

It was all good fun. All except for Robins. He was the referee but hobbled off the field in the first half with what was initially thought to be just a minor muscle strain. He entered the spirit of the celebrations that night but next day when the Lions had moved to Nelson, he was still being troubled by the leg and went off to a doctor. A ruptured Achilles tendon was diagnosed and Robins had a few days in hospital and was put in plaster from ankle to knee.

For the next several weeks, Robins on crutches was a forlorn figure on the touchlines at training.

Generations of excellence. All Black fullbacks Billy Wallace, George Nepia, Bob Scott and Don Clarke together at the charity day in Wellington.

administrator and former prop, said he knew who was to blame. "There is no doubt in my mind that most of the trouble that has erupted on this tour has been initiated by the Lions themselves." Pearce accused a Lion of kicking one of the Auckland players when he was on the ground.

The Auckland brawl began when the Irish No. 8, Noel Murphy, called for a mark and his opposite number, Keith Nelson, tackled him. The Lions players took exception. The trouble was the mark hadn't been given and Nelson was within his rights. The Lions thought otherwise.

The New Zealand council, the game's ruling body, later issued a placatory statement saying it deplored rough play, that the laws of the game had to be adhered to by both sides and the referees respected. What it didn't say, and what it couldn't say, was that there was a gulf between British and New Zealand players about what a ruck was and how to play in them. The New Zealand players and the referees understood the rules, both written and unwritten. The Lions, and not just in 1966, were less sure.

They were also less sure in the tests, perhaps another symptom of the leadership vacuum. The great Otago coach of the 1940s, Vic Cavanagh, could have an acerbic tongue and he was at his best when he dismissed the 1966 Lions as a "nothing team". He made the comment after the first test in Dunedin, which was won by the All Blacks 20–3. It may have been a harsh judgment because the Lions, whatever their faults, had to confront one of the best All Black teams fielded, at least in the forwards. If the Lions had decided, as they said they did, to take the All Blacks on upfront, it was a grave error of judgment. Any battlefield commander, as Campbell-Lamerton had been, knows that the best place to attack an enemy is at his weakest points, not his strongest. Wilson Whineray, retired the year before from international rugby, believed the Lions erred in not playing to their own strengths, the backs. And Whineray knew the All Black forwards like no other: Ken Gray and Jack Hazlett as props, the latter gaining his place on the strength of Southland's win against the

Lions, and Bruce McLeod at hooker; Colin Meads, then in his tenth year of test rugby, locking the scrum with his brother Stan; and three of the best loose forwards to pull on the All Black jersey, Waka Nathan, Kel Tremain and Brian Lochore. Fred Allen retained the same pack for each of the four tests and, since no injuries intruded, why wouldn't he? They were a formidable pack. The Lions were, shall we say, less formidable. Though they had individual players of genuine merit, especially Alun Pask at No. 8 and flankers Jim Telfer and Ron Lamont, they were not in the same league as the All Blacks. New Zealand won the first test by three tries to none and there were many observers who thought the margin of victory could have been greater but for some wasted kicking in the second half.

Such was the completeness of the All Black win that after the game Campbell-Lamerton, as quoted by Terry McLean, muttered, "I'd rather die than go through such an experience again." No such extreme measures would have been seriously contemplated, but Campbell-Lamerton dropped himself for the second test, in Wellington. The Lions pack took on a more solid look with the presence of Willie-John McBride and Delme Thomas at lock, veteran Noel Murphy on the side of the scrum and with Telfer moving to the back in place of Pask. The changes did the trick for the Lions, but not so much that they were able to beat the All Blacks. The New Zealand pack was again superior and though the Lions were able to lead 9–8 at halftime after playing with a brisk southerly at their backs, it was evident the All Blacks were in full control. The All Black win wasn't without some alarms though, and Lions centre Colin McFadyean could well have scored and made it more interesting had referee Pat Murphy applied the advantage law as he later acknowledged to aggrieved Lions he should have. It was a better performance from the Lions, from both backs and forwards, and the All Blacks were not quite as dominant with their 16–12 win as they had been in the first test. They scored three tries to none though, evidence itself of the All Blacks' forward power and evidence too of the strength in the midfield of Ian MacRae in his second test. He almost single-handedly introduced the concept of second-phase possession to New Zealand rugby with his ability to take the tackle, commit defenders, then deliver the ball for the next onslaught. But it was the power of his running and a burst between David Watkins and Mike Gibson that led to the All Blacks' first try, by Kel Tremain.

The Lions should have gained confidence and belief in their selections from their performance in Wellington. But by the time of the third test in Christchurch, it must have dissipated because Campbell-Lamerton put himself back in the scrum and Thomas, who had had such a fine game at lock in the second test, was moved to tighthead prop. It was one of the more curious decisions on a tour that was characterised by curious decisions.

Sandy Hinshelwood dives spectacularly to score in the fourth test at Eden Park. The would-be tackler is Mac Herewini.

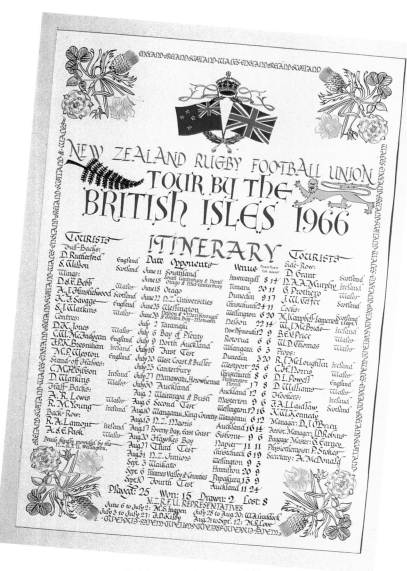

Lions tours spawned this type of memorabilia.

If Thomas had been last man standing, it might have been understandable but three specialist props, Ray McLoughlin, Denzil Williams and David Powell, had to watch from the stand. What they watched was a game in which the All Black pack was again dominant but one which the Lions, with a little more luck and a little more wisdom, might have won. The All Blacks won 19–6, but the Lions at least had the consolation of scoring their first two tries in the series, one of which was a gem to David Watkins. They didn't score at all in the second half but may have done had their finishing not been thwarted by knock-ons and wayward passing.

A combination of injuries and selection peccadillos again brought changes to the Lions for the fourth test while the All Blacks continued their luxury of minimal changes, none to the forwards and Malcolm Dick replacing Ian Smith in the backs. Injuries ruled out Delme Thomas and Noel Murphy from the Lions, Welshman Brian Price went into lock to replace his captain and the peccadillo was the switch in positions between Jim Telfer and Alun Pask. When Des O'Brien was asked why Telfer would be at No. 8 and Pask on the side of the scrum, his reply was a self-contented "wait and see". The waiting-and-seeing didn't last long because Pask had his jaw broken after about 20 minutes and whatever chance the Lions had of gaining at least one test win was well and truly gone. Fourteen average-to-good Lions against 15 very good-to-great All Blacks made for an unbalanced contest. Still, the Lions had some chances which they took well, resulting in tries to Hinshelwood and McFadyean, and other chances which they didn't take at all. The All Blacks were not spectacular but they didn't need to be. Fred Allen drilled them to do the basics well and to eliminate errors and such a simple philosophy was more than adequate against the Lions.

"The All Blacks were formidable," Campbell-Lamerton later recalled, "but even so the second test could easily have gone our way. Selection was often difficult because of injuries and many of us played injured because there was no option. As far as dropping myself for the second and fourth tests was concerned, it doesn't take courage to do that if you loved your team and you knew someone else could do a better job."

O'Brien made some interesting observations about the state of British rugby relative to New Zealand after the tour. Fred Allen, he said, wouldn't last as a coach in Britain. "Mr Allen would be flat on his face if he tried to coach a British team the same way he does an All Black side," he said. O'Brien felt that British players wouldn't stand up to, or for, the type of aggression and competitiveness that characterised New Zealand players.

Just try me, said Allen. He reckoned British players were every bit as hard and tough as New Zealanders and all they lacked was the direction and the coaching. When they get it, he said, watch out New Zealand.

Allen had just five years to be proved right.

1971
When Lions Roared

When the 1971 Lions left New Zealand having won a series for the first time, many were the reasons put forward as British and New Zealanders alike wondered how such a decisive swing in the rugby pendulum could have come about.

Some of the reasons were put down to individual players such as Barry John and Gareth Edwards, or Mike Gibson and Willie-John McBride, all players of rare qualities. Another interpretation was not so much that the Lions won, but that the All Blacks lost — that New Zealand hadn't recovered from the retirement of several key players after the tour of South Africa the year before. One theory was that New Zealand rugby was temporarily in a trough and that the Lions were temporarily at a peak and it was mere fortune, good for one, ill for the other, that the peak and trough coincided. Another was that the Lions were lucky, that the All Blacks in the four tests scored eight tries to the Lions' six and the difference was solely in the kicking of Barry John.

All these offerings had varying validity but none on their own could provide the complete answer as to why a combined British team, having previously won only one test in New Zealand since 1904, and with a success rate not much better in South Africa, could suddenly beat in a series a country that was held to be the most enduringly successful in rugby history. It was more than the bounce of the ball, the fortunes of sport, that beat the All Blacks in 1971.

Perhaps the more telling answer lay not in 1971 but in the 1960s when the Lions went to South Africa in 1962, New Zealand in 1966 and South Africa again in 1968 and did not win a single test (two wins against Australia were their only successes). The British attitude then and before had been an Olympian view:

The 1971 Lions squad. Back row: Dr Doug Smith (manager), Mike Gibson, Chris Rea, Ian McLauchlan, Fergus Slattery, Sandy Carmichael, Derek Quinnell, Mike Roberts, John Spencer, Sean Lynch, Delme Thomas, Mike Hipwell, Peter Dixon, Carwyn James (coach). Middle row: Ray Hopkins, Willie-John McBride, Mervyn Davies, Gordon Brown, John Dawes (captain), Bob Hiller, John Bevan, Alistair Biggar, John Taylor. Front row: Ray Mcloughlin, Arthur Lewis, John Pullin, Gareth Edwards, Barry John, Frank Laidlaw, Gerald Davies, J.P.R. Williams, David Duckham.

that it was not so much the winning that mattered, but the taking part. The Four Home Unions Committee, the multinational body charged with organising Lions tours, had even instructed the 1966 team before coming to New Zealand that playing "Lions-style rugby", however ill defined that may have been, was more important than winning the test matches. But the Four Home Unions found at the end of 1966 when their team hadn't won any of the tests that such warm fuzzy satisfaction wasn't really what they wanted. A change in administration and, more importantly, a change in attitude was due. The seeds of the success of the 1971 Lions were sown with the failure of their predecessors. There was another important factor. It was in the 1960s that the national sides of Britain separately began making tours. Wales went to South Africa in 1964 and to New Zealand in 1969 and England came to New Zealand in 1963. It wasn't the intention, but such tours became "feeling out" tours for the Lions. British players became more accustomed to both the rugby and the rugby environments of New Zealand and South Africa.

They learned of the different ways in which the game was played and refereed and, importantly, they learned of the difference in attitude: the New Zealanders and South Africans played their sport to win and not, as was the British way, for the game's own sake.

Another factor of importance to the success of the Lions was the visit to Britain in 1967 of the All Blacks captained by Brian Lochore, coached by Fred Allen and managed by Charlie Saxton. The All Blacks were unbeaten on that tour and were regarded fondly, and still are, for the adventurous nature — underpinned by organisation — of their play. Those All Blacks, by dominating in the forwards so the backs could play attacking, exciting rugby, played exactly the way in which the Four Home Unions wanted the Lions to play. Crowd-pleasing, winning rugby. And the man behind the success of the team was Fred Allen. Granted the All Blacks had players of genuine merit and the team remains rightly regarded as one of New Zealand's finest, but it was Allen who brought all the various strands together. This was at a time when British rugby was slowly acknowledging the need for proper coaches and that neither selectors nor captain, no matter how effective they may have been in their primary roles, were necessarily also good coaches. Coaching schools had been set up in Ireland and Wales, not without lingering opposition. The Irish prop, Ray McLoughlin, had been sacked as Ireland captain because he told the selectors he did not want them in the dressing room immediately before a game when his players should have been focusing on the task immediately ahead of them.

The Lions of 1966 had appointed a coach, John Robins of Wales, but gave him the title of honorary assistant manager and no mandate to actually coach the team. His brief was more that of a modern fitness trainer and the coaching effectively rested where in Britain it traditionally had, with the captain. The Lions of 1968 in South Africa also had a coach, Ronnie Dawson, who had been the captain in New Zealand in 1959, and while the team was unsuccessful, and while there continued to be ambivalence and confusion about his role, it was at least a step along the way.

British administrators slowly came to realise they had to slough off their hidebound ways. They could not win rugby in the 20th century on the basis of organisation laid down in the 19th. Change in rugby administration comes slowly, and slowly it came. After the disappointment of 1966, the Four Home Unions Committee began to act more quickly than at its previous glacial pace. In November of 1966, it decided that the manager and assistant manager of future Lions teams would be chosen a year out from the tour and then, in March of 1967, it decided that the manager would be chairman of the Lions selection committee, which would otherwise be made up of one (rather than two) selector from each of the four unions. At the same time, the committee gained a new chairman, John Tallent of England, and a new secretary, John Hart of Scotland, both of them more forward-looking than their predecessors. This was the arrangement for the Lions tour of South Africa and it remained unchanged for the Lions tour of New Zealand in 1971. The committee met in May of 1970 to decide on the critical appointments

for New Zealand knowing, from the experiences of 1966 and 1968 that, no matter how talented the players, it was the management that would determine the success or otherwise of the tour. Four men wanted the job of manager and four wanted to be coach. The managerial contenders were Doug Smith of Scotland, Duggie Harrison of England, and Gwilym Treharne and Handel Rogers of Wales. The coaching candidates were Carwyn James of Wales, Martin Underwood of England, Roly Meates of Ireland and Roy Bish of Wales.

Normally the manager would have been appointed first, but it was not straightforward on this occasion. Rogers had managed the Welsh team in New Zealand in 1969 and was therefore considered to be ideal for the Lions role. But the two leading coach contenders were both Welsh and the committee could not countenance both manager and coach being from Wales (this would have been against the principle of nationality balance and also would not have been politically acceptable to the rest of the committee). So the coaching role was decided first and the choice of James was probably the wisest decision any Four Home Unions Committee ever made. A Welsh first five-eighth in 1958–59, James was the successful coach of Llanelli and had coached the West Wales team that had performed so valiantly against the 1967 All Blacks. A 41-year-old bachelor, he was a lecturer at Trinity College in Carmarthen in west Wales, was one of the leading authorities on the Welsh language, and was a man of much personal charm and intellect and with a profound understanding of rugby. As events proved, he was an ideal choice.

With James's selection, the manager's job effectively came down to two: Smith or Harrison. While there was some acknowledgement of the need to appoint the right people to the right jobs, an element of rugby politics and turns for jobs did still exist. England had provided the manager for the 1968 tour so Scotland's Smith was appointed manager. Harrison, a Dorset farmer, had been a popular president of the Rugby Football Union and had made a round-the-world tour at his own expense in 1966–67 promoting rugby in all manner of places and perhaps would have been a successful manager.

But Smith had his own attributes, not least a physical presence that he could use in daunting or avuncular manner, depending on circumstances. A doctor of medicine, he had played eight tests for Scotland on the wing and came to New Zealand with the Lions in 1950 when his play was restricted somewhat by a broken arm. It's said that after the tour, when he resumed playing for London Scottish, he wore a leather brace to protect the arm — something similar to what Colin Meads wore in South Africa in 1970 — and was not averse to belabouring stroppy opponents with it.

The choice of Smith and James was, with hindsight, as perfect a choice as could be made. One step the Four Home Unions had not made by 1970 was the logical one of giving the coach the authority to choose the players he would have to coach. James was not a member of the selection committee but he and Smith were of such like mind that it probably didn't matter. The pair of them decided what they needed to do in New Zealand and which players they needed to make it happen, and set about the planning.

With the English union marking its centenary in the northern season of 1970–71 and the opening of a revamped Arms Park in Cardiff, there was more than the usual rugby activity. All manner of celebration matches were played and Smith and James were at them all, assessing who was worthy of being a Lion. The most important matches were the Five Nations and when Wales won the Grand Slam, it became obvious that the nucleus of the Lions party would be Welsh. It was only slightly less obvious that the captain, the third member of the management triumvirate, would

Carwyn James . . . an ideal choice as coach of the 1971 Lions.

be the Welsh captain, John Dawes. He almost single-handedly over six years had reorganised London Welsh from being largely a social club to one of the most formidable in Europe (he had some assistance from a former All Black, Hugh Burry, who was a doctor in London). Not a player of brilliance, Dawes was a player of presence and had the respect of his teammates for both his playing skills and the manner in which he gained the best from his players. None of the other countries had a captain in the same league.

For a change, Smith and James — not forgetting the other selectors — had the best of British from which to choose. The old bane of Lions tours, players unwilling or unable to take time off work to go to the other side of the world to play some footy, was not a serious factor in the early months of 1971 (though it would continue to affect later tours). Some were unavailable, such as Welsh prop Barry Llewellyn whose experience of being in New Zealand in 1969 would have been invaluable, and England prop Keith Fairbrother. The Irish No. 8, Ken Goodall, had switched to league and England centre Chris Wardlow broke his jaw in a game after being chosen for the Lions.

There were a few murmurings about the final selection of 30 players, especially the selection of the reserve Welsh halfback, Ray Hopkins, and the omission of Irish hooker Ken Kennedy, but the overall impression of the team was that it was nicely balanced and that there were some genuine stars. When they assembled at Eastbourne in southern England, James had the newly appointed Welsh director of coaching, Ray Williams, talk to the team and the essence of the Lions' plan of attack was outlined. New Zealand

The Lion King (Mk II)

For a bloke who didn't regard himself as a regular goalkicker and who didn't want to go to New Zealand anyway, Barry John didn't make a bad impression in 1971.

John scored 180 points in New Zealand, the most by any visiting player, and was lionised, so to speak, from North Cape to the Bluff as "the King". Yet he almost never made it.

John had been injured in a match in France in the Five Nations in 1971 and felt the effects for several weeks afterward. In the meantime, a letter inviting him to join the Lions tour had arrived at his home in March but he just ignored it.

Coach Carwyn James subsequently phoned John and asked him why he hadn't replied and John told him he was still affected by the injury — a broken nose — and that he didn't want to go to New Zealand.

"I had to spend some time with him persuading him to make himself available," James said.

Perhaps only James could have persuaded him. Both James and John came from the tiny Welsh village of Cefneithin near Llanelli so there was a kindred spirit between the two.

James talked to the Lions manager, Doug Smith, and they agreed that John would be a special case. He wouldn't have to train as often as the other players and he could pretty much have his own tour as long as he was available to play. "If you don't want to train, you don't train," James told John. "You will play whenever you want to play, that's a promise."

Aware of the risks he was taking, James told Smith he would square such a promise with captain John Dawes and the rest of the players.

John also was aware of the risks and said he didn't want to be regarded as a prima donna. Ten days before the team was due to assemble, John decided he would go.

James was true to his word and John didn't always attend team trainings and the players were told such things as "Barry's got a sore back" or "Barry's nursing a sore knee". On one occasion, Barry was nursing some supposedly ailing part of his body when the other players watched him playing an impromptu game of soccer.

"What's going on?" one Lion asked another. "Oh, the King's sore again," was the reply.

None of the Lions resented the special treatment for their star. "He played rugby on a different plane from anyone else I ever saw," No. 8 Mervyn Davies once said. "He was on a different, superior wavelength."

John was neither the first-choice goalkicker for his club, Cardiff, nor for Wales before the tour. "I've always considered myself a No. 2 goalkicker, happy to fill in when No. 1 fails," he said at the end of the tour. "Even after kicking all those goals in New Zealand, I don't have any ambition to be a regular kicker." He'd much prefer, he said, to concentrate on his position at first five-eighth.

He didn't do so for much longer after the Lions tour. He played three matches of the Five Nations in 1972 and then, at the age of 27, he quit. Part of the reason, he said at the time, was the celebrity status he acquired as a result of the tour of New Zealand. For all his confidence and seeming cockiness on the field, he liked anonymity off it and that was something he didn't get. He said he tired of people stopping him and talking to him, even just standing and looking at him. "I never sought adulation," he said. "That's probably why I ran away from it."

The inimitable "king" of the 1971 Lions, Barry John.

John Taylor, John Dawes and friend as they leave London for New Zealand.

rugby, the players were told, was obsessed with forward power or, in James's words, perspiration was regarded as more worthy than inspiration. The job of the Lions, James said, would be to at least match the All Blacks in the forwards and to thrash them in the backs. This had always been the aim of Lions teams but in 1971, for the first time, they had the personnel to do it. As James also said, the All Blacks always played as if they expected to win and the Lions played and hoped they'd win. This time, he said, it would be different.

It may sound simplistic, but much of the hard work for the Lions' series win had been done before they even played a game. The evidence was soon apparent in New Zealand after the two-game prelude in Australia when the Lions were beaten by Queensland and Smith introduced a new phrase, circadian disrhythmia, to the rugby lexicon. That was the main reason for the Lions' defeat, he thought, and it was only after much delving into dictionaries that the lay public realised he'd been talking about jet lag. One newspaper headlined the Lions as "woeful" after that first match, but it was a word never to be used again about the Lions in 1971.

From the first match in New Zealand, a 25–3 beating of a combined Counties and Thames Valley — with Counties then among the most enterprising of New Zealand teams — to the last, the drawn fourth test, the Lions made a triumphal march throughout New Zealand. There were hiccups and the occasional deviation along the way, such as the second test in Christchurch and the Canterbury match, but generally the Lions excited and entertained like no other rugby side before them. They were true to the James promise: they were competitive in the forwards and in the backs they chanced their arms much more than New Zealanders were used to seeing. The New Zealand style was to win the ball from the set piece, halfback to kick over the top of the forwards for them to start all over again, or for the ball to go to ground in midfield for the second-phase to start. Outside backs were there essentially for defensive purposes. This was not the James way.

A former Lion turned journalist, Clem Thomas, summed up what the Lions did: "They re-established the fundamental ethos that rugby is an attacking game best enjoyed by fifteen players running and handling at risk. Perhaps their greatest atttributes were their courage in defence and their ability to conquer not only by kicking but by passing. Never were they more dangerous than when they were under pressure. They re-established the aesthetics and ideals of the game, particularly the exquisite nature of the pass which entirely devalued the more physical and rugged attitudes of New Zealand rugby."

They had the coach with the widsom to see and they had the players able to put James's theories into practice. There were the greats of the game such as Edwards, John, Gibson and McBride, but there were many others, in the test side or not, who were as versed in the Lions principles and just about as able to put them into practice. There were wings such as John Bevan and David Duckham, two different types of players but equally effective on attack and defence. There was Gerald Davies, a survivor of the 1966 tour, who belied his slight size with his speed and his intelligent reading of where he needed to be and when. There was Bob Hiller, the England fullback who laboured under the label of "steady" yet he could easily have slipped into the test team but for the presence of J. P. R. Williams — a man ahead of his time as an attacking fullback who was also an aggressive defender. Perhaps the one flaw in Williams's game was his kicking, but wasn't it he who ensured the fourth test was drawn with a mighty dropped goal?

The greatest onus was on the forwards because it was they who had to gain equality with an All Black pack that was, like most All Black packs, formidable. James put a lot of emphasis on scrummaging, knowing the Lions were neither as big nor as strong as the All Blacks, but also knowing that correct technique would make the difference. It was where men such as the Scot,

Ian McLauchlan, and the Irishman, Sean Lynch, came into their own after injury had taken the first-choice Lions props Ray McLoughlin and Sandy Carmichael out of the tour. There was McBride of the many battles against his greatest rival, Colin Meads, and there were Gordon Brown and Delme Thomas. One of the supposed weaknesses in the Lions before the tour was in the loose forwards but if there was weakness among Fergus Slattery, Peter Dixon, Mervyn Davies and Derek Quinnell, it was both rare and illusory.

The nascent power of the Lions was unleashed when they beat the other "Lions", Wellington, 47–9, with a display that was regarded as-near-to-perfect for 80 minutes as it is possible to get. This wasn't a mug Wellington team, but the Lions scored nine tries — a tremendous number for the time — in a display that sent a shudder through New Zealand rugby. It was a match more than any other that stamped Mike Gibson on the consciousness of New Zealanders as one of the greatest backs to play in New Zealand. Terry McLean

One of the most gifted of Lions backs, Mike Gibson.

Tane's Horror

For a few horrible moments, Tane Norton's All Black dream became a nightmare. He was in the dressing room at Carisbrook, counting down the nervous minutes until it was time to go out to play. It was the first test against the Lions in 1971. It was Norton's first test.

"The All Blacks had been named the week before and I thought I had a chance of making the reserves so you can imagine how I felt when I was named in the team," he recalled. "Stories in the papers, people congratulating you in the street, that sort of thing, but it was only when I was in the dressing room at Carisbrook before the game that it really hit me that I was an All Black.

"There in the same dressing room pulling on their black jerseys were Colin Meads, Ian Kirkpatrick, Bryan Williams . . . and I was one of them!"

He pulled on his first boot. Reached for his second. But then Norton's heart flipped.

"First boot, 9½, that was fine. But then the second boot. Far too big. 14½! I thought, 'What the hell is going on here?'"

Players had only one pair of boots in those days and they trained in them as well. The practice the previous day had been wet, so back at the hotel Norton cleaned his boots as best he could and then put them on a heater. Other players did the same.

Sitting in the dressing room with his one boot that fitted and the other that didn't, Norton pondered what to do. "I thought I could stuff some paper in the toe and at least I'd still be able to run around. It wouldn't have been ideal, but it should've worked. I was determined to get out on that paddock, right or wrong. But then I thought if I've got a boot that's too big, some other poor bugger's got a boot that's too small and he wouldn't be able to do anything about it."

It has to be understood that an All Black dressing room before a test is as silent as the grave. There's no idle banter. Such conversations as there are relate only to the game and are conducted in half-whispers. A newcomer such as Norton wasn't about to shout out an expletive and declare he had been landed with odd-sized boots.

But a player with more experience did. As Norton sat and worried and wondered, from across the dressing room Alan Sutherland uttered an oath, threw a boot to the floor and stormed off toward the toilet.

"Aha," thought Norton. While Sutherland was absent, Norton sidled across, picked up Sutherland's discarded boot, ascertained that it was in fact the required 9½, and quietly replaced it with the 14½.

Norton was back in his place, mightily relieved as he laced up both perfectly fitting boots. Sutherland reappeared, sat in his place, picked the boot up off the floor and put it on, showing no outward sign of his surprise that it had somehow grown in size while he was in the toilet.

Both men, their blood pressures back to normal, then went out and played their game. The boots weren't mentioned then or later, not until an All Black reunion in Auckland in 2003. "I hadn't told anyone about it and I'd certainly never discussed it with Alan until I saw him at the reunion. I said to him, 'Remember in Dunedin in 1971 . . . ?'

They had a good laugh about it, how they had both put their boots on the same heater and how somehow one or other, and neither knew who, mixed up the boots when retrieving them.

"That was a moment of sheer panic in the shed at Carisbrook," Norton recalled. "I tell you what, I never made that mistake again. I always checked and rechecked that they were my boots I had in my hands."

1971 test debutant Tane Norton.

in his report of the Wellington match compared Gibson to the great All Black centre of the 1920s, Bert Cooke. It was also a game, so Gibson himself later acknowledged, in which he appreciated for the first time a licence to use his flair and freedom in which to move.

It was games such as that against Wellington, and other displays of like quality, that made the Lions a popular side, that made crowds flock to see them, that made people stand around outside the players' hotels hoping to see them in person, and that made an untold number write to them. They were the entertainers of rugby: the All Blacks were New Zealand's team and naturally had the support of the rugby public, but it was the Lions who captured the imagination.

It wasn't all unrelenting joy. The match against Canterbury is a black mark in rugby history. One of the Lions' philosophies laid down at Eastbourne when they assembled and again when they arrived in Auckland was that they wouldn't take a backward step. They would not be intimidated. They would not turn the other cheek. The Lions didn't have a "99" call as other Lions had had, but they knew that if they were to achieve what they wanted in New Zealand, which was to win the series and win their provincial matches, there would be times when they would have to practise some of the black arts of rugby. Such a time came against Canterbury.

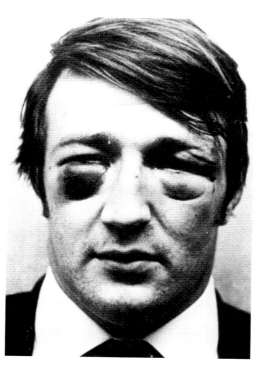

The face of a victim: Sandy Carmichael after the Canterbury match.

In the words of the Christchurch *Press* rugby writer, John Brooks, a seam of sourness ran through the game. Others called it brutal, others the Battle of Lancaster Park. There was violence, there was no doubt. Lions and Canterbury players alike threw punches, some ineffectual, some effective, and Lions and Canterbury players alike indulged in deliberate illegalities of the type that would later be called professional fouls. When the Lions flanker, Mike Hipwell, seemed deliberately to take his time getting back on side — "lazy running" as a modern referee might say — Alex Wyllie gave him a hurry-up. The front rows, it must be said, did not often exchange polite pleasantries and even Fergie McCormick, from fullback, delivered pugnacious comments. Each side blamed the other, as they tend to in such circumstances. Canterbury players were accused of being thugs and of deliberately going out to hurt the Lions, and the Lions were accused, among other things, of indulging in the old British habit of lying on the ball on the wrong side of rucks.

The cost to Canterbury was in bad publicity and in reputation and their coach Jim Stewart said later he resented his side being painted as the sole aggressors. He said he told one of his props, Alister Hopkinson, that in previous games the Lions were doing a lot of damage in the front rows. "What am I going to do about it?" Hopkinson asked his coach. "It's in your hands," Stewart replied, "but I'm not going to have the whole game ruined by the front row."

The cost to the Lions was the loss from the tour of their two first-choice test props, Ray McLoughlin and Sandy Carmichael, and their flanker, Hipwell. Carmichael's broken and battered face was pictured in every New Zealand newspaper and he had to wear dark sunglasses for his remaining few days in New Zealand. True to the props' code, he never said who did what to him. "I don't know how it happened," was his standard response in 1971 and again, years later. There was no doubt what happened to McLoughlin. He both broke and dislocated a thumb when he threw a punch at Wyllie and discovered that Wyllie's skull was much harder than McLoughlin's thumb. Hipwell was also shipped home, but because of a knee injury that wasn't necessarily a direct result of the Canterbury match.

Opposing brilliance: Gerald Davies and Bryan Williams.

Davies Answers Taunts

The 1971 Lions' match against Canterbury has gone down in rugby folklore as a dirty game, one in which players from both sides decided that getting their retaliation in first was one way to intimidate the opposition. The match against Hawke's Bay later in the tour can't have been far behind.

The Lions won 25-6 and wing Gerald Davies scored all four of their tries but it was a match that left a sour taste in the mouth.

Lions coach Carwyn James accused Hawke's Bay of being unnecessarily negative and playing not to lose rather than to win, while the Lions were accused of being wanton aggressors and transgressors.

Halfback Gareth Edwards was said to have taken a kick at the head of prop Hilton Meech which, fortunately for both, missed; Lions hooker John Pullin had to have a gash under an eye stitched; prop Ian McLauchlan ended the match with a bloody nose and other players nursed various ills.

Some of the Lions let taunts such as "soft Poms" and "long-haired pansies" get to them. Bay supporters clustered around the players' tunnel as the teams left the field and booed both the Lions and referee Bob Watson of North Auckland, and a Bay selector, Derek Tomb, muttered to Watson after the game, "You'll never get a test."

It was one of those niggly games that pleased no one and not even the sparkling running of Davies lifted the game from the depths.

Barry John, never the type of player to throw a punch, chose his own form of protest. Late in the game, he slowed to a walk several times when fielding the ball in defence, challenging and teasing the Bay players. Such actions didn't endear him to either the Bay players or spectators, but he left his most outrageous party trick until last.

Back on defence once more, when he gathered the ball he promptly sat down on it, taunting the Bay players.

"Hawke's Bay that day just wanted to take players out," John told Welsh journalist Peter Jackson. "When Gerald scored his four brilliant tries, the crowd did nothing to acknowledge any of them. They were pathetic. So when they kicked downfield with about 10 minutes to go, I ran back to get the ball. I trapped it with my backside and then I sat on it. They were

charging at me and it sounded as if the whole crowd of 25,000 were shouting, 'Kill! Kill!'

"I had taken the precaution of making sure I was inside the twenty-five before sitting on the ball. I left it as late as possible, picked the ball up and slammed it right back behind them so they all had to turn around. I was showing them, in a more subtle way, what I thought of them. I was totally disgusted by what had gone on. If this was rugby, what was the point in playing it?"

John's gestures were not appreciated. He was booed by the crowd and criticised by British and New Zealand journalists alike, being described as petulant and of turning the game into a farce. One paper said his halo was slipping to which John responded, "I never asked anyone to put a halo there in the first place."

John's mocking and the others' fighting took the gloss off Davies's superlative performance, but one of his teammates, Willie-John McBride, never forgot it.

Years later he recalled one of the Davies tries. "He left everybody for dead and the fullback came across and the blindside wing came across and you could see that he was going to be sandwiched and cut to pieces. I can still see it vividly in my mind. He just changed pace and the two guys collided . . . and Gerald had run between the two of them and scored. I've never seen anything like it in my life. He was the best wing threequarter I've seen. He had everything. He had pace, he had change of pace, he had sidesteps, he had swerves, he had hands, he had feet . . . he could do anything."

Gerald Davies against Hawke's Bay
. . . "He left everybody for dead."

The worth of Smith as a manager was borne out in the aftermath. He refused to talk about foul or dirty play, refused to accuse Canterbury of anything, and instead merely described it as "a hard game", which no one could deny. The more emotive words came from, of all people, the All Black coach, Ivan Vodanovich, in Blenheim the next day. If the Lions persisted with illegal play, he said, the first test "could become another Passchendaele".

It was a strange thing for Vodanovich to say. Usually the most charming and mild-mannered of men, he wouldn't have dreamed of deliberately offending anyone. Yet the comparison of a rugby match, however violent it may have been, with the 1917 battle in which 800 New Zealand troops were killed in a single day was an unfortunate analogy for him to draw. The reference to World War I must have been contagious because Terry McLean in his match report for the *New Zealand Herald* chose another World War I battle. "One could never wish to take from the Lions the glory of a defence which was to rugby what Verdun was to the western world."

The effect of the Canterbury match thrust the Lions into a quandary. A week out from the first test, they'd just lost their two best props. One of them, McLoughlin, was the thinking man of the forwards and James's great

ally in devising ways of overcoming the physicality of the All Blacks. It was a devastating blow for them.

The All Blacks had troubles of their own. Several test players from the tour of South Africa had either retired or gone their separate ways. Malcom Dick, Grahame Thorne, Ian MacRae, Brian Lochore and Keith Murdoch of the fourth test against the Springboks were all unavailable. Thorne had returned to South Africa, the others had retired — or Lochore thought he had — and Murdoch had a mysterious injury which was not so severe as to prevent him from being named in teams to play the Lions but was severe enough to stop him actually playing. The net effect of retirements and form meant that there were seven newcomers to test rugby in the All Black team — Bruce Hunter, the only All Black in South Africa not to have played a test, Ken Carrington, Bob Burgess, Alan McNaughton, Peter Whiting, Tane Norton and the man who replaced Murdoch from the original naming, Richie Guy. Bryan Williams, so effective on the wing in South Africa, had been put at centre. The captain was the indomitable Colin Meads.

It was, in effect, an All Black team in transition against a Lions team that, apart from the Canterbury match, had been nigh unbeatable.

Chico and The Man

The Lions' No. 2 halfback in New Zealand in 1971, Ray "Chico" Hopkins, spurned the latest in medical advances when he sought treatment for an injured leg halfway through the tour.

Hopkins had apparently burst a blood vessel in a thigh but had continued playing while the No. 1 halfback, Gareth Edwards, was recovering from a hamstring strain. The injury worsened and, as Hopkins said, the affected area was as hard as a board.

While in Masterton for the game against Wairarapa-Bush, Hopkins met the fabled fullback of the Invincibles, George Nepia, at a reception and told him of his injury and how orthodox treatment so far hadn't worked.

"I know just the thing," Nepia told him, and proceeded to explain how he would fix the problem with ancient Maori remedies.

Hopkins went to the Nepia "surgery" the next day and though the explanation from both men was vague, it appeared to involve oil from the bark of a kowhai tree. Nepia complemented that by applying a hot iron to the affected area. He told Hopkins that he used to treat all his own injuries when he was playing with methods handed down through the generations "and they all worked".

How well Nepia's treatment of Hopkins worked was difficult to discern. The swelling went down eventually but Hopkins played only two more of the remaining matches.

1971 — When Lions Roared

The Lions in 1971 had a bit of a theme song, 'We Shall Overcome', which had come to be the anthem for civil rights campaigners in the United States in the 1960s. They sang it as if they meant it and during one rendition performed in a restaurant in New Zealand before the first test, a group of New Zealanders listened and smirked, implying that singing is one thing, actually doing it another. Ray Hopkins, the Lions halfback, was so worked up he threw a salt shaker at the smirkers.

The Lions sang it in their bus on the way to Carisbrook for the first test. Not for them the silent-as-the-grave bus ride that New Zealand players demand. One who sang, but who had doubts, was Gareth Edwards. He'd damaged a hamstring at training two days before and didn't think he'd be able to play, but was encouraged by James to say nothing publicly and give it a go. Edwards, with his accurate long pass and his familiarity with the foibles of Barry John, was crucial to the Lions' chances.

If Edwards had doubts, well-founded because he didn't last long before being replaced by Hopkins, John had none. An irrepressible spirit for whom confidence was 99 per cent of preparation, John pulled his jersey over his head in the dressing room shortly before the start and announced: "I wouldn't swap anyone in this dressing room for anyone else. I'm happy with my shirt. Let's go."

And go they did. The Lions did not dominate the game, as mellow memory might have it. The All Blacks

Three pivotal figures of the 1971 series: Gareth Edwards, Sid Going and Ian Kirkpatrick.

Barry John doing what he did best — dictating play.

did. It was, more than anything, the Lions' defence that won them the first test 9–3. Time and again the Lions were called upon to stem the All Black tide. "All I can recall is wave after wave of All Black jerseys," Edwards recalled years later. Most Lions agreed, even the only tryscorer of the game and one of the Lions' new heroes, Ian McLauchlan. Small by comparison with international props and especially with Richie Guy and Jazz Muller, McLauchlan earnt himself the nickname of "Mighty Mouse" — and any opposing prop who dared call him Minnie Mouse soon came to regret it.

The two standout features of the game were McLauchlan's try, when he charged down and recovered an attempted clearing kick by Alan Sutherland, and the probing kicks by Barry John that had Fergie McCormick running hither and yon. John effectively kicked McCormick out of the All Blacks, although McCormick also had kicking lapses that may have cost him his place.

The loss of the first test was critical. It sounds trite and obvious, but the first test in a four-test series is the most important: one side goes one up with three to play, the other one down with three to play. There's no choice.

It said much for the All Blacks, and for the leadership of Colin Meads, that they were able to make such a superlative comeback in the second test and inflict, as it turned out, upon the Lions their only defeat. The Lions

Ian Kirkpatrick sets off for his extraordinary try in Christchurch.

after Dunedin had proceeded gaily on with impressive victories, especially against New Zealand Universities, and if the TAB had then been allowed to operate on rugby, it would have had the Lions as favourites. The Lancaster Park surface was tacky and this was later held to have been one of the reasons why the Lions backs didn't fire as they'd fired so much during the tour. That may be so, but the All Blacks were also hungrier and more determined to make up for the first test loss and there was no better example of their determination than the amazing solo try by Ian Kirkpatrick, running almost from halfway for one of the great All Black tries.

Luck didn't run with the All Blacks when they needed it most. In the lead-up to the third test in Wellington, Meads had been troubled with a leg injury and there were doubts — though he probably had none — as to whether he could play. In addition, Peter Whiting had a back injury so Vodanovich decided he needed both a lock and a possible cover for captain. Who better to turn to than Brian Lochore, one of the All Blacks' greatest captains? He'd retired after the South African tour but had continued playing for his club and

Dr Doug's Future Shock

The prophet: Doug Smith.

The manager of the 1971 Lions, Doug Smith, gained great credit as a prophet when he correctly predicted before the tour that his team would win two tests, draw one and lose one.

That was precisely how it finished, adding enormously to the reputation of Smith, not just as a successful manager, but as a seer of merit. But Smith's ability to see into the future didn't impress the All Black captain, Colin Meads. In his speech at the after-match function at Eden Park following the game that confirmed the accuracy of Smith's prediction, Meads had this to say:

"The . . . thing I have to say about Dr Doug . . . is something that annoyed me early in the tour. It was about when he left London. He made the great statement that the Lions would win two tests, lose one and draw one. The press out here rang me up. I'm always out, my wife takes the phone calls, and a persistent man finally got through to me about midnight one night.

"So I said that the Lions wanted to save some of their cockiness until later in the tour. That was splashed all over New Zealand.

"Dr Doug, you're the greatest bloody predicter I've ever met. And I hope to hell you go home to Scotland and all this great hospitality you've had out here has been far too much for you and that we hear no more predictions from you in the future."

A test win apiece, Colin Meads and John Dawes lead their teams out for the third test.

had also played for Wairarapa-Bush against the Lions. Lochore was not then, and has never been, a man to say no when his country calls him. So off he went to Wellington where he locked the scrum with Meads. It was not a happy comeback because the All Blacks lost. They were beaten more thoroughly than they had been in Dunedin. The Lions defence was as good as it had been in Dunedin; John was in superlative touch and just to show he wasn't only a kicker, he also scored a try. The Lions scored all their points in the first half — and this was at Athletic Park and there wasn't even a wind. The only reply the All Blacks could muster in the second was a try by McCormick's replacement at fullback, Laurie Mains.

Such was the success and popularity of the Lions, and such was the newly-acquired celebrity of James, that two of the touring journalists, Terry McLean of the *New Zealand Herald* and Earle Read of the New Zealand Press Association, had lengthy interviews with him about the state of rugby even before the fourth test. Such "tour reviews" generally get written after the last test or at least after the series has been decided. It said much for James's confidence in his side's ability to do well in Auckland that he responded with alacrity to some questions that other coaches would have preferred to leave unanswered until after the last test.

For example:

How can New Zealand benefit from the style of rugby you have played?

"The New Zealand pattern of play is quite predictable. New Zealand's contribution to our rugby has been an emphasis on the ruck. Your forwards have driven from the lineout to get a ruck situation far better than any country in the world has achieved. But I would say this has been overdone, it has meant three things. Firstly, the nurturing of an overall high standard of halfback play. I am amazed at the standard of halfback play in this country. Second, it has unfortunately laid too much emphasis on the kicking first five-eighth, putting in up-and-unders to put the ball in front of the forwards and create another ruck. Third, it has involved

Peter Whiting and Gordon Brown vie for the ball in the fourth test.

the second five-eighth in crossing the advantage line to take the tackle and create the ruck . . . it makes rugby a very physical game here. New Zealand might well benefit from our style because we have only used these ploys as variations within a wider pattern — a pattern which has ensured quick passing from the halfback to the threequarters.

"Furthermore, it is a pattern which realises that wings are semi-fullbacks, that fullbacks are invaluable attackers and that without the counter-attack, the game is very much the poorer."

New Zealand would learn these lessons and James would admire the All Blacks even more, but there was no time to learn such lessons before the fourth test. The All Blacks could only tie the series. The Lions couldn't lose it.

No one likes a draw, least of all the players involved, and there's usually clichéd talk about a draw being a fair result, no one deserved to lose and all that garbage. The All Blacks probably deserved to win the match and they did score two tries to one, but perhaps the difference — and this was a difference that underlined the series — was that the Lions had more flair and took more chances. They were adventurous. Perhaps the best example of that was the outrageous 40-metre dropped goal by J.P.R. Williams that put the Lions in front early in the second half. His kicking was, by his own admission, the weakest weapon in his armoury and he had never before dropkicked a ball. So what better occasion to start than in a test match to ensure the first Lions series victory in New Zealand?

Winners and losers: John Dawes, Doug Smith, Colin Meads, Carwyn James and Gordon Brown after the fourth test.

1977
One Wet Winter

There's an old bit of bush philosophy that relates to the dire consequences of an accumulation of mistakes or omissions. It goes along the lines of: "For the want of a nail, the shoe was lost, for want of a shoe, the horse was lost, for want of a horse, the rider was lost . . ." and so on until it reaches an inevitable conclusion and a kingdom was lost.

If the small things aren't done, the great things can't be achieved. Any single mistake or omission could be overcome, but not the accumulation of many. This then could be the story of the 1977 Lions in New Zealand.

If it's true that the 1971 Lions did pretty much everything right, from the planning stages to the last minutes of every game, then their successors six years later did everything pretty much wrong. They had their own faults to begin with and had others heaped upon them. Everywhere the Lions turned, it seemed, they could do no right. Even the weather was against them and the most common refrain now, nearly 30 years later, from players or anyone associated with that tour was how consistently bad the weather was. And it was a wet winter but it's an almost inescapable conclusion that if other things had gone better, if selection in the first place had been better and if all that followed had been planned and executed better, the weather wouldn't have seemed so bad. It's a poor tour if the abiding memory of it is the weather.

Yet for all the faults, the self-imposed handicaps and the pressures real and imagined, the Lions could have, and nearly did, emulate the success of their predecessors. The All Blacks won the series 3–1, but it

Two of the three key men of the 1977 Lions: John Dawes and George Burrell.

could so easily have been 2–2; even 3–1 to the Lions. The coach of the Lions, John Dawes, remarked rather sourly at the end of the tour that his team had genuinely lost only one of the tests, the third in Dunedin. It's true but sad to say that when the Lions' aircraft took off from Auckland at the end of the tour, the players cheered. Given their views of the tour, it's not difficult to imagine that Dawes and the manager, George Burrell, would also have joined in the cheering. If they did, and if such rejoicing was unanimous, it might have been the only time on tour that the whole party was in unison.

It was a tour the Lions generally were pleased to put behind them; a tour, too, that much of New Zealand was probably pleased had ended.

Much attention centred at the time, and later, on two of three key individuals: Dawes and Burrell. Attention focused also on the captain, Phil Bennett, but for different reasons. Dawes had been the captain of the Lions in 1971. Not a great player by the high Welsh standards of the time, but he was more than competent and he was a good organiser, especially in bringing together the sparkling talents of those around him. He was credited with turning London Welsh from a socialising, disorganised rabble into one of the best-performed clubs in Britain. In 1971, he was affable and gracious. He was a popular captain, saying the right things, doing the right things, acting as a captain should.

Burrell had been the manager in 1975 of the first Scotland team to tour New Zealand. A Borderer, he was quick to pick up and remark on the similarities between Scots and New Zealanders; there was a kinship there. He liked New Zealanders and they him. He was a manager of his times and was the acknowledged boss of the team, even though he had a strong-willed captain, Ian McLauchlan, and a coach, Bill Dickinson who, because of the conservatism of the Scottish union, went by the quaint title of "advisor to the captain". The triumvirate worked well together and the Scottish team was a happy one and may have been more successful than history records had Eden Park not been flooded beyond recognition on the day of their single test. The conditions in Auckland were met not with anger or dismissive patronising, but with rueful humour. Burrell had the well-heeled of Auckland roaring with laughter the day before at a lunch at Ellerslie when he contrived in his speech to link certain passages of rugby's law book with the desired actions of the first night of marriage. (A sample: ". . . it shall be put in without delay . . .")

The humour, the affability, the liking and being liked, was not so apparent in 1977. A few months after the Lions tour, Dawes and I happened to run into one another in a bar in London. "You bastards," he said, "are all the same." It wasn't just the beer that was bitter. During the Five Nations season that followed, I was in Scotland for a match and ran into Burrell. "I never want to see that place again," he said of New Zealand.

Years later, when many more tours had turned into memories and books, Dawes was back to his old, affable self. He stood once at Sophia Gardens in Cardiff watching the All Blacks train and it was as if 1977 had never been. This was the Dawes of smiles and of praise for the All Blacks and for the ethos of rugby as it is, or at least was, practised in New Zealand.

The 1977 tour turned two good men into, for a time, men who harboured bitterness and ill feelings to all people and all things who they felt had conspired against them.

It's probably not possible for bitterness to reside in the soul, even temporarily, of Phil Bennett, the 1977 captain and one of the most genuine, nicest people it's possible to meet. Where there was bitterness and enmity in Dawes and Burrell, in Bennett there was an ineffable sadness, a heartfelt regret that things had turned out the way they did. To listen to Bennett nearly

Phil Bennett: an unhappy brilliance.

30 years after the tour is to recognise and feel his hurt, his deep wish that things had been other than what they were. The other ranks, the players less centre stage than the manager, coach and captain, recall the tour not so much with fondness, for that was not a word that applied in 1977, but with a regret for opportunities which were lost and a wish that things could have been done differently.

How did this come to pass? Lions tours were supposed to be the great adventure for British rugby players, the apogee of a player's career. They were supposed to be enjoyed and if there was success on the field as well, so much the better but enjoyment was the key ingredient. British rugby was flushed with success in the mid-1970s — were not the Welsh at the top of the rugby tree? Had not the Lions won in New Zealand in

1971 and again in South Africa in 1974? Had not British rugby, generally speaking, finally developed forward play to complement the enduring brilliance of its backs? The Lions had been named in March and assembled six weeks later in London, where they were given a round of farewell parties. There was no hint then of what was to come. With characters such as Willie Duggan, the Irish No. 8 who happily announced himself to be the interpreter for his close mate, Moss Keane, the genial Scottish lock, Gordon Brown, who moonlighted as the team's choirmaster, the deep-thinking and charming Mike Gibson, he of so many tours — how could this not be a success?

Lions and any other opponents will always say that there's no such thing as a weak All Black team and that's true but it's equally true that some are stronger

Jack Gleeson coached the All Blacks in tests for the first time in 1977. With him at training are Grant Batty (obscured), Andy Haden and Bill Bush.

than others. The All Blacks in 1977, the Lions believed, were going through a transition phase after the tour of South Africa the year before. Some players were finished, others were on the verge of finishing, and there were yet others on the fringes for whom All Blackdom was not far off. Opponents know the time to get an All Black team is at such a transitional phase, when confidence levels may not be as high as with a team that has performed together successfully for two or more seasons and when combinations haven't had time to work smoothly together and when perhaps there may still be a position or two that's not finally settled. Such was the case in 1977 and the All Blacks also had a new coach, Jack Gleeson, who had taken over from J.J. Stewart. Gleeson had coached (and managed) the All Blacks on an internal tour in 1972 and he'd been a national selector, coached the North Island and trial teams and the second All Black team that went to Argentina toward the end of 1976. It was his time. A new coach, no matter who he may be, brings his own thoughts and his own style to the team. It can be an unsettling time for players until they know whether they fit the new coach's needs or, horror of horrors, don't.

The signs were propitious for the Lions, but the All Blacks won the series 3–1. They won it because of a try from a Lions mistake toward the end of the fourth test and but for that mistake, among others, the series may have been drawn. The Lions lost the first test because of an intercept try by Grant Batty — the type of try that knocks the stuffing from a team. It's almost possible, in film of the match, to see Bennett's head wilt as half-crippled Batty scampered down to the other end of the park. The series turned on such moments. The Lions could argue they were beaten by ill luck; but all teams have luck both good and ill and as anyone involved in top sport knows, it all evens out over time and in any case, there's no point complaining about it. The All Blacks also had ill luck in that series: they lost Batty after the first test for good when he decided his injured knee was just too wonky to carry on in international rugby; they lost their best prop, Kent Lambert, to

Grant Batty scores the try in Wellington that broke Lions hearts. Andy Irvine and Graham Price were just too late.

appendicitis between the first and second tests; and they lost their best back, Bruce Robertson, because of concussion before the second test. Between the first and second tests, Gleeson wrote a letter to a friend in England, told him of Lambert's appendix, and plaintively asked: "What the hell am I going to do?" Gleeson's concerns were well founded because the Lions won the second test, a fairly brutish affair compared with tests today which have undergone video cleansing, and this led to more Gleeson anguish but, more crucially, decisiveness.

These were the days of ruthlessness and wonder. For the first two tests, Gleeson had a young Aucklander, Colin Farrell, at fullback. He's been judged harshly by history and I remember him telling me passionately in Italy a few seasons later how he hadn't been given a fair go. If he meant by Gleeson — selectors aren't there to give people a fair go; but if he meant the New Zealand public,

Colin Farrell takes the field for his first test, followed by Frank Oliver.

Bennett: It's Only a Game

Phil Bennett first came to New Zealand with Wales in 1969, captained the Lions in 1977 and has been an avid follower of the All Blacks whenever they've been in Britain, and sometimes he's thought that New Zealanders just take rugby far too seriously.

Then along came Jonah Lomu to make him think again.

Bennett reminisced on what he thought about New Zealand rugby after the All Blacks had been beaten in the World Cup semi-final by France in 1999.

"I'd never known a nation take defeat like it," he recalled after what was to New Zealanders one of the most harrowing losses of All Black history. "For two or three hours I was with them afterwards and it was like somebody had passed away . . . there had been a great disaster.

"And I was saying, 'Well yeah, but it's a game, you know. Your family are okay and you've got your health.' And they'd say, 'It isn't a game, it's everything.' They were pointing to the fern and they were crying, grown men. So I was looking back and I thought, 'God, '77, no wonder they wanted to win in their own backyard.'"

Bennett recalled in 1977 going into a café in small-town New Zealand and the woman serving looked at him, realised who he was, and said, "Oh, your rucking's terrible. You want to go down to Otago and learn some rucking down there." Bennett, stunned, gaped at the woman and said, "I only wanted a sandwich."

He remembered the images of Colin Meads carrying a lamb under each arm and it somehow seemed to typify New Zealand rugby for him: strength and pride but a little one-dimensional. New Zealanders, he felt, should look beyond rugby. Rugby players in Wales were revered, too, but so were others . . . there was more to life in Wales than just rugby.

For Phil Bennett, there was more than just life with the Lions.

But it was Lomu who caused Bennett to think, not that he may have been wrong, but that perhaps the emphasis was not what he thought it was.

It was after the semi-final loss to France that Bennett ran into Phil Kingsley-Jones, who was then Lomu's manager, at a function. Bennett told him there was a small boy in the tiny village of Felinfoel that Bennett called home who had a similar kidney condition to what Lomu had.

As it happened, the All Blacks were going to be in Wales for the play-off match and Kingsley-Jones said he could arrange for Lomu to meet the boy at the team's hotel.

Bennett was in the designated hotel at the appropriate time, waiting, and the place was thronged with New Zealand supporters, decked out in their black clothing and still lamenting the loss to France. Lomu walked in and Bennett recalled the supporters as "going mad". Half criticised him for blowing the lead in the semi-final (as if he had been personally responsible) and half were telling him what a great rugby player he was.

Lomu interrupted them with a wave of a hand and said, according to Bennett: "I've come to see a little boy and he's my priority."

Bennett's eyes shone when he related what happened next: "He talked to this little boy for half an hour and he made this little boy believe that he was going to get well. I owed Jonah Lomu the greatest thanks in the world.

"Two hundred fans . . . they just wanted to grasp Jonah but his attitude was, 'Yeah, we've been knocked out of the World Cup but there's a little boy there quite ill, I want to talk to him.' And I think there's a lesson for all of us there."

which I suspect he did, he was right. New Zealanders are unforgiving when the All Blacks lose a test and Farrell just happened to be in the wrong place at the wrong time. In his place at fullback was Bevan Wilson, a fullback of orthodox style and the latest in a lengthening line as New Zealand rugby sought a replacement for Joe Karam, who had switched to league at the end of 1975. Farrell could take comfort that he was in fairly select company when he got his rejection slip. So, too, did one of the folk heroes of New Zealand rugby, Sid Going, who was then the All Blacks' most-capped halfback and he'd also had a memorable game for New Zealand Maori against the Lions. But his individualistic style of play did not fit in with Gleeson's idea of getting the ball to his backs and he was replaced by a perennial reserve, Lyn Davis, who had warmed a seat in the stand throughout the 1966 and 1971 series against the Lions. Another change was a portent: Graham Mourie was chosen for his first test in place of Kevin Eveleigh on the side of the scrum. Already, Andy Haden and Stu Wilson had made their debuts in the series so Gleeson was giving shape to the All Blacks of the future at the same time as trying to win in the present.

The All Blacks won the third test 19–7 and it was the one test outcome the Lions did not dispute. They were outplayed but not outplayed so much as to make the fourth test in Auckland a foregone conclusion. Crucial differences for the All Blacks came with reliable goalkicking from Wilson and alert and supportive play in the loose by Mourie and Ian Kirkpatrick. Even though Kirkpatrick scored within the first minute the Lions remained within scoring range of the All Blacks and if Bennett had been more accurate with a couple of penalty goal attempts, the outcome may have been different. But the All Blacks led throughout and just to ram home the advantage, Bruce Robertson dropkicked a goal in the last seconds.

One up and one to play for the All Blacks. Tests stick in the memories of players and of the teams' supporters for different reasons. For one a loss, for the other a win, every so often a draw. So it was in Auckland. The Lions remember the fourth test in 1977 like a fisherman

remembers the almost greatest moments: it was the one that got away. The All Blacks and New Zealanders generally remember the fourth test for Lawrie Knight's winning try and for the humiliation of an All Black team being so weak in the forwards they felt compelled to put down a three-man scrum. Not for nothing did the English journalist, John Reason, write about strong men sitting in the stands putting their heads in their hands. New Zealand rugby, so proud of its forward prowess even if sometimes the pride has been more romantic than realistic, had been reduced to conceding forward power to, of all things, a British team. To South Africans yes, to the French maybe, but to the British? It was an affront to New Zealand machismo and gave the lie to the myth of craggy farmers coming down out of the hills in search of a scrum and a lineout. New Zealand won the test 10–9 because of Knight's try, but also because they deserved to. They made better use of the ball they had, and surely that is one of the most telling factors in any game of rugby. The Lions could have drawn the series but they lost it 3–1. It could be said, too, that the Knight try came not so much out of nothing, but out of a Lions error which may have been the story of their tour. Bennett, hapless to the last, missed touch and Bill Osborne happily took the ball and returned it with interest. Steve Fenwick, the Lions' Welsh centre, took the Osborne kick but rather than return it, he looked around for support and all he found was the Lions hooker, Peter Wheeler. By the time Wheeler had the ball, he had Mourie as well and the ball popped out of Wheeler's arms into the waiting clutches of Knight and all he had to do was to gallop off into the corner. "We outscrummaged, outjumped, out-everythinged them, yet we lost the game," Burrell commented sadly afterward.

But the Lions didn't lose that test because of Bennett's missed kick or because Wheeler didn't secure the ball. They didn't lose the series because of such errors. There were many more reasons than those.

Overleaf: Take-off — Lions halfback Brynmor Williams gets airborne in the second test. Earthbound are Bill Beaumont, Willie Duggan, Lawrie Knight and Terry Cobner (behind Knight).

The series could have been lost before it was even played. As with other Lions tours, the outcome could have been decided with the original selections. For a start, players who would have made a difference were not available, and that's a recurring endnote in the Lions' history. In the words of John Reason, the Lions in 1977 made do with artisans while the artists stayed at home. The Lions were not able to call on the services of players such as the England flanker, Peter Dixon, and a Welsh trio of brilliance, Gareth Edwards, J.P.R. Williams and Gerald Davies. All, for various reasons, did not want another Lions tour: they had tasted success already. Another who had been a key member of the 1971 and 1974 Lions, prop Ian McLauchlan, was not chosen, but would have gone like a shot. McLauchlan, the "Mighty Mouse" of 1971 and not a man to call a spade by any other name, was livid that he was not chosen, especially when props demonstrably inferior to him were. His absence may have been critical. Not only was he a sound scrummager but he was a keen follower of New Zealand rugby and would have revelled in the harsh conditions; his value off the field would have been as great as his value on it. The Lions also had to do without Roger Uttley, the England No. 8 and captain, the Welsh lock, Geoff Wheel, the hard-tackling and laugh-a-minute Welsh centre, Ray Gravell, and the Irish flanker, Fergus Slattery. Missing in action also, and this may have been the most critical of the lot, was Mervyn Davies, the "Merv the Swerve" of 1971.

Fourteen months before the tour, Dawes had told Davies he wanted him as captain of the Lions. In 1976 Dawes was coach of Wales and had already been appointed coach of the Lions. He approached Davies at the end of the Five Nations in 1976 and told him he wanted him as captain. But then tragedy. Playing for Swansea a few weeks later, Davies collapsed on the field with a brain haemorrhage. Paralysed on his left side, he was a week in the neurological ward of the University of

Showing Real Spine

All Blacks and Lions have generally got on well over the years, some of them forming lifelong friendships after their battles on the field. But however close the friendship, it wasn't the done thing to talk to the opposition before matches, especially not test matches. It was an unwritten requirement to go to some lengths to avoid running into opponents until battle commenced.

In 1977 Tane Norton was the All Black captain. The All Blacks had won the first test in Wellington and were preparing for the second in Christchurch.

"I had a bit of a crook back and I went off to see the physiotherapist, Brian McKenzie. You can imagine my surprise when I walked into his waiting room and there were three Lions sitting there. Graham Price was one of them but I can't recall who the other two were. I gave them a bit of a nod and fortunately, Brian came out more or less straightaway and ushered me into his rooms."

McKenzie, who became the first physiotherapist to tour with the All Blacks when he went to Britain with Graham Mourie's team in 1978, had in his rooms a model of a spine on a stand, cervical vertebrae down to coccyx, the whole thing.

"When Brian finished treating me, I told him I was going to borrow his spine model for a while. So I carried the spine out through the waiting room where the Lions were still sitting and just said quietly to them as I walked past: 'Well, good luck, I've had my spine replaced.'"

One of Norton's special pals was Bobby Windsor, the Welsh hooker and a fabled character.

"We got on really well," Norton said, "except for one game. We were both caught at the bottom of a ruck. It was out in the middle of the ground on the cricket block area and it was muddy. Bloody awful actually. Bobby and I were the last up and as I stood I scooped up a handful of the mud. As we were running to catch up with play, I just shoved the handful of mud into Bobby's face. He spluttered a bit, called me something not very nice and then started to chase me, cursing and swearing at me. He was a good bloke."

This photo of muddied Fran Cotton during the match against the Junior All Blacks became one of the best-known images of the tour.

Wales hospital before he was removed from the danger list. It was, obviously, the end of his rugby career. It was the end of any sort of physical endeavour.

Had Davies been the captain as Dawes wished, the Lions' tour may have turned out differently. He was a dominant figure, unlike the slightly built Bennett. He was gregarious, unlike the more retiring Bennett. Davies liked to move around, to socialise, he didn't mind the haul of a long tour. Bennett was homesick. As ideal a man as he is, and as great a player as he was, Bennett is the first to admit he shouldn't have been captain and he concedes he should never have agreed to it. He was miserable from first to last; it affected his play, it affected his team. "I am well aware," he says candidly, "that as a captain, I was a failure."

The faults of the Lions tour should not be laid solely at his feet though. The senior players left at home would have rallied in support, as senior players do, or are supposed to do, on tours. Did Bennett have support? Of course he did, but it seems not enough by players senior enough to command respect.

Terry McLean wrote at the end of the tour for the *New Zealand Herald* that the 1977 Lions tour mirrored in some ways the All Blacks' tour of Britain in 1972–73. There was a significant difference though. The Lions lost their series: the All Blacks went within a whisker of becoming the first New Zealand team to secure a Grand Slam. What McLean meant though was this: "They considered themselves, as did the Lions, to be moving in hostile territory and they too believed that because they had a good team spirit among themselves that was the answer to everything." In other words, they circled the wagons and looked inward while at the same time keeping a jaundiced eye on the outside world. Any team on tour that does that is bound to fail. Bennett and others complained often after the tour that the incessant rain of the 1977 winter meant they stayed inside more often than was good for them and that they didn't mix with New Zealanders as much as they should have or even could have. But did the rain, no matter how depressing, become a convenient excuse? There were ample tales after the tour of the Lions

turning up reluctantly and briefly at functions arranged for them or, worse, not turning up at all. Or at after-match functions, standing within their own group and, stony-faced, refusing to mix with the locals. Any rugby player anywhere will happily talk of the "heavies" and the "fishheads" who could open the batting for the World Boring XI. These people get in the players' ears and give them the benefit of their cutting wit and astute wisdom. They are a part of rugby and, as such, need to be tolerated. What the Lions (speaking generally, because there were exceptions among the players) failed to do was to acknowledge the need to project their image, to show a friendly face when that, after all, was all that was required of them. All Blacks have been guilty of the same discourteous insularity and when that happens, it's a management fault.

Some of the Lions' hostility could be understood; some couldn't. Burrell and Dawes both rightly condemned *Sunday News* and *Truth* for the type of stories written about the Lions. In the week the Lions had their best comeback win of the tour, against New Zealand Maori (they trailed 6–19 early in the second half then won 22–19), *Truth* slammed into the team's behaviour: "The Lions make a great pack — of animals. The touring British Isles rugby side is a disgrace to its members and their homeland. There has been only one word to describe their behaviour since the team arrived here — disgusting."

The paper continued with anonymous reports of players urinating down stairwells, ripping hotel doors off hinges, throwing glasses, turning over tables, uncoiling fire hoses and similar mayhem. Some incidents did occur, as Burrell acknowledged, and reparation was made. The story was an exaggeration of the degree, painting the 1977 team in the same colour as the 1968 Lions in South Africa who were known as "The Wreckers".

Dawes was naturally incensed: "The hostility over here to the boys is so great. I've never known anything like it. They're not angels, mind, but when I think back to the 1972–73 All Blacks and try to think of what has gone wrong, I can't. The All Blacks had some nasty players. We don't have any like that."

Scotland's champion, Andy Irvine, during the third test. The Lions in the background are Willie Duggan and replacement halfback Doug Morgan.

His reference to the All Blacks raised an interesting theory, postulated years later by a Lion who felt the New Zealand public, led by some newspapers, was hostile toward the Lions because of the way they perceived the All Blacks had been treated in Britain. Prominent in the memory banks was the public vilification of Keith Murdoch — even the phraseology was similar. Murdoch, like the Lions, was accused of being an animal.

Even worse for the Lions was a *Sunday News* story headlined: "They're lousy lovers". It went on to quote a woman who purportedly had sex with four of the players. "I found them boring, self-centred, ruthless, always on the make and anything but exciting bedmates," she supposedly said. It did not explain why she had to try out four to reach her conclusion; perhaps she wanted a better sample to lessen the margin for error. The Lions were, understandably, angry. It can't be

The front page that incensed the Lions.

Singalong With the Lions

What better time for a rugby team to have a sing-song than after a good win? That's what the 1977 Lions decided after what was generally agreed to be their best win outside of the second test, a 34–15 beating of Auckland.

But rather than just a sing-song, the tuneful Lions went the whole hog — they cut a record.

The team had a week off between the Auckland match and the third test in Dunedin and on the Sunday morning, they headed off from Auckland for a few days of rest in Waitangi, where the 1971 Lions also spent some time away.

Rugby wasn't part of the plan and coach John Dawes even banned talking about the game. It was only music on their minds.

The Lions had been enthusiastic singers on bus trips and in their hotel team rooms and the idea of cutting a record for sale was put to them by journalist Terry Godwin on behalf of the International Sportswriters' Club, which had farewelled the Lions from London in lavish style in May. It was the Queen's Silver Jubilee year and Godwin thought what better way for the Lions to mark it than to make the record and give any profits to the Silver Jubilee Trust Fund. (The Lions also played a rare home game in September to mark the jubilee.)

Team management agreed, players agreed and the planning began. Scottish lock Gordon Brown, never far from a smile and a song, was designated choirmaster and he supervised the players as they chose their repertoire, though that was pretty much determined by what they sang already anyway.

Musicians and various technicians were called in and the Waitangi Hotel became the recording studio.

The choice of music might be called eclectic: a mixture of traditional and pop with a bit of folk and some religion, all songs to which the players would probably have already known the words and tune. With Brown as the choirmaster, 'Flower of Scotland' must have been an automatic choice and not far behind would have been 'You Are My Sunshine' and 'Take Me Home Country Roads', songs that have been sung on rugby tours almost since they were first written. 'The Wild Mountain Thyme', a song also liked by All Black choristers over the years, had to have been a must and the 23rd Psalm and 'Amazing Grace' were there for the religious content. Since the Lions had been accused of being animals, perhaps they deliberately chose 'House of the Rising Sun' and since they were also accused of being ungrateful guests and homesick, 'Show Me the Way to Go Home' may also have been a natural choice.

The full list: 'Lion Blue', 'You Are My Sunshine', 'Take Me Home Country Roads', 'The Wild Mountain Thyme', 'Island of Dreams', 'House of the Rising Sun', 'The Rose of Tralee', 'Summer Holiday', 'The Flower of Scotland', 'Where Have All the Flowers Gone?', 'There's a Goldmine in the Sky', 'The Lord is My Shepherd', 'Amazing Grace', 'The Canoe Song', 'Banks of the Ohio', medley — 'Moonlight Bay', 'For Me and My Girl', 'Abie My Boy', 'Wait Till the Sun Shines Nellie', 'I Don't Want to Go Home', 'Bye Bye Blackbird', 'Show Me the Way to Go Home'.

A record 18 Welsh players were on the tour, plus Dawes, and for all their justified singing prowess, not one Welsh song made the final cut.

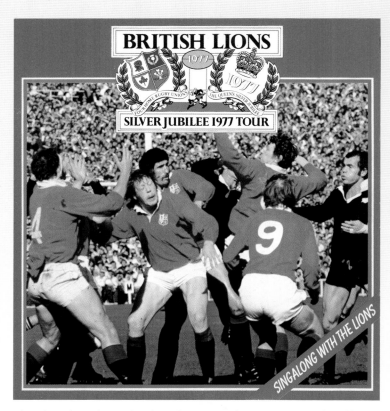

The Lions lost the series, but they were always on song: the album cover for the long-playing record they cut in Waitangi.

Lions outnumbered: Sid Going has a choice of options — Lawrie Knight, Andy Haden, Ian Kirkpatrick and Kevin Eveleigh.

pleasant for a testosteroned male to have his sexual shortcomings shouted out in headlines, but it was unsettling, too, for those players entirely innocent who had calls from anxious wives in Britain wanting to know what was going on.

With such stories, it's no wonder the Lions turned inward and no wonder Dawes treated journalists with disdain.

Unwelcome such stories may have been and stretching the truth they surely were, but they should not have made the difference between winning and losing a test series. There were deeper reasons for that.

The great irony of the tour was that two more significant factors in the Lions' loss were also two of the Lions' great strengths. One was their record of having won their last two series, in New Zealand and South Africa, and the other was a forward strength which sometimes shaded, sometimes beat, the All Blacks.

The Lions tour of 1971, rather than being a battle honour to be borne proudly and, if possible, emulated, became a millstone around the Lions' necks in 1977. Burrell once tore down a photo of the 1971 team from a clubhouse wall, saying it had no place in the current tour. Players were told not to mention 1971. Bennett related a story about Dawes's reaction to an analysis of the Lions' play by the 1971 coach, Carwyn James. "Who the hell is he?" Dawes demanded with as much asperity as he could muster.

The saddest 1977 tale of all came at the end of the tour when Mervyn Davies, Dawes's first choice as captain, was told to leave a reception for the team after the fourth test. The story has been told in various ways but it was most graphically told by Davies himself in Peter Jackson's insightful *Lions of Wales*. Davies had recovered sufficiently to follow the tour as a columnist for the *Daily Mirror* and to do some public speaking. He and another former Lion, Clem Thomas, of the *Observer*, had been invited to the reception by the New Zealand union. It was common in those days for the union to handpick journalists, rather than invite all, to attend dinners and receptions. Davies and Thomas were at the bar when Dawes went to them and said, "Merv, no press in here."

"I said, 'John, I'm leaving but the only reason I'm leaving is that I don't want to cause any hassle. You haven't invited me here. The New Zealand union has invited me. It's got fuck-all to do with you.'

"I've never blamed John for that and it hasn't affected our friendship. I honestly believe that Burrell had a tremendous influence on him."

The other Lions asset that became a liability was their forward power. They became so obsessed with the power of the pack that the backs were neglected and there was no better example of that than in the fourth test when, with the Lions in a position to win, they attempted a series of pushover tries, all of which failed, rather than give the ball to the backs. Granted the backs were Reason's artisans rather than artists, but they were more than competent and with some, such as the Scottish fullback, Andy Irvine, or the Irish centre, Mike Gibson, who was somewhat neglected on the tour, there was more than a touch of brilliance. It was another irony of the tour that as a superior back himself, and one of the best organisers of backs, Dawes neglected the backs at a time their presence was desperately needed.

Gleeson's predecessor as the All Black coach, J.J. Stewart, as usual got straight to the point: "They have lost that quality I have always admired so much about the play of British and French backs — the ability to run on to the ball from deep positions . . . the 1971 Lions were terrific runners and passers but this lot are not." From being the Lions' traditional strength, the backs in 1977 became their weakness. The emphasis on forward power did not go unnoticed elsewhere either. In 1979, at a flash dinner in London, the All Black manager, Russ Thomas, had to speak on behalf of the team. Rather than the normal platitudes, heartfelt nevertheless, about touring Britain and the quality of the game, Thomas uncharacteristically climbed into British rugby for its obsession with forward play and said that by putting all its efforts into the forwards it was neglecting the backs and this would be the undoing of British rugby.

Dawes, with help from Welsh flanker Terry Cobner, undoubtedly had the Lions forwards performing to their optimum and the team's confidence soared. It all came plummeting down though when they were beaten in Christchurch by New Zealand Universities just before the first test. "The students outwitted and outfought us; they worried and harassed us into making elementary mistakes," Bennett said. "We were well beaten. And then John Dawes murdered us. When I'm old and grey I shall still remember that morning after the Universities game with total clarity. It was the most painful training session I've ever encountered."

Bennett said the players begged for mercy, some vomited and some cried. "After what seemed an eternity, he then sent us on a half-mile run. But still Dawes wasn't finished. Then came 50 press-ups."

The players were so shattered most of them splashed their way across the Avon rather than walk along the bank to a bridge to get back to their hotel.

John Hopkins, who covered the tour for the British *Sunday Times*, knew Dawes well and he summed up the tour: "I personally believe that one of the most important reasons why the Lions failed was because Dawes would not believe that his way of doing things was not the right way. Like Frank Sinatra, Dawes did it his way and I believe that his way was wrong."

Knight Wrapped in Cotton

All Black No. 8 Lawrie Knight was the headliner of the day with his try that gave New Zealand the 10–9 victory against the Lions in the fourth test in 1977, sealing a 3–1 series win.

But Knight may not have been in a position to score the try but for helpful advice and a protective arm from one of the dominant British forwards, Fran Cotton.

This was the test in which the Lions did everything but win the game, such was their control in the forwards. It was the test in which the All Blacks put down a three-man scrum in an effort to play away from the Lions' strengths — a startling admission by a country that more often than not prided itself on its forward play.

British journalist John Reason wrote of the three-man scrum, which had been practised in training on the Thursday: ". . . strong men sitting in the stands put their heads in their hands. Most of them were wearing black ties with silver ferns and they all looked as if they thought the silver ferns should be removed so that they could lead the whole nation in a proper period of mourning."

Carwyn James, the great Welsh coach who had masterminded the Lions' 1971 victory, called the All Black ploy undignified.

Knight was in the middle of it all. It came about when John McEldowney had to leave the field early in the second half because of a neck injury. Referee David Millar told the players to carry on while a doctor certified McEldowney was indeed injured and unable to continue. It was six or seven minutes before his replacement, Bill Bush, was allowed on and in the meantime Knight moved in to tighthead. It was during this period that the three-man went down with flanker and captain Graham Mourie putting the ball in. Ironically, it resulted in the quickest and cleanest possession the All Blacks gained from a scrum all day.

It was in the more orthodox scrums that Knight found reason to thank Cotton.

"I was lifting a lot of weights in Gisborne and I thought I was a strong guy," Knight recalled. "I thought I'd go into the front row at tighthead against Cotton."

At the first scrum, Knight said he felt his back go "the wrong way".

"Cotton didn't really know I was there. He just flicked me round and did what he wanted. But on one occasion we had a 10-metre scrum. It was our put-in and they had an eight-man shove. They

Young fans rush onto the field to celebrate Lawrie Knight's winning try in the fourth test.

don't even strike for the ball. They just drive and we're about seven metres from the line and all I could do was collapse the scrum. And I collapsed on Cotton's boot and he came down on top of me and whispered, 'Stay on your feet Lawrie and you'll be all right'. I was very grateful because he could have done a lot of damage had he not been the gentleman he is."

As a result of Cotton's concern for the front-row interloper, Knight was still in one piece and able to score the try that won the test and stopped the Lions from squaring the series.

He admits he was still exhausted from his front-row stint when the decisive moment came. Phil Bennett missed touch and Bill Osborne returned the ball high over the forwards. It went down to Steve Fenwick who had Mourie, Knight and Osborne bearing down on him. Fenwick had the Lions hooker, Peter Wheeler, in support and, rather strangely, chose to pass it back to him rather than take the All Blacks' tackle and set up a maul. Mourie tackled Wheeler so forcefully the ball shot out of his arms into Knight's gleeful grip and Knight, his stride hardly checked, galloped on to the corner for the try to win the match. It was a great moment for New Zealand rugby; a galling one for the Lions, who knew they'd done enough to win.

Dawes clearly took his rugby seriously, and was passionate about the game and about the Lions, yet Hopkins said one of his stock phrases was, "Never mind, it's only a game."

When this was referred to Gleeson, he responded: "Sure, it's only a game and I do understand what he means when he says that and to a degree it's true." Then Gleeson added with sad prescience: "I am speaking to you, I am alive and well, I have not got cancer — I hope. Sure it's only a game but it's a game that everyone wants to win." (Gleeson died of cancer two years later.)

For various reasons — none of them were, on their own, sufficient to cause irreparable damage, but all of them, cumulatively, were more than enough — the Lions lost the series. "For the want of a nail, a shoe was lost, for the want of a shoe, a horse was lost . . ."

Top: Bill Beaumont about to scoop up the ball in the fourth test. Others are Fran Cotton, Andy Haden, Gordon Brown, Frank Oliver, Bill Bush and Graham Price.

Inset: A sight the All Blacks and the crowd at Eden Park were happy to see.

1983
That Eighties Show

The Lions tour of New Zealand in 1983 wasn't the end of the beginning — that milestone had long since been passed — but it might have been the beginning of the end: the end of rugby tours as we used to know them.

Change was definitely in the air when Irishman Ciaran Fitzgerald brought his Lions to New Zealand. There were signs for those who had the vision to see. There were several issues as the Lions made their less than triumphal progress and it was later analyses of those issues, rather than realisation at the time, that led to far-reaching changes in the way in which the game was organised.

Some of the issues, such as violence in games and the yawning gap between European and New Zealand refereeing styles and interpretations, were publicly debated. There were differences, too, between what players regarded as hard play and foul play. Sometimes it was a fine line, sometimes the two opinions were divided by a motorway.

The century-old true-blue amateurism concept became an issue, too, especially for the players. Administrators, both in New Zealand and Britain, toed the Corinthian party line of amateurism being the single most distinguishing feature of rugby and even as the Lions toured, the New Zealand union continued to hunt down any transgressor, especially if his name was Andrew Maxwell Haden. But the players and the administrators were not as one. Haden, in his first book published just after the Lions tour, and others had argued for change. The essence of their argument was that they were increasingly having to give up work to play international rugby and while the national unions reaped the financial benefits, the players didn't.

Coach Jim Telfer shows how it's done.

Willie-John McBride wasn't always this happy in 1983.

Haden, Graham Mourie and others had argued for a World Cup, a bringing together of the rugby world in Olympic-like competition, but the International Rugby Board, even as late as 1983, saw this as the thin end of the professional wedge — which of course it was. While the Lions were in New Zealand, an Australian man-about-town, David Lord, who had been sportsman, journalist, broadcaster, friend to the stars and foe to the administrators, dreamt up an idea for a professional rugby circus. "A circus is for clowns," growled the Lions manager, the redoubtable Willie-John McBride. But at least the clowns would be paid for their efforts and as Lord's proposals circulated among British and New Zealand players alike, eyes gleamed. There were wildly contrasting reports of who had signed, who hadn't and who wanted to but hadn't been asked. In the end, nothing happened because Lord couldn't front up with the one ingredient to make it happen — money. But the seed had not just been sown: it was germinating healthily and would sprout not too many years hence.

It could be argued that it was another 12 years before rugby went professional. That's true, but it was a combination of Lord's pipe dream and the advocacy by players for a World Cup that created the climate for what happened in 1995 when the International Rugby Board not just bowed to the inevitable, but fell over in their indecent haste to embrace it. The World Rugby Corporation professional plan of 1995, the effects of

Super League, and the hurried case for cash taken to News Ltd by New Zealand, Australia and South Africa used the climate that had already been created. By 1995, the Lord seeds had sprouted.

The Lions tour of 1983 was the catalyst for change of an entirely different kind, but one which would have equally far-reaching repercussions. British rugby then was organised pretty much the way it always had been and consisted mainly of clubs involved in "friendly" competitions, that is, with no real end-purpose in mind other than enjoyment of the game and perhaps, for the individual, of playing well enough to be noticed by national or Lions selectors. Competitiveness was almost as dirty a word in British rugby, or at least in English rugby, as professionalism. The amateur view, with its origins locked away in Victorian England, was that rugby was for the players and not for the spectators and, for heaven's sake, not a game to be played to win. Wales had a cup competition but for the most part, clubs arranged their own fixtures, journeyed hither and yon to play them, often in front of no one, then had a jolly good time afterward. To play games for competition points and for that competition then to culminate in semi-finals and final was tantamount to surrendering to the dark forces. It was this belief, as odd as it may sound now, that underpinned the International Rugby Board's reluctance to adopt the World Cup until it was more or less forced to by New Zealand and Australia.

The successes of the Lions in New Zealand in 1971 and in South Africa in 1974 had brought a great deal of pride to British rugby but it also induced complacency. If the Lions could beat the two most competitive sides in world rugby, the All Blacks and the Springboks, the theory went, then surely there was nothing wrong with British rugby. There were two holes in that argument. One was that both those tours relied on the confluence of some extremely talented players and coaches and the other was that British rugby relaxed in the afterglow of those results rather than exploited and built on them. The best coach of the 1970s in Britain, and one of the best of all time, Carwyn James, was cast aside after his greatest triumph and left to ply his trade with lesser lights. If ever a prophet was without honour in his own country, it was he. It was at once gratifying and sad to see the great James coaching in Italy when the All Blacks were first there in 1977.

Not everyone in British rugby was blind to what needed to happen. One administrator, John Burgess, compiled a lengthy report that said, in essence, if English rugby was to develop so that its international team could regularly be on a par with the best, it needed to introduce competitive structures which, with typical English irony, were called "leagues". Burgess's report was filed along with other reports which saw a future that administrators didn't like.

Such were the undercurrents when the Lions were in New Zealand in 1983, but as is often the way, it was what was happening on the surface that took the eye and concentrated the mind. And on the surface was a Lions side that in essence reflected British rugby as it was then — a side with some extremely talented players, but a side that lacked cohesion and didn't seem to believe it was good enough to beat the All Blacks. As a result, it fashioned a losing record second only to the 1966 Lions. Admittedly, it was against a strong All Black team. New Zealand then was blessed with an extremely experienced and powerful forward pack and had behind it one of the best halfbacks to wear the black jersey, Dave Loveridge. Outside him were backs who, and this is not meant unkindly, were tradesmanlike: in other words, they could be relied upon to do the job for which they were chosen. Some, such as the back three of Allan Hewson, Stu Wilson and Bernie Fraser, could be seen as the forerunners of the back threes that so lit up the All Blacks 10 and 15 years later.

The Lions, as so often in the past, created some of their own problems. Selection was again criticised though the rugby selection that has totally escaped criticism has yet to be chosen. The case for a touring position for players such as the England hooker, Peter Wheeler, England centre Paul Dodge, and even the England No. 8 and captain, John Scott, did seem compelling. Both Wheeler and Scott fitted the New Zealand mould of being gnarly competitive forwards

If the Cap Fitz

Not for the first time, the Lions in 1983 had a captain who did not have universal approval. When the Lions were chosen, critical comment zeroed in on the choice of Ciaran Fitzgerald of Ireland as captain.

Yet Fitzgerald was eminently qualified for the job. He was an army officer trained in leadership, as was another much-criticised Lions captain, Mike Campbell-Lamerton, in 1966, and he had worked wonders with Ireland.

When Fitzgerald took over the leadership of Ireland in 1981, they had lost seven matches in a row. Under Fitzgerald, they then won the Five Nations tournament in 1982 for the first time in 33 years and in the season preceding the Lions tour, they shared the championship with France.

The issue was not so much Fitzgerald's credentials, but the fact his presence kept out Peter Wheeler, the England hooker who had limited captaincy experience and whose side had finished last in the Five Nations.

The British press, largely based in London and largely Anglocentric, was aghast at Wheeler missing the captaincy and, even worse, not even being chosen for the tour; the other hooking position going to Colin Deans of Scotland.

The thrust of the Fleet Street tirade against Fitzgerald was that he was not among the best two hookers in Britain or Ireland and that he was not the best captain. His record of the previous two seasons seemed not to have mattered.

The constant barrage of criticism of Fitzgerald unsettled the side, as another Irishman, Donal Lenihan, explained. "Touring New Zealand is a difficult assignment in the best of circumstances but regardless of what was said, when you get off on a negative note like that it does have an effect on the tour party. It certainly did not help the morale of the squad." (Lenihan was originally chosen for the tour but had to pull out because of injury, then joined later as a replacement.)

Fitzgerald acknowledged the burden under which he laboured but said after the initial outburst, it didn't affect him. "I wasn't really surprised to get the captaincy because I knew I was going to be in there with a chance because of our record over the previous two seasons . . . I was very surprised by the criticism that followed though, by the level and intensity of it. But I think if it was going to affect me it would have been more likely to if it was a more gradual process . . . if it had been less intense, it might have affected me more, but it was so intense so quickly that it was 'something's wrong here'. My view was that it wasn't based on the way I was playing, so so be it."

Another of the Irish Lions, Ollie Campbell, thought in retrospect that the Irish players could have done more for Fitzgerald on the tour. "He was probably under a lot more pressure than we realised at the time," Campbell said.

Fitzgerald, like other captains before him, conducted himself with a quiet uncomplaining dignity.

The Lions manager, Willie-John McBride, was in no doubt about who should have captained the team.

"If you look at the qualities of leadership displayed consistently in the Four Home Unions over the past two seasons," he said, "then Ciaran's selection was a foregone conclusion."

Captain in his day job, too: Ciaran Fitzgerald.

but perhaps, as had happened in the past, they both fell victim to the imperatives of nationalistic compromise in the selection process. The names of both Wheeler and Scott would surely have come up when the selectors — again, representing each country — were mulling over who they'd take because they chose as their captain the Irish leader and hooker, Ciaran Fitzgerald. His selection as both hooker and captain may well have consigned to Wheeler and Scott their "not wanted on voyage" tags. Fitzgerald was a controversial choice — at least in the eyes of the majority of the British press — because it was felt he was chosen as a captain first rather than as a hooker first. He was cast in the same mould as Mike Campbell-Lamerton had been in 1966: a fine leader of men, trained as a leader (Fitzgerald, like Campbell-Lamerton, was an army officer) but not up to the mark as a test player. As with Campbell-Lamerton, such criticisms of Fitzgerald were harsh. He had after all captained Ireland in 1982 and 1983 when they had won the mythical triple crown in the Five Nations after coming last in 1981. Such criticisms, too, seemed to overlook the influence of Willie-John McBride. Fitzgerald conducted himself throughout the tour much as Campbell-Lamerton had in 1966, displaying a dignity that was not matched by some of his critics.

The Lions' downfall could not be attributed to original selection, of captain or of anyone else, but rather primarily to the strength of the All Blacks at the time and, a distant second and third, to injuries which were the bane of any touring team and an itinerary that seemed planned to please administrators rather than those actually charged with the success of the tour. Clem Thomas, the former Lion turned journalist, called the itinerary suicidal. It had the Lions playing seven matches in the first three weeks, including those against Auckland, Wellington and Manawatu and culminating in the first test. The Lions could not have it both ways, however. They and the International Rugby Board had agreed on shorter tours in the late 1970s and the Lions' visit to South Africa in 1980 was the first of the new breed when they played 18 matches including four tests.

The tour in 1983 followed a similar pattern with McBride and the coach, Jim Telfer, complaining that the shortened lead-up did not allow for full and proper preparation for the first test. McBride, whose Irish charm in 1983 was sometimes blunted by the demands of being a manager, really put his foot in it after the third test when he publicly damned the itinerary, saying it had been badly put together and could be partly blamed for his side's poor performance. McBride made the comments at the test dinner and sitting listening was Mickey Steele-Bodger, then chairman of the Four Home Unions Tours Committee and one of the most powerful men in British rugby. Steele-Bodger, also a man whose charm could be blunted, was not amused. His committee, he said tartly, had only agreed to the draft itinerary submitted by the New Zealand union once it had been approved by the Lions management, i.e. McBride. Furthermore, Steele-Bodger said, had the Lions won the series the reason probably would have been offered that the itinerary gave the team the hard games it needed. "Judgment tends to be governed by hindsight and is based on results that occur," he said. By then, it was 3–0 to the All Blacks and 1–0 to Steele-Bodger. (As an aside, Steele-Bodger was the inheritor of the Victorian amateur dream but he combined his rigid if sometimes anachronistic principles with a twinkling humour. During the All Blacks' tour of Britain in 1978 Steele-Bodger was leaving the All Blacks' hotel in London early one morning just as Haden was arriving back at the hotel. Haden, seeing Steele-Bodger approaching, tried to hide his unmistakable frame behind a column in the hotel foyer. But Haden knew you had to get up early to beat Steele-Bodger. With a twinkle in his eyes and a wagging finger, Steele-Bodger gazed at Haden and said: "One day I'm going to get you Haden, one day.")

As had become the norm on Lions tours, violence was one of the issues of the day and, as always, it stemmed not so much from the nefarious motivations of players but from a different understanding of what was hard and what was dirty. And as usual, the ruck was at the centre of the ruckus. British forwards of whatever era had garnered a reputation of not appreciating the niceties of rucking and, when found lying on the ball on the wrong side of a ruck (or sometimes not lying on the ball at all) they took great exception to New Zealand studs raking their backs or their legs. New Zealanders of most eras until the present knew precisely what rucking was. By a backward raking movement with the feet, it was a means of getting the ball back to the halfback. And if an opposition body was in the way, well, that was the price the opponent paid for being on the wrong side of a ruck. Some of the Lions' matches in 1983 were criticised for being overtly dirty by the British while New Zealanders saw no wrong. (This is not to say that some New Zealanders did not deliberately indulge in foul play — of course they did; but what was at issue was whether their actions crossed the bounds of unwritten laws. A friendly punch to remind an opponent who's boss was acceptable; deliberately kicking an opponent was not.)

The Lions' match against Manawatu in 1983 was one example of the type of game that led to headlines in Britain saying things such as, "Pack of raging bulls" (this was three years after the Robert De Niro film was released) or "Send off thugs". Fitzgerald argued that some of his players were injured because they'd been attacked off the ball. Colin Meads, who knew hard play when he saw it, was at the Manawatu match and said he didn't see anything that would make him blanch. He accused the Lions of playing politics, figuring if they screamed loud enough about New Zealand rucking the French referee for the tests, Francis Palmade, would eventually hear. The Manawatu halfback against the Lions was Mark Donaldson and he knew well the code of conduct that players imposed upon themselves. Playing for the All Blacks in Glasgow in 1979, he became mightily peeved at lineout time with a Scottish forward who continually charged through the All Black line in an effort to upset the delivery of the ball to him. Inevitably, the next time was one too many and Donaldson whacked him, a neat little straight right to the jaw. After the referee had cooled things down, Donaldson knew not to expect any mercy next time he got caught in a ruck. Sure enough, he was caught with

the ball soon after. The Scottish forwards piled in on top of him and Donaldson eventually emerged with a ripped jersey, souvenirs on his back and a bit of blood here and there. Such was the players' code. Honour had been satisfied. Now it's the citing commissioner or some other gimlet-eyed official who has to be satisfied and rugby is a much more politically correct, sanitised version of the game than it once was.

The Lions had lost only one match in the lead-up to the first test, 12–13 to Auckland in a defeat that was engineered by the lineout prowess of Haden and Gary Whetton and by a dropped goal from a tousle-haired youngster of whom more would be heard, Grant Fox. The Lions had no reason to be despondent going into the first test though because they'd had a good 27–19 win against Wellington which more or less settled their test team. They had players of genuine quality in the backs such as Terry Holmes at halfback and Ollie Campbell at first-five and in the forwards, Graham Price and Ian Stephens as the props and loose forwards Jeff Squire and Peter Winterbottom, the latter a flanker who was regarded as being in the New Zealand mould.

Ollie Campbell, one of the Lions' backline stars.

The All Blacks, even though they won the first test by only 16–12, were far more formidable than anything Lions coach Jim Telfer could put onto the field to confront them. Telfer in an extraordinary *cri de coeur* at the end of the tour lamented the poor state of British rugby and wondered aloud whether New Zealand dominance would ever be broken. New Zealand had hardened test experience to call on with a front row of captain Andy Dalton, props John Ashworth and Gary Knight, locks Haden and Whetton and loose forwards Mark Shaw and Murray Mexted. The only test newcomer in the forwards was Jock Hobbs, who'd taken over the openside flanker's role from Graham Mourie, who'd retired after the Australian series the year before. The backs were similarly experienced, with only Ian Dunn brought in at first five-eighth for the injured Wayne Smith and Warwick Taylor introduced at second five-eighth.

When the All Blacks trained for the first test at the Burnham army camp, John Brooks of the *Press* in Christchurch gently inquired of Dalton whether he was concerned about the geriatric look of the pack. Dalton paused a little, then said the more experienced, the better they were. But the comment stuck and Dalton obviously reported it to his teammates because a day or two later one of the "geriatrics", Gary Knight, thrust an ungeriatric arm around the neck of a reporter and asked, "Geriatrics, are we?" The front row must have liked the ring of their new monicker though because when they combined in a book two years later, it was called *The Geriatrics*.

The Lions would have scoffed at such a title. For all the All Blacks' unflattering margin of victory in the first test, their forwards had too much strength and too many wiles for the Lions. The Lions' only points came from three penalty goals and a dropped goal from Ollie Campbell, one of the few backline stars, and the All Blacks scored the only try. It was scored by Mark Shaw and that was only right and proper because it was he who

The spry geriatrics: Gary Knight, Andy Dalton and John Ashworth.

The face of a fighter: Andy Haden in the third test.

Mark Shaw looks for support as Peter Winterbottom zeroes in on him.

began the move when he worked the ball free of a maul and got the backs moving in one of the few fluent backline movements of the test. During the breakout, Steve Pokere passed to Stu Wilson and there were many in the British press who howled that the pass was forward, Shaw shouldn't have scored and if he hadn't, the Lions would have won. Perhaps so. But referee Palmade didn't call it forward and if the All Blacks benefited then, that's the nature of the rub of the green. Refereeing has never been — and God forbid if it ever was — an exact science. Neither has passing a football, come to that. For all the All Blacks' forward dominance, the game, which was fairly dreary, did hang in the balance and some of the All Blacks must have been worried about giving Campbell another shot at goal. In the event though, it was Allan Hewson who put it out of reach for the Lions with a 45-metre dropped goal with just a minute to go.

It became something of a rallying call for touring teams in the 1970s and 80s that if ever the All Blacks were to be beaten, it would be in the first test. That was when they were at their most vulnerable, so the theory went, and there were some close scrapes to support it. All Black teams then didn't have warm-up games and assembled only on the Tuesday or Wednesday before the test, having probably only two full training runs before a match. The touring teams, by contrast, had the advantage of being together all the time and living as professional rugby players. Coming ready or not, the touring teams would cry, and sometimes the All Blacks weren't quite ready. The All Black machine had gathered momentum by the time of the second test, however. That certainly was the case in 1983. While the All Blacks ironed out their kinks, with Smith coming back in for Dunn as the only change, the Lions

Gary Whetton shows the forward control that characterised the All Blacks' performance in the second test.

had to have an injury roll call to see who was fit. Their best halfback, Holmes, had gone home after damaging a knee in the first test and two of their better forwards, Stephens and Squire, were also out injured. They couldn't have arrived in Wellington brimming with confidence, even though they'd had three fairly comfortable provincial wins since Christchurch.

In 95 years of tests at Athletic Park, the weather was frequently a factor. Some of the wettest, windiest tests played by the All Blacks were at the venerable old park which, despite its reputation, had a certain charm. A rugby-specific ground, spectators were close to the action — aside from those who braved the heights and the elements in the towering edifice known as the Millard Stand. It was a rare test in Wellington when the

weather wasn't a factor. The second test in 1983 wasn't one of them. New Zealand and British journalists gathered for a few drinks in the old Hotel St George in the city on the night before and the stayers among them were amazed to see snow falling as they left. Even in their befuddled state, they knew the weather would determine the outcome. There was a freezing southerly, sweeping in off Cook Strait and howling down the ground. When Dalton won the toss, he did what anyone who lived in Wellington would have done and chose to play with the wind at his back in the first half. Use the elements when you can, was the theory. Wellingtonians — and there were four of them in the All Blacks — had become expert at attributing points values to the wind. "That's a 10-point wind," they'd say, or "That wind is

The man who dominated the Wellington test, Dave Loveridge.

worth 20 points." The wind on 18 June 1983, was seen as being worth more than the nine points the All Blacks had gathered by halftime through a try by Loveridge, cutting neatly through on the blindside, and a conversion and penalty goal from Hewson. The Lions, as they said later, thought so too. Nine points with a stiff southerly at the All Blacks' backs wasn't seen as enough.

What happened in the second half was one of the most complete performances by an All Black pack and it elevated Loveridge from being a very good halfback to the exalted status of being one of the best to pull on an All Black jersey. Sid Going was the best runner, Bryan Williams once remarked, and Chris Laidlaw was the best passer, but Loveridge combined the attributes of both. The All Black tactic in the second half was

simple. Get the ball, hang on to it and keep it tight. It became nine-man rugby down the tramlines, Loveridge as a sheepdog with the forwards as the flock. It was complete mastery and the Lions, striving as mightily as they could, had no answers.

Loveridge predictably and typically didn't want to know about the praise that went his way. It was the forwards, he said, who made all the difference and made his life so much easier than it was for the Lions halfback, Roy Laidlaw. But his coach, Bryce Rope, had no intention of Loveridge's light staying under the bushel. "This match will go down in history as Dave Loveridge's test," he said. "I believe that his was one of the finest exhibitions of halfback play in the history of test rugby. The way he changed the direction of our

Cold Comfort

Think of a test in Dunedin and most people north of Otago, and especially North Islanders, tend to think of cold. Television's affectation of calling anywhere vaguely south of Timaru "the deep south" (despite the contradictory American origin of the "deep south" term) adds to the imagery of Carisbrook as being just a decent dropkick away from the Antarctic.

It's no colder in Dunedin at test time than other places in New Zealand a lot of the time. Rugby is still, for all the great changes that have been wrought, a winter game. But then, there have been some tests at Carisbrook when the word "cold" has been almost an understatement.

Such a test was in 1983 when the Lions played the third in their series. It was a day of icy blasts, of snow flurries, of putting on every item of clothing it was possible to put on.

So it was for the All Blacks. It may not have been the first time players wore thermal vests under their jerseys, but it was certainly the most publicised. Some of the players wore mittens as well, an occasion for at once complimenting them on their practical sense and of bemoaning the lost state of New Zealand manhood.

The three gloved ones were Stu Wilson, Steve Pokere and Allan Hewson. The last-named, it may be recalled, had played in similar conditions at Carisbrook two years previously in the inter-island match and had had

to leave the field for what was described at the time as exposure.

While much was made of the wearing of mittens, some people with longer memories wondered what all the fuss was about. Some of the Original All Blacks wore mittens on occasions in Britain and others did, too, from time to time, and former Lion Vivian Jenkins recalled that wearing mittens used to be all the rage when he played in the 1930s.

"I remember wearing them myself a few times," he recalled. "Why, I wonder, did the habit die out? It should be revived. Anyway, it helped Hewson to give a classic display."

It didn't die out, as it happened, it merely lies dormant every so often before fashion or the elements bring them back into play.

Curiously enough, it was at the same ground 20 years later that mittens were reintroduced to a regular place in the game. Impressed with the light fabric used in players' protective wear, Highlanders captain Taine Randell worked with the manufacturer to have mittens made. He became a firm advocate of them, several other of the Highlanders also wore them and players from other teams also picked up the habit.

One other effect of the weather at Carisbrook in 1983 was that the two teams, by agreement, took the rare step of staying in their snug dressing rooms during the playing of the two national anthems.

Allan Hewson and his mittens in the third test. Forwards Gary Knight, Andy Haden and John Ashworth stayed barehanded.

play when we turned into the wind was superb and his use of the blindside was inspirational."

Even 20 years later, those whose memories encompassed the match still referred to it as "Trapper's test" ("Trapper" because he looked bedraggled after one wet Taranaki training and was told he looked like a rat trapper, whatever that might be).

Two down and two to play, things were not looking good for the Lions. For the All Blacks, it was quite the opposite and for the third test in Dunedin they were, shades of 1966, able to field an unchanged team. The Lions, who'd had a week's break in the Bay of Islands and beaten North Auckland and lost to Canterbury, lost another key forward because of injury and made other changes they hoped might reverse their declining fortunes.

Above: Roy Laidlaw gets a pass away to Ollie Campbell in the third test.

Top: The programme for the test in Dunedin in which the All Blacks clinched the series.

Bernie Fraser gets away from Gwyn Evans in the All Blacks' dominant win in Auckland.

Inset: Stu Wilson scores the second of his three tries. He ended the test as the All Blacks' record tryscorer.

Andy Haden and Maurice Colclough contest lineout possession in the fourth test. Steve Bainbridge reaches, too, while Roy Laidlaw waits.

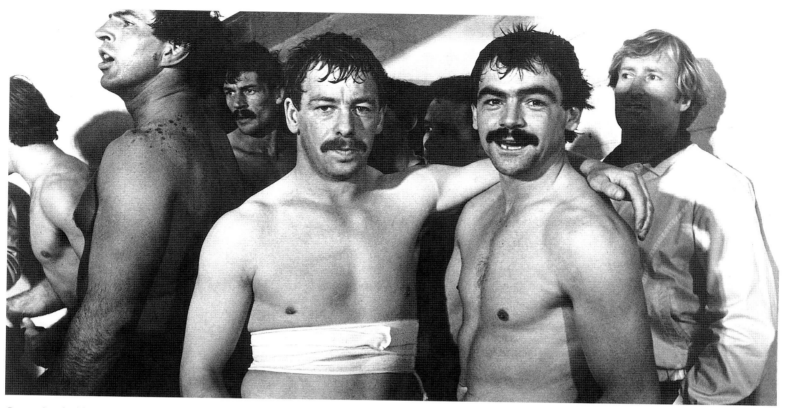

Opposing halfbacks Roy Laidlaw and Dave Loveridge meet up after the fourth test.

They didn't. They were competitive in Dunedin, scoring two tries to the All Blacks' one, but they were again outplayed in the forwards, though not, curiously enough, in set play. The Lions had all the possession they needed to win but lacked the talent. The All Blacks' one try was scored by Stu Wilson, slithering over for his 16th test try to equal the record held by Ian Kirkpatrick and it had been set up by the man who became the man of the series, Loveridge.

The series safely locked away, the All Blacks — with Ian Dunn back in place of the injured Smith — caned the Lions in the final test in Auckland. They'd been expected to win and achieve the first whitewash of the Lions since 1966 but no one could have expected the final victory scoreline of 38–6. It was a rout. Six tries to none was as comprehensive a test victory as could be wished for. All the Lions could mount were two penalty goals. It was as one-sided a test match as later games would be against sides such as Italy or the South Pacific states. The All Black outside backs so enjoyed the experience that at one point Stu Wilson ran as close to the New Zealand pack as he dared and cried out, "Come on you boofheads, we want more nut!"

Various factors were advanced for the Lions' poor performances — the itinerary got a lot of the blame even though the Lions had agreed to it, injuries as always played a part in a touring team's make-up, New Zealand forwards' ruggedness — a euphemism for violence — was held as one of the reasons and even the difficulty of bringing together the players of four different rugby cultures into one team was lamely offered. The real reason, the overriding reason, why the All Blacks won and the Lions lost was that the All Blacks were good and the Lions were poorly organised. They had talent, but no cohesion. They had marginally a better record than the 1966 team.

Jim Telfer was not afraid to confront the reality. "We have kidded ourselves for 12 years," he said. "In 1971 the Lions beat the All Blacks and we thought we had conquered the world. I said after the Scotland tour here two years ago that All Black rugby was more physical and aggressive. It is time we stopped kidding ourselves

The vanquished and the victor: Ciaran Fitzgerald and Andy Dalton.

about the standard of rugby in the Five Nations. You could not have a more dedicated, committed team than these Lions but they were not good enough — they were like lambs to the slaughter."

Clem Thomas made a brutal assessment when he said the Lions were the worst of the British teams to come to New Zealand. Some of the forwards, he said, were up to test standard but the tragedy of the tour was that the backs, with the exceptions of John Carleton, Roger Baird and Geoff Evans, tarnished the image of traditional Lions back play. Even Ollie Campbell, of whom great things had been expected, failed to live up to his reputation, Thomas thought, though, to be fair to Campbell, he seemed throughout the tour to have trouble with one or other of his hamstrings.

The British *Daily Telegraph* writer on the tour, John Mason, was just as unhappy as Thomas. "New Zealand rugby, the best in the world, growled and we cowered," he said. Mason thought wrong test selections were a decisive factor and he would have had Colin Deans as hooker and Jeff Squire as captain but if Telfer had been thinking along those lines, it became an irrelevance when Squire went home because of a shoulder injury. So Fitzgerald stayed as hooker and captain, but to blame him alone for the losses would have been ultra-myopic: the Lions were not good enough.

"I have failed," Telfer said in that mournful way he can sometimes adopt. The failure was not his alone. The failure was a system in Britain that had failed to adapt to the changing times, a system that was administered by men who still thought Twickenham was the Vatican of rugby: that there resided power and infallibility. It took the failure of the Lions tour and then the World Cup four years later to force such entrenched attitudes to change.

1993
Enduring Tradition

The Lions leave footprints that the rugby tracker can read. The signs left by the 1993 team were similar in some respects and identical in others to those left by their predecessors.

Disagreements about refereeing have been endemic to Lions tours; so, too, has the odd controversy, whether it's about the captaincy — muted in 1993 — the attitude of players who don't make the test teams or some off-field incident that becomes briefly a cause célèbre to be eventually discarded and forgotten among the detritus of rugby tours. And in 1993, as with so many previous Lions tours, there was the most indelible footprint of them all: so near but yet so far. Like other Lions teams, the class of 1993 went home with those burning phrases of sport ringing in their ears: could have, should have. They were also left with the most dispiriting phrase of all: did not.

Their coach, Ian McGeechan, the most widely respected coach in British rugby since Carwyn James, wrote a short book after the tour. It was called *So Close to Glory*. If ever the Lions are pensioned off, as some people still want, as being an anachronism in modern rugby — and what a dumb, short-sighted move that would be — those words could be the Lions' epitaph. The Welsh journalist and former Lion Clem Thomas thought McGeechan's book could have been equally called *Same Old Story* because that was pretty much what it was.

It was a tour and a team that promised much against an All Black team that was in the throes of reasserting its international rugby authority and in a country grappling with the dying days of the game's outdated, old-fashioned and misplaced amateur regulations.

The Lions, the last of the amateurs, had their house in order. McGeechan, himself a Lion in 1974 and 1977 and coach in Australia in 1989, had been appointed the previous August and had all the authority he needed. Gone were the days, finally, when the appointment of coach was determined by sectional national interests or, even worse, that it was someone's turn. Gone were the days when the coach was coach in name only and sometimes not even that, reduced to the role of directing players in runs around the park at training. Gone were the days when the coach didn't have a say in which players were chosen. Gone were the days when the brief for the Lions was to go and enjoy themselves and not worry about the results.

The last of the amateurs maybe, but the Lions were professional in their approach — from the administrative level back in Britain to the management of the tour to the players or, at least, most of the players. There were some, sadly for McGeechan and sadly for the Lions, who saw the tour as a free jaunt around New Zealand that also included some rugby.

The Lions came to New Zealand at a time of transition in All Black rugby. The great teams that had won the World Cup in 1987 and dominated world rugby for the remainder of the 1980s had withered and died, interred at the old Arms Park in Cardiff where they had played the cup play-off match in 1991 against Scotland. Some players knew they had outlived their usefulness, others would soon learn that they had. Laurie Mains became the All Black coach in 1992 to succeed the unsuccessful compromise of having Alex Wyllie and John Hart as co-coaches at the cup. It wasn't stated publicly but it was implied that Mains's brief was not just to maintain the All Blacks' winning tradition, but also to build a squad capable of winning the cup in South Africa in 1995. The four-year cycle of international rugby, from one cup to the next, had been introduced by stealth. Mains set about his task in 1992 with a series against a hastily put together World XV to mark the New Zealand union's centenary, two tests against Ireland, a three-test series against Australia and a quick trip to South Africa to welcome the Springboks back into the world game after their years of apartheid isolation. One match against the World XV was lost, the series in Australia was lost but the All Blacks were on their way back. If the Lions are the ultimate test for the All Blacks, as they should be but haven't always been, Mains would probably have preferred another year before confronting them. But each must play with the cards that are dealt.

It wasn't just on the field that changes were occurring in New Zealand rugby. The whispers against amateurism had become a clamour and as a means of somehow compensating the players for their endeavours, while still obeying the letter of the amateur laws if not the spirit, a money-raising venture called the All Black Club was launched. It was a New Zealand equivalent of the quaint tradition in other strong rugby countries of stuffing banknotes into the toes of players' boots, itself an equivalent of the plain brown envelopes which were so much a part of other sports that tried vainly to cling to amateur principles laid down in a different country in a different century in different circumstances.

Against this background in New Zealand, there had been talk in Britain that the Lions tour might be the last. The idea of combining the three British countries with Ireland for occasional tours to New Zealand, South Africa

Laurie Mains, coach of the All Blacks in 1993.

and Australia had outlived its usefulness, some argued, and now stood as a potential impediment to the individual countries' preparations for the World Cup. One Lions tour every four years, it was said, would take out one year in which any one of the national teams could tour themselves and build for the cup. The arguments then were exacerbated later after the introduction of professionalism and the valid concerns by the British clubs which not only paid the players but also developed and nurtured new generations of players. Some of the talk that the Lions had run their course was newspaper talk, but there was also some in official circles. Fortunately for world rugby, such talk came to nothing.

McGeechan, for whom a passion for the Lions is embedded in his soul, wrote a report for his bosses after the New Zealand tour and didn't hold back: "The Lions must continue — the test matches provide an arena which is completely different from any other experience the players get and the response in New Zealand is completely different from any other national tour. As they kept reminding us, the Lions are the biggest thing which ever happens to New Zealand, and South Africa for that matter. We must not underestimate the Lions'

role and their significance on the world rugby stage. Whatever we think nationally, we cannot provide what the Lions provide and although there will be inherent difficulties of bringing four countries together, the advantages far outweigh any problems, and British rugby will always benefit from the existence of the Lions."

McGeechan's passion for the Lions and his frank admiration of and respect for New Zealand rugby were what drove him in the months before the tour. A Scotsman schooled in England, McGeechan saw the 1967 All Blacks as a teenager. Their manner of play and their dedication to winning so impressed him that he wrote a university dissertation about the All Blacks. (It irks McGeechan that he loaned the thesis to another student and hasn't seen it since — a document now of historical interest, it could lurk still on some undusted shelf somewhere.)

Unlike most of his predecessors, McGeechan benefited from an enlightened approach by administrators to the tour. He was appointed coach in August of 1992 and was joined by Dick Best of England as assistant coach — Best, incidentally, was a close friend of the New Zealand assistant coach, Earle Kirton — and by the England manager, Geoff Cooke, as the manager.

The two central figures of the 1993 tour, Geoff Cooke (left) and Ian McGeechan.

Dooley Decision Irked

The British Four Home Unions Tours Committee, the body that used to be responsible for Lions tours, was often portrayed as being starchy, antediluvian and unbending in its fixation with rules being adhered to.

Lions lock Wade Dooley would agree with such an assessment. Dooley's passion in his rugby life was to play a test for the Lions against the All Blacks. But a week before the first test in 1993, his father died suddenly and Dooley raced home, expecting to return after the funeral.

The New Zealand union chairman, Eddie Tonks, extended his condolences and told Lions manager Geoff Cooke that Dooley would be welcomed back.

But no.

Dooley was met at Heathrow by the Four Home Unions Committee secretary, Bob Weighill, a former air commodore and the most charming and efficient of men. Weighill arranged for Dooley to be met at Manchester and had a wreath sent to his father's funeral.

About a week later, Dooley phoned Weighill and told him he was ready to go back to New Zealand. At about the same time, Weighill had had a phone call from Cooke asking when Dooley would be available.

Weighill, as it happened, was preparing to go to New Zealand so he booked Dooley on to the same flight. But then the difficulties began. Weighill reported what he had gone to his committee and was told Dooley could not return. It would be in breach of the tour's agreement, he was told, and was not covered by insurance.

Dooley was told he could return to New Zealand to watch the Lions, but not to play. On those terms, he chose to stay at home. "I couldn't come back and play," he said, "so I'd be there as a non-player. I was so looking forward to playing a test match against New Zealand for the Lions."

Dooley's only test in New Zealand was as a replacement for England in 1985. He had also played against the All Blacks in the World Cup in 1991.

Weighill meanwhile went to New Zealand and walked into a frosty reception from the players, who blamed him for Dooley's continued absence.

It wasn't just the players who were upset. "It's an appalling way to treat a person who has given such a lot to the game," Cooke said.

Captain Gavin Hastings said in his autobiography that the decision had incensed the players at a time when the Lions were at a low ebb — it was after they had lost to Otago and lost the first test, and Scott Hastings had had to go home injured.

"It gave us something to bitch about during a low point of the tour," he said.

Wade Dooley . . . denied a Lions test against the All Blacks by red tape.

Modern managements didn't bring a complete break from the past, however. The three were joined by a selector from each country: Derek Morgan of England, David Richards of Wales, Ken Reid of Ireland and Bob Munro of Scotland. They met, they talked, they planned, they watched club play, they talked to players, they watched the Five Nations and on 22 March they met for six hours at a hotel near Heathrow to finalise the touring party of 30. It was made public the next day and, not for the first time, there was a fuss about the captain.

McGeechan and his team had opted for Gavin Hastings as captain ahead of the man most widely touted for the job, Will Carling of England. The case for Carling was strong. He'd captained England for five years and led them to two Grand Slams in the Five Nations as well as the World Cup final against Australia in 1991. Hastings, by contrast, had captained Scotland for just one season and they had been beaten by England.

McGeechan conceded that had the captain been named in August when the management appointments had been made, Carling would have been an automatic choice. Yet the factors which counted so heavily for Hastings in March the following year had also applied in August of 1992. These were his experience with the Lions — he'd been in Australia in 1989 — and his knowledge of and experience in New Zealand. The latter was a persuasive factor in McGeechan's mind because he knew the value of a captain who would be respected by New Zealanders. Aside from his visits to

New Zealand with Scotland and with the World XV in 1992, Hastings also played club rugby in Auckland in 1987. He had stayed behind after the World Cup and played for the University club and had made the Auckland squad, sitting on the bench for two matches (one of which was a Ranfurly Shield challenge).

Hastings was the best fullback in Britain at the time, and among the best in the world, was also sure of his place in the Lions test side and McGeechan was determined not to repeat the errors of the past when a captain either missed tests or, even worse, played in them because he was captain rather than because he deserved a place on playing merit. Carling, as it turned out, could not guarantee a test place but he also lacked the New Zealand and Lions experience that Hastings had. Carling also had in New Zealand a slightly unfortunate reputation of being afflicted by excessive self-esteem and of being the type of patronising Englishman not held dear in earthy New Zealand circles.

This was demonstrably unfair on the man, who could be as charming and unaffected as the best of them.

The timing of the naming of the team was unfortunate for McGeechan. Of the 30 players, 16 were from England and just two from Ireland yet two days before the announcement Ireland had beaten England. This naturally enough caused a few anguished questions, especially from reporters from across the Irish Sea, but McGeechan in his quiet, calm way was able to assure them that selections

Gavin Hastings, the popular captain of the 1993 team.

Halfback Dewi Morris — English despite his Welsh name — clears during the first test in Christchurch.

were based on several matches and not just one.

The captaincy and the Irish aside, it was accepted as the best it could be. There was experience, and none more than flanker Peter Winterbottom, the sole survivor of the tour of New Zealand 10 years previously, and there was rare promise, especially the England lineout forward, Martin Bayfield. There were competitive match-ups for positions, especially at first five-eighth, between the England duo of contrasting styles and temperament, Rob Andrew and Stuart Barnes, and in midfield where Carling and his England teammate, Jeremy Guscott, had to vie with the Welshman, Scott Gibbs, and Hastings' brother Scott. The Lions were seen as having competent if not brilliant backs and forwards expected — or at least hoped — to be the match of New Zealand's.

If McGeechan or any players were under any illusions about what they faced in New Zealand, they didn't last long. They won their first four matches — against North Auckland, North Harbour, New Zealand Maori and Canterbury — but none was what might be called a runaway victory and all underlined what McGeechan had been telling his players: no matter how much better than them you might think you are, New Zealand players are hard and they'll all be out to beat you. There are no soft games in New Zealand. And if any players had lingering doubts, and they shouldn't have, they would have been finally dispelled when the Lions were thumped 37–24 by Otago. The loss couldn't have come at a worse time for the Lions — it was the last Saturday before the first test and not only had they lost, Bayfield had been carried off on a stretcher after being upended in a lineout, Scott Hastings ended up in hospital with a broken cheekbone after a collision with one of Josh Kronfeld's knees, Carling had strained a leg

The try the Lions say wasn't. Frank Bunce gets over the line in an embrace with the ball and Ieuan Evans. Walter Little, Gavin Hastings and Will Carling look on — Va'aiga Tuigamala celebrates.

muscle and the leading lock, Wade Dooley, had gone home because of the sudden death of his father.

In diversity, good teams triumph. The Lions didn't triumph in the first test in Christchurch, but they thought they should have. They were convinced then, and remain convinced now, they should have won. It might have been in the late afternoon of 12 June 1993, that some of the Lions first heard an old New Zealand rugby cry, "Look at the scoreboard." For all the Lions' continuing anguish, the scoreline now remains what it was at the end of the first 80 minutes of Lions test rugby in New Zealand for 10 years: All Blacks 20, Lions 18.

The Lions pointed to three incidents in the game that they said cost them victory. The first was in the first minute when Grant Fox, with that laser accuracy of his, put up an up-and-under. It came down just out from the Lions' goal-line and just in from the corner.

The Welsh wing, Ieuan Evans and the All Black centre, Frank Bunce, both claimed it. Both certainly had arms around it. Over the line they crashed and Australian referee Brian Kinsey thought Bunce had gained the necessary downward pressure and awarded the All Blacks the try. Vigilant video analysis may have deemed otherwise but that wasn't a luxury available to Kinsey then and he had to call it as he saw it. The Lions saw it differently, as defending teams tend to do. "If the whole situation had been reversed and the Lions were attacking," McGeechan said, "I would have been delighted if we had been awarded a try but I would not have expected it. To most people at the game and to the millions of armchair critics watching on television there seemed to have been an element of doubt and, to the best of my knowledge, if the referee has any doubt he should award a five-metre scrum."

The second incident was more ill luck than anything else. Guscott had attacked down the left wing with only the fullback, John Timu, to beat. Guscott had Carling inside him and as he went to pass, Michael Jones pulled Carling back. Guscott was then forced to chip over Timu and the ball bounced into touch. Kinsey penalised Jones for the illegal tackle and Hastings kicked the goal, but the Lions reckoned Jones's early tackle probably prevented a try being scored. They didn't argue for a penalty try though. The Lions in that instance may have been right but there are many incidents in a game — and especially in a test match — which could mean the difference between winning and losing. Spilled balls in the loose, uncontrolled lineout taps, wrong options, missed tackles — all can have unknowable effects on the outcome.

The third incident had the Lions more riled than the others. Ten minutes from the end, Hastings had put the Lions in front with a superb kick into the wind. The Lions by then seemed to have the better of the All Blacks and all they needed for their win was not to offend anywhere within Fox's range. But the big Lions No. 8, Dean Richards, dumped Bunce and turned him toward the Lions' side. The Lions halfback, Dewi Morris, had the ball but Kinsey blew his whistle. Penalty. Fox, as he did throughout his stellar career, obliged. Hastings was furious out on the field: McGeechan was furious in the stand. An explanation wasn't forthcoming. "It appeared an outrageous decision at the time and one that I was simply at a loss to explain," McGeechan said. "Having watched it again a hundred times on the video I am still unable to explain satisfactorily why we were penalised."

The All Blacks and New Zealanders generally were relieved. They knew it had not been a commanding performance by the All Blacks and they knew also that

Gavin Hastings is upset, Sean Fitzpatrick listens and Brian Kinsey explains while Grant Fox just gets ready to nail the winning goal for the All Blacks in the first test.

the Lions, for all their troubles in the provincial matches, had made the transition to test level admirably. Their forwards in particular were more competitive than had been expected — Bayfield, recovered from his Carisbrook spill, was dominant in the lineouts and the loose trio of Winterbottom, Ben Clarke and Richards was at least the equal of All Blacks Jones, Zinzan Brooke and Jamie Joseph. It was said the All Blacks had been lucky to win; perhaps the All Blacks were counting their lucky stars when they slumped in their dressing room afterward but isn't there another old New Zealand rugby saying about sides making their own luck?

The Lions were devastated and, on top of their vicissitudes of the week before, their tour could have been in danger of collapsing. It says much for the leadership of McGeechan and Hastings, plus influential figures such as Cooke and Best and senior players, that far from feeling sorry for themselves and sliding further down a slippery slope, the Lions' resolve hardened.

This wasn't evident at the time because between tests the Lions beat Taranaki but lost to both Auckland and Hawke's Bay and it was after the loss in Napier that the Lions' chances in the test in Wellington were all but written off. It was a trap for the unwary, however, this basing test prospects on a midweek result by a team that had few test players. It was in the nature of the old-style tours — though the Lions' 13-match itinerary was more new-style — that games preceding tests were often stinkers, partly because it was the lesser players involved and partly because some minds were on the greater challenge of the test match earlier than they should have been.

Overleaf: Jamie Joseph storms away from a scrum in the second test and Dean Richards and Jason Leonard head to try to cut him off. Others are Jon Preston (extreme left), Grant Fox (background), Sean Fitzpatrick, Mark Cooksley (head down), Martin Johnson (4) and Michael Jones.

Mooreish Moment

England and British Isles hooker Brian Moore, known for his competitive tangles with Sean Fitzpatrick, offered an insight into the subtleties of front-row play after the Lions beat the All Blacks in the second test in 1993.

The match in Wellington was, Fitzpatrick ruefully recalled, his worst in an All Black jersey.

It was he who dropped the ball in the second half that led to the try by Rory Underwood that secured the win for the Lions.

Moore gleefully takes some credit for that.

The All Blacks had had a scrum five metres out from the Lions' line and went for a pushover try. But the Lions didn't buckle. In fact, they heaved back and the All Blacks retreated and No. 8 Zinzan Brooke was left scrambling to clear the ball.

"At that point in the game," Moore recalled, "if we in fact had got pushed over there we would have lost that test."

Not just because the All Blacks would have scored, but psychologically it would have damaged the Lions, Moore said.

"We scrummaged more for the ball and that was obviously a dent to their psyche because they had gone for it expecting to do us. No one who's not a forward understands the huge significance of small events and that was almost imperceptible to most people. But it was a big turning point because shortly after that was a turnover and Rory Underwood . . . [scored]. I remember going back to the halfway line and waving to the crowd nicely and cans rained down . . .

"One that landed on me was actually full. Now I don't know why I did this but I opened it and drank it and threw it away. Just waved it . . . it upset everyone more."

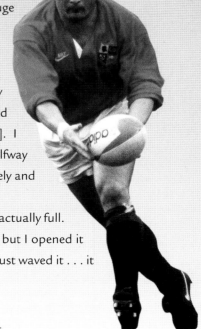

Combative hooker Brian Moore.

McGeechan's focus was in the right place. Though he had injury concerns — most notably to Hastings — he drilled and drilled again the test players, most often in scrums but also in prolonged lineout sessions in which variety was the key. The Lions lineout had been bolstered by the arrival of Martin Johnson, who had replaced Dooley. Johnson was then young and green but New Zealanders who knew their rugby knew his potential and among them was John Hart, who had had Johnson in the New Zealand Colts when Johnson did a stint in the King Country. By including Johnson in the test team at the expense of Andy Reed, the Lions went into the Wellington test with four genuine jumpers: Bayfield, Johnson, Clarke and Richards. The All Blacks had also made a change in the lineout, with Mark Cooksley, who had been impressive for the Maori against the Lions, replacing Ian Jones. There were other changes in both teams, coaches of both knowing that the first test performances were far from flawless. For the Lions, Gibbs replaced Carling at centre, Brian Moore took over at hooker from Ken Milne and Jason Leonard went to tighthead, even though he hadn't played on that side of the scrum since his schooldays.

John Kirwan, by then in the twilight of his career, had missed the first test because he'd been late arriving home from overseas, went back into the team in place of Eroni Clarke, who moved to second-five in place of the injured Walter Little. Halfback Jon Preston regained a place at the expense of Ant Strachan.

McGeechan's biggest concern on the eve of the second test was Hastings, who had strained a hamstring and who had said he couldn't play. Without him, the Lions' chances would be considerably reduced. His goalkicking was almost as unerring as Fox's, he was easily the best fullback in the Lions party and his leadership was irreplaceable. McGeechan tried to talk him into changing his mind, even if he lasted just 10 or so minutes (shades of similar entreaties to Gareth Edwards before the first Lions test in 1971). McGeechan went to Guscott and Carling and asked them to try to persuade Hastings. Eventually, at the lunchtime on the Friday, Hastings said he'd give it a go.

Another big decision was required of the Lions. A brisk northerly whistled down Athletic Park and most captains would play with it if they won the toss, figuring to get points up and then just stop their opponents in the second half. But McGeechan and Hastings figured they'd play into the wind, even though it meant also looking up into a bright sun. They figured that players from both sides in the first test had taken most of the first half to settle down and the Lions, who had played with the wind in Christchurch, had not been able to take full advantage of it. Therefore, the theory went, play into the wind and that would concentrate the minds wonderfully.

It worked, more or less. The Lions led 9–7 at halftime from two Hastings penalties and a neat dropped goal from Andrew. The All Blacks' seven points had come from a try by Clarke that was a direct result of the sun. Fox had sent up another high kick, Hastings lost it in the sun and though he made a grab at it the ball spilled into the in-goal area and Clarke fell onto it. Fox had converted the try but the two-point lead playing into the wind delighted the Lions. The gamble had worked. The All Blacks were less than delighted. The forwards had been nowhere near dominant and had been beaten in lineouts, especially by Bayfield and Johnson. Mains was so concerned at halftime that Jones replaced Cooksley, who had suddenly developed an injury severe enough to allow him to be replaced in those non-substitution days.

The All Blacks were better in the second half and mounted some promising moves but their hands and accuracy failed them too often to make inroads. Midway through the half, the Lions retreated in the face of an effective All Black rolling maul but as Sean Fitzpatrick broke off from it, the ball spilled from his hands. Such opportunities come rarely in test matches against opponents of equal calibre. Morris scooped it up on the Lions' 10-metre line and flicked the ball out to Guscott, who clapped on the pace and outflanked Bunce. Guscott changed pace and wrong-footed Kirwan then flung the ball out to Rory Underwood, who was at full pace. His spectacular dive across the line didn't end

Rory Underwood dives for the try that took the Lions out to a 17–7 lead midway through the second half. John Timu is the All Black defender.

the match but it sealed it for the Lions. It was a comprehensive victory for them, one of the best by a Lions team in New Zealand.

In the aftermath, the All Black forwards and especially the tight five were given most of the blame. The New Zealand newspaper reaction against the All Blacks stunned the Lions, who thought the All Blacks were the darlings of New Zealand newspapers. Fitzpatrick had known what was coming. As he and Hastings walked off Athletic Park, he muttered: "You watch the country turn against us now."

Fitzpatrick later conceded he'd had a shocker of a game. "I have no doubt it was my worst game in an All Black jersey," he said. "They had not a bad team and

we were still developing. Maybe that was one of the factors. Laurie Mains was into his second year as coach and we were developing as a unit but some way off what we wanted to become. I can't say why I in particular didn't play well in that game. Perhaps it had something to do with me taking my position for granted. Perhaps there wasn't enough of the fear of losing."

In the days that followed, criticism of the tight five rolled on and Mains put the pressure on them at training. Fitzpatrick felt the heat. He knew the All Blacks wouldn't play like that again.

The Lions, buoyed by their success and knowing they could have won the first test, hardly dared hope they might become just the second Lions team to win a series in New Zealand. They knew the All Blacks would strike back with a vengeance. McGeechan, the student of All Black rugby, knew precisely what to expect. Mains called Andy Haden in to help out with lineout tactics and McGeechan correctly deduced this would have something to do with crowding Bayfield and Johnson and limiting if not stopping their supply of ball. Correctly deducing is one thing, McGeechan wryly noted later, doing something about it was altogether different. During training, while the All Blacks worked at nullifying Bayfield, the Lions worked at protecting him. It was as if the third test would come down solely to the freedom afforded one man, Bayfield.

But it was more than that. One of the most effective ways of nullifying an opponent's lineout strengths is not to allow him to use them. The All Blacks therefore chose not to kick to touch unless in the more dire circumstances. With Fox, they had the ideal man to

The Lions' lineout revelation, Martin Bayfield.

Michael Jones and Dean Richards clash in the third test.

"Winters" of Discontent

It might have been one of the saddest, if most telling, moments of any Lions tour. At the end of the tour in 1993, the players got together and were required to sit in a circle and each of them had to make a brief statement about the tour.

It's a common enough practice for rugby teams after tours and sometimes after matches. Only a few sentences are required and the comments usually are along the lines of, "Well, we didn't win the series but we gave it a great crack and I'm proud to have been a part of it." That sort of stuff.

During the 1993 tour, and especially after midweek losses to Hawke's Bay and Waikato, there were rumours of a split in the touring party: there was the test team, otherwise known as the Saturday team, and there were some of the midweekers.

After the tour, the rumours were confirmed.

At the team meeting, according to hooker Brian Moore, it came to flanker Peter Winterbottom, a hardened and respected player who was the only survivor of the 1983 tour.

Winterbottom stood up and said his piece: "I'm enjoying myself and if I made new friends it was a mistake." He then sat down.

Moore continued: "Winters played really well on that tour and [he] is a hard, straight and honest man. And he doesn't say things like that . . . without cause. And I'm not sure I had the bottle to say that, but that was the way it was."

Far too many players in 1993, according to Moore, "cocked up and went on the piss. It was unforgiveable."

The split was confirmed by captain Gavin Hastings. "At the end of the tour there were two distinct tour parties. There was a tour party that was playing test matches and trying to win a test series and there were guys that had jumped off the train . . . there were some guys that just didn't front up. That's why I believe New Zealand is the hardest place to go on tour because you have to front up there every week and when you're down in the pissing wet rain of Invercargill on the Tuesday night before one of the test matches and you're going to get your head kicked in, you've got to be prepared to take it. I think there were probably three or four guys who just weren't prepared and weren't hard enough and prepared to work hard enough."

Coach Ian McGeechan wasn't happy either with some of the midweek players though he said England captain Will Carling, who had played in the first test but was then dropped, was a notable exception.

McGeechan wrote of the Waikato loss: "The stark reality was that rightly or wrongly, with the exception of Will Carling, the midweek players all felt that they had no real chance of making the test team and therefore the biggest single incentive to produce the best was missing."

McGeechan also remarked, "We had a very good test side but we had a lot of players who were quite happy to enjoy the tour but not for the rugby."

Peter Winterbottom, twice a Lion in New Zealand.

Jon Preston heads for the goal-line in the third test after evading Gavin Hastings.

One of the Lions' best loose forwards, Ben Clarke, during the third test.

Dean Richards was quick, but Grant Fox was quicker. This is in the third test, two tests away from the end of Fox's glittering career.

bring the ball down in the tramlines and either have it bounce back infield, or ensure that All Black loose forwards were up quickly to harass the Lions defender and if possible force him into touch. Preston and Timu were also adept at kicking for touch and not finding it. It was a tactic the Lions had used with effect in Wellington; now it was the All Blacks' turn. Having correctly deduced the All Blacks' tactics, McGeechan also correctly deduced the All Blacks' resolve. It is a fearsome thing, this resolve, when motivated by humiliation as it had been. When men such as Fitzpatrick, Craig Dowd and Olo Brown, plus locks Ian Jones and Robin Brooke, not to mention loosies Joseph, Michael Jones and Arran Pene, get their dander up and determine not to back down, woe betide whoever gets in their way.

It was an emphatic All Black win in Auckland: 30 points to 13; three tries to one, even though the Lions led 10–0 after a quarter of the match. It was as decisive as any test win between such opponents could be. McGeechan felt the All Blacks were flattered by the score; but some with memories of the All Blacks' fourth test win 10 years previously thought the All Blacks could have matched that.

The Lions acknowledged the All Blacks' superiority. They knew they'd done all they could and that in the face of such a unified All Black performance, they could do no more. Instead, they took solace in their victory in Wellington and looked back at what could have been a victory in Christchurch. To have won the series in Auckland, they would have had to have beaten

Jerseys were swapped but the trophy was New Zealand's. Gavin Hastings and Sean Fitzpatrick. In the background, photographer Paul Estcourt appears to be enjoying the moment.

the All Blacks twice in a row — not even the Lions of 1971 were able to manage that. No team since the Australians in 1949 had done that, though that was against a New Zealand C team. A year later, in 1994, France became the next team to beat the All Blacks twice in a row and did so only because of that extraordinary try "from the ends of the earth" scored by Jean-Luc Sadourny.

McGeechan made a string of recommendations to the British Four Home Unions Tours Committee at the end of the tour, among them one that perhaps a second coach should have responsibility for the midweek matches so the head coach could concentrate on the Saturday games and, specifically, the tests. He also suggested that a captain be chosen specifically for the midweek matches.

He left those who appointed him in no doubt about the demands of a tour of New Zealand: "The New Zealand environment is intimidating simply because, from waking up in the morning and talking to waiters and waitresses, the key note is rugby. Outside the hotel, people talk in the shops about rugby and at the receptions the talk was also obviously about rugby. Some players found this almost too intrusive and did not feel totally comfortable with the atmosphere. Others, and in particular Ben Clarke, Martin Bayfield and Scott Gibbs, found it challenging and their progress throughout the tour was dramatic."

Hastings summed up the tour thus: "It was the trip of a lifetime, a tour to a rugby-mad nation, never to be forgotten. I wish we had won the test series but at least we gave it our very best shot and we came very close. Long live Lions' tours!"

Statistics

British teams in New Zealand
(British team scores first)

	1888	1904	1908	1930	1950	1959	1966	1971	1977	1983	1993
Ashburton County-North Otago					29–6						
Auckland	6–3 0–4 3–0 1–1	0–13	0–11	6–19	32–9	15–10	12–6	19–12	34–15	12–13	18–23
Bay of Plenty							6–6	20–14	23–16	34–16	
Bay of Plenty-Thames Valley						26–24					
Buller					24–9						
Canterbury	14–6 4–0 8–0		8–13	8–14	16–5	14–20	8–6	14–3	14–13	20–22	28–10
Canterbury-South Canterbury-West Coast		5–3									
Counties										25–16	
Counties-Thames Valley							13–9	25–3	35–10		
H. Roberts' XV	4–1										
Hawke's Bay	3–2		25–3	14–3	20–0	52–12	11–11	25–6	13–11	25–19	17–29
King Country-Counties						25–5					
Manawatu										25–18	
Manawatu-Horowhenua			12–3	34–8	13–8	26–6	17–8	39–6	18–12		
Marlborough-Nelson Bays								31–12	40–23		
Mid Canterbury										26–6	
Nelson-Golden Bay-Motueka-Marlborough				41–3	24–3	64–5	22–14				

All Blacks v Lions

British teams in New Zealand
(British team scores first)

	1888	1904	1908	1930	1950	1959	1966	1971	1977	1983	1993
Nelson–Marlborough			12–0								
New Zealand		3–9	5–32 3–3 0–29	6–3 10–13 10–15 8–22	9–9 0–8 3–6 8–11	17–18 8–11 8–22 9–6	3–20 12–16 6–19 11–24	9–3 12–22 13–3 14–14	12–16 13–9 7–19 9–10	12–16 0–9 8–15 6–38	18–20 20–7 13–30
New Zealand Juniors						29–9	9–3		19–9		
New Zealand Maori				19–13	14–9	12–6	16–14	23–12	22–19		24–20
New Zealand Universities						25–13	24–11	27–6	9–21		
North Auckland				38–5	8–6	35–13	6–3	11–5	18–7	21–12	30–17
North Harbour											29–13
Otago	8–3 4–3 0–0		6–9	33–9	9–23	8–26	9–17	21–9	12–7		24–37
Otago-Southland		14–8									
Poverty Bay			26–0								
Poverty Bay-East Coast						23–14	9–6	18–12	25–6		
Poverty Bay-East Coast-Bay of Plenty				25–11	27–3						
South Canterbury			12–6		27–8						
South Canterbury-Ashburton County-North Otago				16–9							
South Canterbury-Mid Canterbury-North Otago						21–11	20–12	25–6	45–6		
South Island	5–3 6–0										
Southland			14–8	9–3	0–11	11–6	8–14	25–3	20–12	41–3	34–16
Taranaki			0–5	23–7	25–3	15–3	12–9	14–9	21–13		49–25
Taranaki Clubs	0–1 7–1										
Taranaki-Wanganui-Manawatu		0–0									
Waikato						14–0	20–9	35–14	18–13	40–13	10–38
Waikato-King Country-Thames Valley				40–16	30–0						
Wairarapa	5–1										
Wairarapa-Bush			17–3	19–6	27–13	37–11	9–6	27–6	41–13	57–10	
Wanganui	1–1		9–6	19–3	31–3	9–6				47–15	
Wanganui-King Country							6–12	22–9	60–9		
Wellington	3–3		13–19	8–12	12–6	21–6	6–20	47–9	13–6	27–19	
West Coast					32–3					52–16	
West Coast-Buller			22–3	34–11		58–3	25–6	39–6	45–0		

Statistics

New Zealand v British combined teams

Date	Ground	City	Team	Score	Team	Score	Halftime
13.8.1904	Athletic Park	Wellington	New Zealand	9	Great Britain	3	3–3
6.6.1908	Carisbrook	Dunedin	New Zealand	32	Anglo-Welsh	5	21–0
27.6.1908	Athletic Park	Wellington	New Zealand	3	Anglo-Welsh	3	0–0
25.7.1908	Potter's Park	Auckland	New Zealand	29	Anglo-Welsh	0	12–0
21.6.1930	Carisbrook	Dunedin	Great Britain	6	New Zealand	3	GB 3–0
5.7.1930	Lancaster Park	Christchurch	New Zealand	13	Great Britain	10	NZ 8–5
26.7.1930	Eden Park	Auckland	New Zealand	15	Great Britain	10	5–5
9.8.1930	Athletic Park	Wellington	New Zealand	22	Great Britain	8	NZ 6–3
27.5.1950	Carisbrook	Dunedin	New Zealand	9	British Isles	9	BI 3–0
10.6.1950	Lancaster Park	Christchurch	New Zealand	8	British Isles	0	8–0
1.7.1950	Athletic Park	Wellington	New Zealand	6	British Isles	3	BI 3–0
29.7.1950	Eden Park	Auckland	New Zealand	11	British Isles	8	NZ 8–3
18.7.1959	Carisbrook	Dunedin	New Zealand	18	British Isles	17	BI 9–6
15.8.1959	Athletic Park	Wellington	New Zealand	11	British Isles	8	NZ 6–0
29.8.1959	Lancaster Park	Christchurch	New Zealand	22	British Isles	8	14–8
19.9.1959	Eden Park	Auckland	British Isles	9	New Zealand	6	3–3
16.7.1966	Carisbrook	Dunedin	New Zealand	20	British Isles	3	8–3
6.8.1966	Athletic Park	Wellington	New Zealand	16	British Isles	12	BI 9–8
27.8.1966	Lancaster Park	Christchurch	New Zealand	19	British Isles	6	6–6
10.9.1966	Eden Park	Auckland	New Zealand	24	British Isles	11	NZ 10–8
26.6.1971	Carisbrook	Dunedin	British Isles	9	New Zealand	3	3–3
10.7.1971	Lancaster Park	Christchurch	New Zealand	22	British Isles	12	NZ 8–6
31.7.1971	Athletic Park	Wellington	British Isles	13	New Zealand	3	13–0
14.8.1971	Eden Park	Auckland	New Zealand	14	British Isles	14	8–8
18.6.1977	Athletic Park	Wellington	New Zealand	16	British Isles	12	16–12
9.7.1977	Lancaster Park	Christchurch	British Isles	13	New Zealand	9	13–6
30.7.1977	Carisbrook	Dunedin	New Zealand	19	British Isles	7	10–4
13.8.1977	Eden Park	Auckland	New Zealand	10	British Isles	9	BI 9–3
4.6.1983	Lancaster Park	Christchurch	New Zealand	16	British Isles	12	BI 9–6
18.6.1983	Athletic Park	Wellington	New Zealand	9	British Isles	0	9–0
2.7.1983	Carisbrook	Dunedin	New Zealand	15	British Isles	8	NZ 6–4
16.7.1983	Eden Park	Auckland	New Zealand	38	British Isles	6	16–3
12.6.1993	Lancaster Park	Christchurch	New Zealand	20	British Isles	18	NZ 11–9
26.6.1993	Athletic Park	Wellington	British Isles	20	New Zealand	7	9–7
3.7.1993	Eden Park	Auckland	New Zealand	30	British Isles	13	14–10

British and Irish test players in New Zealand

Surname	First name	Country/Club	Year(s)/Tests	Total tests	Tries	Cons	Pens	DGs	GMs	Total points
Aarvold	Carl	England	1930 1,2,3,4	4	3					9
Ackerman	Robert	Wales	1983 1,4r	2						
Andrew	Rob	England	1993 1,2,3	3				1		3
Archer	Herbert	Guy's Hospital	1908 1,2,3	3						
Ashcroft	Alan	England	1959 2	1						
Bainbridge	Steve	England	1983 3,4	2						
Baird	Roger	Scotland	1983 1,2,3,4	4	1					4
Bassett	Jack	Wales	1930 1,2,3,4	4						
Bayfield	Martin	England	1993 1,2,3	3						
Beamish	George	Ireland	1930 1,2,3,4	4						
Beattie	John	Scotland	1983 2r	1						
Beaumont	Bill	England	1977 2,3,4	3						
Bebb	Dewi	Wales	1966 1,2,3,4	4						
Bennett	Phil	Wales	1977 1,2,3,4	4			6			18
Bevan	John	Wales	1971 1	1						
Bevan	Sid	Wales	1904	1						
Black	Angus	Scotland	1950 1,2	2						
Black	Brian	England	1930 1,2,3,4	4		2				4
Bowcott	Harry	Wales	1930 1,2,3,4	4	1					3
Brown	Gordon	Scotland	1971 3,4 1977 2,3,4	5						
Budge	Grahame	Scotland	1950 4	1						
Burcher	David	Wales	1977 3	1						
Burnell	Paul	Scotland	1993 1	1						
Bush	Percy	Cardiff	1904	1						
Calder	Jim	Scotland	1983 3	1						
Campbell	Ollie	Ireland	1983 1,2,3,4	4			4	1		15
Campbell-Lamerton	Mike	Scotland	1966 1,3	2						
Carleton	John	England	1983 2,3,4	3						
Carling	Will	England	1993 1	1						
Chapman	Fred	Westoe	1908 3	1						
Clarke	Ben	England	1993 1,2,3	3						
Cleaver	Billy	Wales	1950 1,2,3	3						
Clifford	Tom	Ireland	1950 1,2,3	3						
Cobner	Terry	Wales	1977 1,2,3	3						
Colclough	Maurice	England	1983 1,2,3,4	4						

Statistics

British and Irish test players in New Zealand

Surname	First name	Country/Club	Year(s)/Tests	Total tests	Tries	Cons	Pens	DGs	GMs	Total points
Cotton	Fran	England	1977 2,3,4	3						
Crowther	S	Lennox	1904	1						
Davey	James	England	1908 1	1						
Davies	Clifton	Wales	1950 4	1						
Davies	Dai	Wales	1950 3,4	2						
Davies	Gerald	Wales	1971 1,2,3,4	4	3					9
Davies	Mervyn	Wales	1971 1,2,3,4	4						
Davies	Terry	Wales	1959 2,4	2		1	1			5
Dawes	John	Wales	1971 1,2,3,4	4						
Dawson	Ronnie	Ireland	1959 1,2,3,4	4						
Dibble	Robert	England	1908 1,2,3	3						
Dixon	Peter	England	1971 1,2,4	3	1					3
Dobson	Denys	England	1904	1						
Down	Percy	Bristol	1908 1,2,3	3						
Duckham	David	England	1971 2,3,4	3						
Duggan	Willie	Ireland	1977 1,2,3,4	4	1					4
Edwards	Gareth	Wales	1971 1,2,3,4	4						
Edwards	Reg	Ireland	1904	1						
Evans	Bob	Wales	1950 1,2,3,4	4						
Evans	Gareth	Wales	1977 2,3,4	3						
Evans	Gwyn	Wales	1983 3,4	2			1			3
Evans	Ieuan	Wales	1993 1,2,3	3						
Evans	Trevor	Wales	1977 1	1						
Evans	William	Wales	1959 1,2,3	3						
Farrell	James	Ireland	1930 1,2,3,4	4						
Faull	John	Wales	1959 1,3,4	3		1	1			5
Fenwick	Steve	Wales	1977 1,2,3,4	4						
Fitzgerald	Ciaran	Ireland	1983 1,2,3,4	4						
Gabe	Rhys	Wales	1904	1						
Gibbs	Reg	Wales	1908 1,2	2	1					3
Gibbs	Scott	Wales	1993 2,3	2	1					5
Gibson	Mike	Ireland	1966 1,2,3,4 1971 1,2,3,4	8						
Guscott	Jeremy	England	1993 1,2,3	3						
Harding	Arthur	Wales	1904, 1908 1,2,3	4			1			3
Hastings	Gavin	Scotland	1993 1,2,3	3		1	12			38

British and Irish test players in New Zealand

Surname	First name	Country/Club	Year(s)/Tests	Total tests	Tries	Cons	Pens	DGs	GMs	Total points
Hayward	Don	Wales	1950 1,2,3	3						
Henderson	Noel	Ireland	1950 3	1						
Hewitt	David	Ireland	1959 1,3,4	3	1		1			6
Hind	Guy	Guy's Hospital	1908 2,3	2						
Hinshelwood	Sandy	Scotland	1966 2,4	2	1					3
Hodgson	John	Northern	1930 1,3	2						
Holmes	Terry	Wales	1983 1	1						
Hopkins	Ray	Wales	1971 1r	1						
Horrocks-Taylor	Phil	England	1959 3	1						
Irvine	Andy	Scotland	1977 1,2,3,4	4			2			6
Irwin	David	Ireland	1983 1,2,4	3						
Jackett	Edward	England	1908 1,2,3	3						
Jackson	Fred	Leicester	1908 1	1		1				2
Jackson	Peter	England	1959 1,3,4	3	2					6
Jeeps	Dick	England	1959 1,2,3	3						
John	Barry	Wales	1971 1,2,3,4	4	1	3	5	2		30
John	Roy	Wales	1950 1,2,3,4	4						
Johnson	Martin	England	1993 2,3	2						
Jones	"Ponty"	Pontypool	1908 1,2,3	3	1					3
Jones	"Tuan"	Guy's Hospital	1908 2,3	2						
Jones	David	Wales	1966 1	1						
Jones	Ivor	Wales	1930 1,2,3,4	4		1				2
Jones	Ken	Wales	1950 1,2,4	3	2					6
Jones	Lewis	Wales	1950 4	1		1	1			5
Jones	Staff	Wales	1983 2,3,4	3						
Keane	Moss	Ireland	1977 1	1						
Kennedy	Ken	Ireland	1966 1,4	2						
Kiernan	Michael	Ireland	1983 2,3,4	3						
Kininmonth	Peter	Scotland	1950 1,2,4	3						
Kyle	Jack	Ireland	1950 1,2,3,4	4	1					3
Kyrke	Venables	Marlborough	1908 1	1						
Laidlaw	Frank	Scotland	1966 2,3	2						
Laidlaw	Roy	Scotland	1983 1r,2,3,4	4						
Lamont	Ron	Ireland	1966 1,2,3,4	4	1					3
Lane	Mick	Ireland	1950 4	1						

Statistics

British and Irish test players in New Zealand

Surname	First name	Country/Club	Year(s)/Tests	Total tests	Tries	Cons	Pens	DGs	GMs	Total points
Laxon	H	Cambridge Uni	1908 1	1						
Leonard	Jason	England	1993 2,3	2						
Lewis	Allan	Wales	1966 2,3,4	3						
Llewellyn	Willie	Wales	1904	1						
Lynch	Sean	Ireland	1971 1,2,3,4	4						
Macdonald	Ranald	Scotland	1950 1	1						
MacNeill	Hugo	Ireland	1983 1,2,4r	3						
Marques	David	England	1959 2	1						
Martin	Alan	Wales	1977 1	1						
Matthews	Jack	Wales	1950 1,2,3,4	4						
McBride	Willie-John	Ireland	1966 2,3,4 1971 1,2,3,4	7						
McEvedy	Pat	Guy's Hospital	1904, 1908 2,3	3						
McFadyean	Colin	England	1966 1,2,3,4	4	1					3
McGeechan	Ian	Scotland	1977 1,2,3r,4	4						
McKay	Bill	Ireland	1950 1,2,3,4	4						
McLauchlan	Ian	Scotland	1971 1,2,3,4	4	1					3
McLeod	Hugh	Scotland	1959 1,2,3,4	4						
McLoughlin	Ray	Ireland	1966 4	1						
Millar	Syd	Ireland	1959 2	1						
Milne	Ken	Scotland	1993 1	1						
Moore	Brian	England	1993 2,3	2						
Morgan	Doug	Scotland	1977 3r,4	2	1	1	1			9
Morgan	Edgar	Swansea	1908 2,3	2						
Morgan	Haydn	Wales	1959 3,4	2						
Morgan	Ted	Wales	1904	1						
Morgan	William	London Welsh	1908 2,3	2						
Morley	Jack	Wales	1930 1,2,3	3	1					3
Morris	Dewi	England	1993 1,2,3	3						
Mulcahy	Bill	Ireland	1959 4	1						
Mullen	Karl	Ireland	1950 1,2	2						
Mulligan	Andy	Ireland	1959 4	1						
Murphy	Noel	Ireland	1959 1,2,4 1966 2,3	5						
Murray	Paul	Ireland	1930 1,2,4	3						
Neary	Tony	England	1977 4	1						
Nelson	Jimmy	Ireland	1950 3,4	2						

All Blacks v Lions

British and Irish test players in New Zealand

Surname	First name	Country/Club	Year(s)/Tests	Total tests	Tries	Cons	Pens	DGs	GMs	Total points
Norris	Charles	Wales	1966 1,2,3	3						
Norster	Robert	Wales	1983 1,2	2						
Novis	Anthony	England	1930 2,4	2	1					3
O'Brien	Arthur	Guy's Hospital	1904	1						
O'Driscoll	John	Ireland	1983 2,4	2						
Oldham	Bill	England	1908 1	1						
O'Neill	Henry	Ireland	1930 1,2,3,4	4						
O'Reilly	Tony	Ireland	1959 1,2,3,4	4	2					6
Orr	Phil	Ireland	1977 1	1						
Parker	David	Wales	1930 1,2,3,4	4			1			3
Pask	Alun	Wales	1966 1,3,4	3						
Patterson	Bill	Sale	1959 2	1						
Paxton	Iain	Scotland	1983 1,2,3,4	4						
Poole	Howard	Cardiff	1930 3	1						
Popplewell	Nick	Ireland	1993 1,2,3	3						
Preece	Ivor	England	1950 1	1						
Prentice	Douglas	England	1930 2	1		2				4
Price	Brian	Wales	1966 1,4	2						
Price	Graham	Wales	1977 1,2,3,4 1983 1,2,3,4	8						
Price	Malcolm	Wales	1959 1,2,3	3	2					6
Prosser	Roy	Wales	1959 4	1						
Pullin	John	England	1971 1,2,3,4	4						
Quinnell	Derek	Llanelli/Wales	1971 3 1977 2,3	3						
Reed	Andy	Scotland	1993 1	1						
Rees	Elgan	Neath	1977 4	1						
Reeve	Jim	England	1930 1,3,4	3	1					3
Rew	Henry	England	1930 1,2,3,4	4						
Richards	Dean	England	1993 1,2,3	3						
Rimmer	Gordon	England	1950 3	1						
Ringland	Trevor	Ireland	1983 1	1						
Risman	Bev	England	1959 1,4	2	1	1				5
Ritson	John	Northern	1908 1	1						
Robins	John	Wales	1950 1,2,3	3			2			6
Rogers	R	Bath	1904	1						
Rutherford	John	Scotland	1983 3	1	1					4
Scotland	Ken	Scotland	1959 1,3,4	3						

Statistics

British and Irish test players in New Zealand

Surname	First name	Country/Club	Year(s)/Tests	Total tests	Tries	Cons	Pens	DGs	GMs	Total points
Smith	George	Scotland	1959 1,3	2						
Smith	Tom	Leicester	1908 2,3	2						
Spong	Roger	England	1930 1,2,3,4	4						
Squire	Jeff	Wales	1977 4 1983 1	2						
Squires	Peter	England	1977 1	1						
Stephens	Ian	Wales	1983 1	1						
Swannell	Blair	Northampton	1904	1						
Taylor	John	Wales	1971 1,2,3,4	4						
Teague	Mike	England	1993 2r	1						
Telfer	Jim	Scotland	1966 1,2,4	3						
Thomas	Delme	Llanelli/Wales	1966 2,3 1971 1,2,4r	5						
Thomas	Malcolm	Wales	1950 2,3 1959 2	3						
Traill	D	Guy's Hospital	1904	1						
Underwood	Rory	England	1993 1,2,3	3	1					5
Vassall	Henry	England	1908 1,2,3	3						
Vile	Tom	Newport	1904	1						
Watkins	David	Wales	1966 1,2,3,4	4	1			1		6
Watkins	Stuart	Wales	1966 3	1						
Welsh	William	Scotland	1930 4	1						
Wheeler	Peter	England	1977 2,3,4	3						
Williams	Bleddyn	Wales	1950 2,3,4	3						
Williams	Brynmor	Cardiff	1977 1,2,3	3						
Williams	Denzil	Wales	1966 1,2,4	3						
Williams	John F	Wales	1908 3	1						
Williams	John J	Wales	1977 1,2,3	3	1					4
Williams	John L	Wales	1908 1,2	2						
Williams	JPR (John)	Wales	1971 1,2,3,4	4				1		3
Williams	Rhys	Wales	1959 1,2,3,4	4						
Willis	Rex	Wales	1950 4	1						
Wilson	Stewart	Scotland	1966 1,2,3,4	4		1	5			17
Windsor	Bobby	Wales	1977 1	1						
Winterbottom	Peter	England	1983 1,2,3,4 1993 1,2,3	7						
Wood	Ben	Ireland	1959 1,3	2						
Young	John	England	1959 2	1	1					3
Young	Roger	Ireland	1966 1	1						
Totals					38	16	44	6		305

NZ test players against British teams

Surname	First name	Provinces	Year(s)/Tests	Total tests	Tries	Cons	Pens	DGs	GMs	Total points
Ashworth	John	Canterbury	1983 1,2,3,4	4						
Batty	Grant	Bay of Plenty	1977 1	1	1					4
Batty	Walter	Auckland	1930 1,3,4	3	1					3
Beatty	George	Taranaki	1950 1	1						
Bevan	Vince	Wellington	1950 1,2,3,4	4						
Briscoe	Kevin	Taranaki	1959 2	1						
Brooke	Robin	Auckland	1993 1,2,3	3						
Brooke	Zinzan	Auckland	1993 1,2,3r	3						
Brown	Olo	Auckland	1993 1,2,3	3						
Brown	Ross	Taranaki	1959 1,3	2						
Bruce	Doug	Canterbury	1977 2,3,4	3						
Bunce	Frank	North Harbour	1993 1,2,3	3	2					10
Burgess	Bob	Manawatu	1971 1,2,3	3	2					6
Burns	Paddy	Canterbury	1908 2	1						
Bush	Bill	Canterbury	1977 2,3,4r	3						
Cameron	Donald	Taranaki	1908 1,2,3	3	1					3
Carrington	Ken	Auckland	1971 1,3,4	3						
Casey	Steve	Otago	1908 1	1						
Caulton	Ralph	Wellington	1959 2,3,4	3	4					12
Cherrington	Nau	North Auckland	1950 1	1						
Clarke	Adrian	Auckland	1959 4	1						
Clarke	Don	Waikato	1959 1,2,3,4	4	1	3	9	1		39
Clarke	Eroni	Auckland	1993 1,2	2	1					5
Clarke	Ian	Waikato	1959 1,2	2						
Colman	John	Taranaki	1908 1,3	2		1				2
Conway	Dick	Otago	1959 2,3,4	3						
Cooke	Bert	Wellington	1930 1,2,3,4	4	2					6
Cooksley	Mark	Counties	1993 2,3r	2						
Cooper	Matthew	Waikato	1993 1r,3r	2						
Corner	Merv	Auckland	1930 2,3,4	3						
Cottrell	"Beau"	Canterbury	1930 1,2,3,4	4						
Cottrell	Wayne	Canterbury	1971 1,2,3,4	4	1					3
Cross	Tom	Wellington	1904	1						
Crowley	Pat	Auckland	1950 1,2,3,4	4	1					3
Cunningham	Bill	Auckland	1908 1,2,3	3						

NZ test players against British teams

Surname	First name	Provinces	Year(s)/Tests	Total tests	Tries	Cons	Pens	DGs	GMs	Total points
Dalton	Andy	Counties	1983 1,2,3,4	4						
Davis	Lyn	Canterbury	1977 3,4	2						
Deans	Bob	Canterbury	1908 3	1	1					3
Diack	"Tup"	Otago	1959 2	1						
Dick	Malcolm	Auckland	1966 4	1	1					3
Dowd	Craig	Auckland	1993 1,2,3	3						
Duncan	Mick	Hawke's Bay	1971 3r,4	2						
Dunn	Ian	North Auckland	1983 1,4	2						
Elvidge	Ron	Otago	1950 1,2,3	3	2					6
Eveleigh	Kevin	Manawatu	1977 1,2	2						
Fanning	Bernard	Canterbury	1904	1						
Farrell	Colin	Auckland	1977 1,2	2						
Finlay	Brian	Manawatu	1959 1	1						
Finlayson	Bunny	North Auckland	1930 1,2	2						
Fitzpatrick	Sean	Auckland	1993 1,2,3	3	1					5
Ford	Brian	Marlborough	1977 3,4	2						
Fox	Grant	Auckland	1993 1,2,3	3		4	8			32
Francis	"Bolla"	Auckland	1908 1,2,3	3	1	1	1			8
Fraser	Bernie	Wellington	1983 1,2,3,4	4						
Fryer	Frank	Canterbury	1908 2	1						
Gallaher	Dave	Auckland	1904	1						
Gard	Phil	North Otago	1971 4	1						
Gillett	George	Auckland	1908 1,3	2	1	2				7
Glasgow	Frank	Southland	1908 3	1	1					3
Glenn	Billy	Taranaki	1904	1						
Going	Sid	North Auckland	1971 1,2,3,4 1977 1,2	6	2					7
Gray	Donaldson	Canterbury	1908 2	1						
Gray	Ken	Wellington	1966 1,2,3,4	4						
Guy	Ritchie	North Auckland	1971 1,2,3,4	4						
Haden	Andy	Auckland	1977 1,2,3,4 1983 1,2,3,4	8	2					8
Haig	Laurie	Otago	1950 2,3,4	3		1				2
Hamilton	Don	Southland	1908 2	1						
Harper	Eric	Canterbury	1904	1						
Hart	George	Canterbury	1930 1,2,3,4	4	2					6
Harvey	Lester	Otago	1950 1,2,3,4	4						

All Blacks v Lions

NZ test players against British teams

Surname	First name	Provinces	Year(s)/Tests	Total tests	Tries	Cons	Pens	DGs	GMs	Total points
Harvey	Peter	Canterbury	1904	1						
Hayward	"Circus"	Auckland	1908 3	1	1					3
Hazlett	Bill	Southland	1930 1,2,3,4	4						
Hazlett	Jack	Southland	1966 1,2,3,4	4						
Hemi	Ron	Waikato	1959 1,3,4	3						
Henderson	Peter	Wanganui	1950 2,3,4	3	1					3
Herewini	Mac	Auckland	1966 1,2,3,4	4				2		6
Hewson	Allan	Wellington	1983 1,2,3,4	4	1	6	9	1		46
Hill	Stan	Canterbury	1959 1,2,3,4	4						
Hobbs	Jock	Canterbury	1983 1,2,3,4	4	1					4
Hore	Jack	Otago	1930 2,3,4	3						
Hughes	Arthur	Auckland	1950 1,2,3,4	4						
Hughes	Ned	Southland	1908 1	1						
Hunter	Bruce	Otago	1971 1,2,3	3						
Hunter	Jimmy	Taranaki	1908 1,2,3	3	2					6
Irvine	"Bull"	Wairarapa	1930 1	1						
Irwin	Mark	Otago	1959 3,4	2						
Jaffray	Lyn	Otago	1977 2	1						
Johnstone	Brad	Auckland	1977 1,2	2	1					4
Johnstone	Peter	Otago	1950 1,2,3,4	4						
Jones	Ian	North Auckland	1993 1,2r,3	3						
Jones	Michael	Auckland	1993 1,2,3	3						
Jones	Peter	North Auckland	1959 1	1						
Joseph	Howard	Canterbury	1971 2,3	2						
Joseph	Jamie	Otago	1993 1,2,3	3						
Kirkpatrick	Ian	Poverty Bay	1971 1,2,3,4 1977 1,2,3,4	8	2					7
Kirwan	John	Auckland	1993 2,3	2						
Knight	Gary	Manawatu	1983 1,2,3,4	4						
Knight	Lawrie	Poverty Bay	1977 1,2,3,4	4	1					4
Laidlaw	Chris	Otago	1966 1,2,3,4	4						
Lambert	Kent	Manawatu	1977 1,4	2						
Lilburne	Herb	Canterbury	1930 1,4	2						
Lineen	Terry	Auckland	1959 1,2,3,4	4						
Lister	Tom	South Canterbury	1971 4	1	1					3
Little	Walter	North Harbour	1993 1	1						

Statistics

Surname	First name	Provinces	Year(s)/Tests	Total tests	Tries	Cons	Pens	DGs	GMs	Total points
Lochore	Brian	Wairarapa	1966 1,2,3,4 1971 3	5	1					3
Loveridge	David	Taranaki	1983 1,2,3,4	4	1					4
Lucas	Fred	Auckland	1930 1,2,3,4	4	1					3
MacEwan	Nev	Wellington	1959 1,2,3	3						
MacRae	Ian	Hawke's Bay	1966 1,2,3,4	4	1					3
Mains	Laurie	Otago	1971 2,3,4	3	1	3	3			18
McCormick	Fergie	Canterbury	1971 1	1			1			3
McCullough	John	Taranaki	1959 2,3,4	3						
McDonald	Alex	Otago	1908 1	1						
McEldowney	John	Taranaki	1977 3,4	2						
McGregor	Dick	Auckland	1904	1						
McGregor	Duncan	Wellington	1904	1	2					6
McLean	Hugh	Wellington	1930 3,4	2	2					6
McLeod	Bruce	Counties	1966 1,2,3,4	4	1					3
McMinn	Paddy	Manawatu	1904	1						
McMullen	Frank	Auckland	1959 1,2,3	3						
McNab	Jack	Otago	1950 1,2,3	3						
McNaughton	Alan	Bay of Plenty	1971 1,2,3	3						
McPhail	Bruce	Canterbury	1959 1,4	2						
McWilliams	Ruben	Auckland	1930 1,2,3,4	4						
Meads	Colin	King Country	1959 2,3,4 1966 1,2,3,4 1971 1,2,3,4	11	2					6
Meads	Stan	King Country	1966 1,2,3,4	4						
Meates	Bill	Otago	1950 1,2,3,4	4						
Mexted	Graham	Wellington	1950 4	1						
Mexted	Murray	Wellington	1983 1,2,3,4	4						
Mill	Jimmy	Wairarapa	1930 1	1						
Mitchinson	Frank	Wellington	1908 1,2,3	3	5					15
Mourie	Graham	Taranaki	1977 3,4	2						
Muller	Brian	Taranaki	1971 1,2,3,4	4						
Murray	Peter	Wanganui	1908 2	1						
Nathan	Waka	Auckland	1966 1,2,3,4	4	3					9
Nepia	George	East Coast	1930 1,2,3,4	4						
Nicholls	Mark	Wellington	1930 2,3	2		2		1	1	11
Nicholson	George	Auckland	1904	1						

NZ test players against British teams

Surname	First name	Provinces	Year(s)/Tests	Total tests	Tries	Cons	Pens	DGs	GMs	Total points
Norton	Tane	Canterbury	1971 1,2,3,4 1977 1,2,3,4	8						
Oliver	Don	Wellington	1930 1,2	2	1					3
Oliver	Frank	Southland	1977 1,2,3,4	4						
Osborne	Bill	Wanganui	1977 1,2,3,4	4						
Paterson	Sandy	Otago	1908 2,3	2						
Pene	Arran	Otago	1993 3	1						
Pickering	Rex	Waikato	1959 1,4	2						
Pokere	Steve	Southland	1983 1,2,3,4	4						
Porter	Cliff	Wellington	1930 1,2,3,4	4	2					6
Preston	Jon	Wellington	1993 2,3	2	1					5
Rangi	Ron	Auckland	1966 1,2,3,4	4						
Reedy	Bill	Wellington	1908 2,3	2						
Roberts	Fred	Wellington	1908 1,3	2	2	1	1			11
Robertson	Bruce	Counties	1977 1,3,4	3				1		3
Robertson	Duncan	Otago	1977 1	1						
Roper	Roy	Taranaki	1950 1,2,3,4	4	2					6
Scott	Bob	Auckland	1950 1,2,3,4	4		1	2	1		11
Seeling	Charlie	Auckland	1904, 1908 1,2,3	4						
Shaw	Mark	Manawatu	1983 1,2,3,4	4	1					4
Simpson	Johnny	Auckland	1950 1,2,3	3						
Skinner	Kevin	Otago	1950 1,2,3,4	4						
Smith	Ian	North Otago	1966 1,2,3	3						
Smith	Wayne	Canterbury	1983 2,3	2						
Stead	Billy	Southland	1904, 1908 1,3	3						
Steel	Tony	Canterbury	1966 1,2,3,4	4	3					9
Steere	Dick	Hawke's Bay	1930 1,2,3,4	4						
Stensness	Lee	Auckland	1993 3	1						
Stewart	Ron	Canterbury	1930 2	1						
Stone	Arthur	Waikato	1983 3r	1						
Strachan	Ant	North Harbour	1993 1	1						
Strang	Archie	South Canterbury	1930 3,4	2	1	3				9
Sutherland	Alan	Marlborough	1971 1	1						
Tanner	John	Auckland	1950 4	1						
Taylor	Mark	Bay of Plenty	1977 2,4r	2						
Taylor	Warwick	Canterbury	1983 1,2,3,4	4						

Statistics

NZ test players against British teams

Surname	First name	Provinces	Year(s)/Tests	Total tests	Tries	Cons	Pens	DGs	GMs	Total points
Thomson	"Mona"	Wellington	1908 1	1	1					3
Timu	John	Otago	1993 1,2,3	3						
Tremain	Kel	Hawke's Bay	1959 2,3,4 1966 1,2,3,4	7	1					3
Tuigamala	Va'aiga	Auckland	1993 1,2,3	3						
Tyler	George	Auckland	1904	1						
Urbahn	Roger	Taranaki	1959 1,3,4	3	1					3
Wallace	Billy	Wellington	1904, 1908 2	2			1			3
Walsh	Pat	Counties	1959 1	1						
Webb	Des	North Auckland	1959 2	1						
Whetton	Gary	Auckland	1983 1,2,3,4	4						
Whineray	Wilson	Auckland	1959 1,2,3,4	4						
White	"Tiny"	Poverty Bay	1950 1,2,3,4	4						
Whiting	Peter	Auckland	1971 1,2,4	3						
Williams	Bryan	Auckland	1971 1,2,4 1977 1,2,3,4	7		2	3			13
Williment	Mick	Wellington	1966 1,2,3,4	4	1	8	6			37
Wilson	"Ranji"	Wellington	1908 1,2	2						
Wilson	Bevan	Otago	1977 3,4	2		1	4			14
Wilson	Hec	Otago	1950 4	1	1					3
Wilson	Stu	Wellington	1983 1,2,3,4	4	4					16
Wood	Morris	Auckland	1904	1						
Wyllie	Alex	Canterbury	1971 2,3,4	3						
Totals					84	39	48	7	1	524
									penalty try	527

All Blacks v Lions

All combined British Teams

Year	Name	Opponents	Played	Won	Drawn	Lost	Test matches Won	Test matches Drawn	Test matches Lost
1888	Great Britain	Australia	16	14	2	0	0	0	0
		New Zealand	19	13	4	2	0	0	0
1891	Great Britain	South Africa	19	19	0	0	3	0	0
1896	Great Britain	South Africa	21	19	1	1	3	0	1
1899	Great Britain	Australia	21	18	0	3	3	0	1
1903	Great Britain	South Africa	22	11	3	8	0	2	1
1904	Great Britain	Australia	14	14	0	0	3	0	0
		New Zealand	5	2	1	2	0	0	1
1908	Anglo-Welsh	Australia	9	7	0	2	0	0	0
		New Zealand	17	9	1	7	0	1	2
1910	British Isles	South Africa	24	13	3	8	1	0	2
	British Isles	Argentina	6	6	0	0	1	0	0
1924	British Isles	South Africa	21	9	3	9	0	1	3
1927	British Isles	Argentina	9	9	0	0	3	0	0
1930	British Isles	New Zealand	21	15	0	6	1	0	3
		Australia	7	5	0	2	0	0	1
1936	British Isles	Argentina	10	10	0	0	1	0	0
1938	British Isles	South Africa	23	17	0	6	1	0	2
1950	British Isles	New Zealand	23	17	1	5	0	1	3
		Australia	6	5	0	1	2	0	0
1955	British Isles	South Africa	24	18	1	5	2	0	2
1959	British Isles	Australia	6	5	0	1	2	0	0
		New Zealand	25	20	0	5	1	0	3
		Canada	2	2	0	0	0	0	0
1962	British Isles	South Africa	24	15	4	5	0	1	3
1966	British Isles	Australia	8	7	1	0	2	0	0
		New Zealand	25	15	2	8	0	0	4
		Canada	2	1	0	1	0	0	0
1968	British Isles	South Africa	20	15	1	4	0	1	3
1971	British Isles	Australia	2	1	0	1	0	0	0
		New Zealand	24	22	1	1	2	1	1
1974	British Isles	South Africa	22	21	1	0	3	1	0
1977	British Isles	New Zealand	25	21	0	4	1	0	3
		Fiji	1	0	0	1	0	0	0
		London (v Barbarians)[1]	1	0	0	1	0	0	0

Statistics

All combined British Teams

Year	Name	Opponents	Played	Won	Drawn	Lost	Test matches Won	Drawn	Lost
1980	British Isles	South Africa	18	15	0	3	1	0	3
1983	British Isles	New Zealand	18	12	0	6	0	0	4
1986	British Isles	Cardiff (v The Rest)[2]	1	0	0	1	0	0	0
1989	British Isles	Australia	12	11	0	1	2	0	1
1993	British Isles	New Zealand	13	7	0	6	1	0	2
1997	British Isles	South Africa	13	11	0	2	2	0	1
2001	British Isles	Australia	10	7	0	3	1	0	2
Totals			**610**	**458**	**30**	**122**	**42**	**9**	**52**

[1]Played to mark the 25th anniversary of the Queen's accession to the throne.
[2]Played to mark the centenary of the International Rugby Board.

Lions' national representation in New Zealand

(English, Scottish, etc. clubs indicates uncapped players)

Club	Players (indicates replacement players)
1888	
England	2
Wales	1
English clubs	15
Scottish clubs	2
1904	
England	2
English clubs	11
Ireland	1
Irish clubs	1
Scotland	1
Wales	6
Welsh clubs	2
1908	
England	5
English clubs	13
Wales	6
Welsh clubs	4
1930	
England	11
English clubs	13
Ireland	5
Scotland	1
Wales	6
Welsh clubs	5

Club	Players (indicates replacement players)
1950	
England	3
Ireland	9
Scotland	5
Wales	14 (1)
1959	
England	8 (1)
English clubs	1 (1)
Ireland	10 (1)
Scotland	5
Wales	9
1966	
England	5
Ireland	9 (1)
Scotland	6
Wales	11 (1)
Welsh clubs	1
1971	
England	6 (1)
Ireland	6
Scotland	7 (1)
Wales	13 (1)
Welsh clubs	1

Club	Players (indicates replacement players)
1977	
England	6 (1)
English clubs	1 (1)
Ireland	4
Scotland	5
Wales	15 (1)
Welsh clubs	2
1983	
England	9 (2)
English clubs	1 (1)
Ireland	9 (2)
Scotland	8
Wales	9 (1)
1993	
England	17 (1)
Ireland	4 (2)
Scotland	8 (1)
Wales	5

Composite British Isles teams in New Zealand

1888 Great Britain

Name	Club/Country	Games	Points
Fullbacks			
J.T.Haslam	Batley	14	3
A.G.Paul	Swinton	18	24
Threequarters			
J.Anderton	Salford	14	10
H.Brooks	Edinburgh University	12	
H.C.Speakman	Runcorn	17	9
A.E.Stoddart	England	13	11
Halfbacks			
W.Bumby	Swinton	18	2
W.Burnett	Hawick	11	
J.Nolan	Rochdale Hornets	11	10
Forwards			
T.Banks	Swinton	6	1
R.Burnett	Hawick	16	
J.P.Clowes	Halifax	–	
H.Eagles	Swinton	19	3
T.Kent	Salford	16	2
A.J.Laing	Hawick	13	
C.Mathers	Bramley	12	2
A.P.Penketh	Douglas	14	1
R.L.Seddon	England	9	3
D.J.Smith	Edinburgh University	5	
A.J.Stuart	Dewsbury	15	1
W.H.Thomas	Wales	15	
S.Williams	Salford	17	

Captain: Seddon.
Played 19, won 13, drew 4, lost 2

1904 Great Britain

Name	Club/Country	Games	Points
Fullback			
C.F.Stranger-Leathes	Northern	2	
Threequarters			
J.L.Fisher	Hull and East Riding	–	
R.T.Gabe	Wales	5	
W.F.Jowett	Wales	1	
W.M.Llewellyn	Wales	4	
P.F.McEvedy	Guy's Hospital	4	
E.Morgan	Wales	4	
A.B.O'Brien	Guy's Hospital	5	4
Halfbacks			
P.F.Bush	Cardiff	5	9
F.C.Hulme	England	–	
T.H.Vile	Newport	5	
Forwards			
D.R.Bedell-Sivright	Scotland	1	3
T.S.Bevan	Wales	5	
S.N.Crowther	Lennox	5	
D.D.Dobson	England	5	3
R.W.Edwards	Ireland	4	
A.F.Harding	Wales	5	3
B.F.Massey	Hull and East Riding	–	
C.D.Patterson	Malone	–	
R.J.Rogers	Bath	3	
S.M.Saunders	Guy's Hospital	4	
J.T.Sharland	Streatham	1	
B.I.Swannell	Northampton	4	
D.H.Traill	Guy's Hospital	3	

Captain: Bedell-Sivright.
Played 5, won 2, drew 1, lost 2

Statistics

Composite British Isles teams in New Zealand

1908 Anglo-Welsh

Name	Club/Country	Games	Points
Fullbacks			
J.C.M.Dyke	Wales	8	9
E.J.Jackett	England	11	9
Threequarters			
F.E.Chapman	Westoe	9	18
R.A.Gibbs	Wales	10	28
R.B.Griffiths	Newport	3	3
J.P. (Ponty) Jones	Pontypool	13	15
J.P. ("Tuan") Jones	Guy's Hospital	11	6
P.F.McEvedy	Guy's Hospital	12	9
H.H.Vassall	England	7	
J.L.Williams	Wales	12	27
Halfbacks			
J.Davey	England	9	9
H.Laxon	Coventry	7	
W.L.Morgan	London Welsh	10	
G.L.Williams	Liverpool	3	
Forwards			
H.A.Archer	Guy's Hospital	11	6
R.Dibble	England	13	
P.J.Down	Bristol	13	
R.K.Green	Neath	2	
A.F.Harding	Wales	11	7
G.R.Hind	Guy's Hospital	10	
F.S.Jackson	Leicester	6	14
G.V.Kyrke	Marlborough Nomads	5	3
E.Morgan	Swansea	14	
W.L.Oldham	England	8	3
J.A.S.Ritson	Northern	9	6
T.W.Smith	Leicester	12	6
L.S.Thomas	Penarth	8	
J.F.Williams	Wales	8	6

Captain: Harding.
Played 17, won 9, drew 1, lost 7

1930 Great Britain

Name	Club/Country	Games	Points
Fullbacks			
J.A.Bassett	Wales	13	
W.G.M.Bonner	Bradford	5	2
Threequarters			
C.D.Aarvold	England	15	18
H.M.Bowcott	Wales	16	18
R.Jennings	Redruth	6	18
T.E.Jones-Davies	Wales	8	28
J.C.Morley	Wales	13	24
P.F.Murray	Ireland	11	3
A.L.Novis	England	14	36
J.S.R.Reeve	England	12	21
Halfbacks			
W.H.Sobey	England	1	
R.S.Spong	England	12	12
T.C.Knowles	Birkenhead Park	10	6
H.Poole	Cardiff	10	
Forwards			
G.R.Beamish	Ireland	16	6
B.H.Black	England	15	65
M.J.Dunne	Ireland	7	3
J.L.Farrell	Ireland	13	3
J.McD.Hodgson	Northern	10	3
I.E.Jones	Wales	14	28
H.C.S.Jones	Manchester	7	
D.A.Kendrew	England	10	3
S.A.Martindale	England	8	6
H.O'H.O'Neill	Ireland	14	
D.Parker	Wales	15	35
F.D.Prentice	England	8	49
H.Rew	England	11	
H.Wilkinson	England	9	27
W.B.Welsh	Scotland	12	6

Captain: Prentice.
Played 21, won 15, lost 6

Composite British Isles teams in New Zealand

1950 British Isles

Name	Club/Country	Games	Points
Fullbacks			
W.B.Cleaver	Wales	13	4
B.L.Jones	Wales	7	63
G.W.Norton	Ireland	3	9
Threequarters			
N.J.Henderson	Ireland	12	18
K.J.Jones	Wales	16	48
M.F.Lane	Ireland	7	12
R.Macdonald	Scotland	11	18
J.Matthews	Wales	15	15
D.W.C.Smith	Scotland	2	
M.C.Thomas	Wales	12	73
B.L.Williams	Wales	15	30
Halfbacks			
A.W.Black	Scotland	8	
J.W.Kyle	Ireland	16	18
I.Preece	England	8	9
G.Rimmer	England	7	
W.R.Willis	Wales	9	3
Forwards			
G.M.Budge	Scotland	12	
J.T.Clifford	Ireland	15	14
C.Davies	Wales	10	3
D.M.Davies	Wales	11	
R.T.Evans	Wales	12	
D.J.Hayward	Wales	16	3
E.R.John	Wales	17	3
P.W.Kininmonth	Scotland	14	
J.S.McCarthy	Ireland	11	12
J.W.McKay	Ireland	10	21
K.D.Mullen	Ireland	13	
J.E.Nelson	Ireland	13	6
V.G.Roberts	England	10	9
J.D.Robins	Wales	12	29
J.R.G.Stephens	Wales	8	

Captain: Mullen.
Played 23, won 17, drew 1, lost 5

1959 British Isles

Name	Club/Country	Games	Points
Fullbacks			
T.J.Davies	Wales	9	72
K.J.F.Scotland	Scotland	17	45
Threequarters			
N.H.Brophy	Ireland	–	
J.Butterfield	England	6	
D.Hewitt	Ireland	13	65
P.B.Jackson	England	14	48
A.J.F.O'Reilly	Ireland	17	51
W.M.Patterson	Sale	9	18
M.J.Price	Wales	14	33
M.C.Thomas	Wales	15	56
J.R.C.Young	England	10	33
Halfbacks			
S.Coughtrie	Scotland	–	
M.A.F.English	Ireland	1	
J.P.Horrocks-Taylor	England	4	5
R.E.G.Jeeps	England	11	
A.A.Mulligan	Ireland	12	
A.B.W.Risman	England	9	33
G.H.Waddell	Scotland	10	21
Forwards			
A.Ashcroft	England	14	6
A.R.Dawson	Ireland	14	3
W.R.Evans	Wales	14	
J.Faull	Wales	16	48
H.F.McLeod	Scotland	14	
R.W.D.Marques	England	14	
B.V.Meredith	Wales	9	3
S.Millar	Ireland	14	3
H.J.Morgan	Wales	16	12
W.A.Mulcahy	Ireland	10	3
N.A.A.Murphy	Ireland	15	12
T.R.Prosser	Wales	11	3
G.K.Smith	Scotland	13	3
R.H.Williams	Wales	17	
B.G.M.Wood	Ireland	13	6

Captain: Dawson.
Played 25, won 20, lost 5

Statistics

Composite British Isles teams in New Zealand

1966 British Isles

Name	Club/Country	Games	Points
Fullbacks			
T.G.Price	Wales	3	17
D.Rutherford	England	6	26
S.Wilson	Scotland	15	62
Threequarters			
D.I.E.Bebb	Wales	15	27
F.P.K.Bresnihan	Ireland	9	15
A.J.W.Hinshelwood	Scotland	13	21
D.K.Jones	Wales	11	3
C.W.McFadyean	England	18	15
K.F.Savage	England	8	9
J.C.Walsh	Ireland	–	
S.J.Watkins	Wales	9	6
M.P.Weston	England	10	6
First five-eighths			
C.M.H.Gibson	Ireland	19	33
D.Watkins	Wales	14	27
Halfbacks			
A.R.Lewis	Wales	13	3
R.M.Young	Ireland	12	3
Loose forwards			
D.Grant	Scotland	8	
R.A.Lamont	Ireland	13	18
N.A.A.Murphy	Ireland	12	
A.E.I.Pask	Wales	16	6
G.J.Prothero	Wales	7	
J.W.Telfer	Scotland	16	
Locks			
M.J.Campbell-Lamerton	Scotland	14	
W-J.McBride	Ireland	15	
B.Price	Wales	12	3
W.D.Thomas*	Llanelli/Wales	14	
Props			
R.J.McLoughlin	Ireland	11	
C.H.Norris	Wales	13	
D.L.Powell	England	12	
D.Williams	Wales	12	
Hookers			
K.W.Kennedy	Ireland	12	
F.A.L.Laidlaw	Scotland	13	

Captain: Campbell-Lamerton.
Played 25, won 15, drew 2, lost 8
* Denotes uncapped at time of selection

1971 British Isles

Name	Club/Country	Games	Points
Fullbacks			
R.Hiller	England	10	102
J.P.R.Williams	Wales	14	16
Threequarters			
J.C.Bevan	Wales	13	51
A.G.Biggar	Scotland	9	27
T.G.R.Davies	Wales	10	30
S.J.Dawes	Wales	17	15
D.J.Duckham	England	15	33
A.J.Lewis	Wales	9	6
C.W.W.Rea	Scotland	10	9
J.S.Spencer	England	9	9
First five-eighths			
C.M.H.Gibson	Ireland	15	23
B.John	Wales	16	180
Halfbacks			
G.O.Edwards	Wales	15	9
R.Hopkins	Wales	10	3
No. 8s			
T.M.Davies	Wales	13	9
P.J.Dixon	England	14	6
Flankers			
R.J.Arneil	Scotland	5	
M.Hipwell	Ireland	5	
D.L.Quinnell*	Llanelli/Wales	9	3
J.F.Slattery	Ireland	12	
J.Taylor	Wales	14	12
Locks			
G.L.Brown	Scotland	13	
T.G.Evans	Wales	6	3
W-J.McBride	Ireland	14	
M.G.Roberts	Wales	10	
W.D.Thomas	Wales	14	
Props			
A.B.Carmichael	Scotland	5	3
J.F.Lynch	Ireland	14	
J.McLauchlan	Scotland	16	3
R.J.McLoughlin	Ireland	4	3
C.B.Stevens	England	6	
Hookers			
F.A.L.Laidlaw	Scotland	10	
J.V.Pullin	England	15	

Captain: Dawes.
Played 24, won 22, drew 1, lost 1
* Denotes uncapped at time of selection

All Blacks v Lions

Composite British Isles teams in New Zealand

1977 British Isles

Name	Club/Country	Games	Points
Fullbacks			
B.H.Hay	Scotland	11	20
A.R.Irvine	Scotland	18	87
Threequarters			
D.H.Burcher	Wales	14	16
G.L.Evans	Wales	17	24
S.P.Fenwick	Wales	12	15
C.M.H.Gibson	Ireland	11	24
I.R.McGeechan	Scotland	15	12
H.E.Rees*	Neath/Wales	12	32
P.J.Squires	England	9	20
J.J.Williams	Wales	14	40
First five-eighths			
P.Bennett	Wales	14	112
J.D.Bevan	Wales	11	4
Halfbacks			
A.D.Lewis	London Welsh	2	
D.W.Morgan	Scotland	15	98
D.B.Williams*	Cardiff/Wales	12	12
No. 8s			
W.P.Duggan	Ireland	15	8
D.L.Quinnell	Wales	14	8
Flankers			
A.Neary	England	13	
T.P.Evans	Wales	13	
T.J.Cobner	Wales	11	12
J.Squire	Wales	14	
Locks			
N.E.Horton	England	4	
M.I.Keane	Ireland	12	
G.L.Brown	Scotland	14	4
A.J.Martin	Wales	13	6
W.B.Beaumont	England	9	4
Props			
F.E.Cotton	England	16	
A.G.Faulkner	Wales	2	
P.A.Orr	Ireland	12	4
G.Price	Wales	14	
C.Williams	Wales	9	4
Hookers			
P.J.Wheeler	England	13	4
R.W.Windsor	Wales	13	4

Captain: Bennett.
Played 25, won 21, lost 4

Denotes uncapped at time of selection

1983 British Isles

Name	Club/Country	Games	Points
Fullbacks			
W.H.Hare	England	6	88
H.P.MacNeill	Ireland	9	8
Wings			
G.R.T.Baird	Scotland	11	24
J.Carleton	England	11	36
G.Evans	Wales	12	21
T.M.Ringland	Ireland	9	20
Centres			
R.A.Ackerman	Wales	10	4
D.G.Irwin	Ireland	11	24
M.J.Kiernan	Ireland	10	11
C.R.Woodward	England	7	3
First five-eighths			
S.O.Campbell	Ireland	11	124
J.Y.Rutherford	Scotland	10	23
Halfbacks			
T.D.Holmes	Wales	4	4
R.J.Laidlaw	Scotland	13	8
N.D.Melville*	Wasps/England	2	8
S.J.Smith	England	2	
No. 8s			
J.R.Beattie	Scotland	9	16
E.T.Butler	Wales	1	
I.A.M.Paxton	Scotland	9	16
Flankers			
J.H.Calder	Scotland	7	12
N.C.Jeavons	England	6	
J.B.O'Driscoll	Ireland	8	
J.Squire	Wales	6	8
P.J.Winterbottom	England	12	4
Locks			
S.Bainbridge	England	11	
S.B.Boyle	England	6	
M.J.Colclough	England	11	
D.G.Lenihan	Ireland	2	
R.L.Norster	Wales	6	
Props			
S.T.Jones	Wales	13	
G.A.J.McLoughlin	Ireland	2	
I.G.Milne	Scotland	8	4
G.Price	Wales	10	
I.Stephens	Wales	4	4
Hookers			
C.T.Deans	Scotland	7	8
C.F.Fitzgerald	Ireland	11	

Captain: Fitzgerald.
Played 18, won 12, lost 6

Denotes uncapped at time of selection

Composite British Isles teams in New Zealand

1993 British Isles

British losses outside of tests

Name	Club/Country	Games	Points
Fullbacks			
A.G.Hastings	Scotland	9	101
A.Clement	Wales	7	13
Wings			
I.C.Evans	Wales	7	20
I.G.Hunter	England	1	
R.Underwood	England	7	15
T.Underwood	England	6	10
R.Wallace	Ireland	5	5
Centres			
W.D.C.Carling	England	7	8
V.J.G.Cunningham	Ireland	3	10
I.S.Gibbs	Wales	7	10
J.C.Guscott	England	9	10
S.Hastings	Scotland	3	5
First five-eighths			
C.R.Andrew	England	7	24
S.Barnes	England	8	33
Halfbacks			
C.D.Morris	England	8	
R.N.Jones	Wales	6	5
A.D.Nichol	Scotland	1	
No. 8s			
D.Richards	England	6	5
B.B.Clarke	England	8	
Flankers			
M.J.Galwey	Ireland	7	5
M.C.Teague	England	8	5
R.E.Webster	Wales	7	10
P.J.Winterbottom	England	7	
Locks			
M.C.Bayfield	England	7	
D.F.Cronin	Scotland	6	5
W.A.Dooley	England	3	
M.O.Johnson	England	4	
A.I.Reed	Scotland	6	5
Props			
A.P.Burnell	Scotland	7	
J.Leonard	England	8	
N.J.Popplewell	Ireland	7	
P.H.Wright	Scotland	6	
Hookers			
K.S.Milne	Scotland	8	
B.C.Moore	England	7	

Captain: A.G. Hastings.
Played 13, won 7, lost 6

Team	Losses	Score	Date
Auckland	6	0–4	1888
		0–13	1904
		0–11	1908
		6–19	1930
		12–13	1983
		18–23	1993
Canterbury	4	8–13	1908
		8–14	1930
		14–20	1959
		20–22	1983
Hawke's Bay	1	17–29	1993
NZ Universities	1	9–21	1977
Otago	5	6–9	1908
		9–23	1950
		8–26	1959
		9–17	1966
		24–37	1993
Southland	2	0–11	1950
		8–14	1966
Taranaki	1	0–5	1908
Taranaki Clubs	1	0–1	1888
Waikato	1	10–38	1993
Wanganui-King Country	1	6–12	1966
Wellington	3	13–19	1908
		8–12	1930
		6–20	1966

Records

New Zealand

Record	Name	Tour
Most matches		
11	Colin Meads	1959,66,71
8	Andy Haden	1977,83
	Ian Kirkpatrick	1971,77
	Tane Norton	1971,77
7	Kel Tremain	1959,66
	Bryan Williams	1971,77
Most points		
46	Allan Hewson	1983
39	Don Clarke	1959
37	Mick Williment	1966
32	Grant Fox	1993
18	Laurie Mains	1971
Most tries		
5	Frank Mitchinson	1908
4	Ralph Caulton	1959
	Stu Wilson	1977
3	Tony Steel	1966
	Waka Nathan	1966
Most penalty goals		
9	Don Clarke	1959
	Allan Hewson	1983
8	Grant Fox	1993
6	Mick Williment	1966
Most conversions		
8	Mick Williment	1966
6	Allan Hewson	1983
4	Grant Fox	1993
Most dropped goals		
2	Mac Herewini	1966

British teams

Record	Name	Tour
Most matches		
8	Mike Gibson	1966,71
	Graham Price	1977,83
7	Willie-John McBride	1966,71
	Peter Winterbottom	1983,93
5	Gordon Brown	1971,77
	Noel Murphy	1959,66
	Delme Thomas	1966,71
Most points		
38	Gavin Hastings	1993
30	Barry John	1971
18	Phil Bennett	1977
17	Stewart Wilson	1966
15	Ollie Campbell	1983
Most tries		
3	Carl Aarvold	1930
	Gerald Davies	1971
2	Peter Jackson	1959
	Ken Jones	1950
	Tony O'Reilly	1959
	Malcolm Price	1959
Most penalty goals		
12	Gavin Hastings	1993
6	Phil Bennett	1977
5	Barry John	1971
	Stewart Wilson	1966
4	Ollie Campbell	1983
Most conversions		
3	Barry John	1971
2	Brian Black	1930
	Douglas Prentice	1930
Most dropped goals		
2	Barry John	1971

Match Records

New Zealand

Record	Name	Test	Tour
Most points			
18	Don Clarke	1st	1959
	Allan Hewson	4th	1983
15	Grant Fox	1st, 3rd	1993
Most tries			
3	Frank Mitchinson	3rd	1908
	Stu Wilson	4th	1983
Most penalties			
6	Don Clarke	1st	1959
5	Grant Fox	1st	1993
Most conversions			
4	Allan Hewson	4th	1983
Biggest wins			
38–6		4th	1983
29–0		3rd	1908
32–5		1st	1908
Biggest winning margins			
32		4th	1983
29		3rd	1908
27		1st	1908

British teams

Record	Name	Test	Tour
Most points			
18	Gavin Hastings	1st	1993
12	Gavin Hastings	2nd	1993
10	Barry John	3rd	1971
Most tries			
2	Carl Aarvold	2nd	1930
	Gerald Davies	2nd	1971
	Malcolm Price	1st	1959
Most penalties			
6	Gavin Hastings	1st	1993
4	Gavin Hastings	2nd	1993
Most conversions			
2	Barry John	3rd	1971
	Doug Prentice	2nd	1930
Biggest wins			
20–7		2nd	1993
13–3		3rd	1971
Biggest winning margins			
13		2nd	1993
10		3rd	1971

Bibliography

Alley, Geoff. *With the British Rugby Team in New Zealand 1930* (Christchurch: Simpson and Williams, 1930).

Barr, R.A. *With the British Rugby Team in Maoriland* (Dunedin: *Otago Daily Times*, 1908).

Cameron, Don. *On the Lions' Trail* (Auckland: Rugby Press, 1983).

Chester, R.H. and McMillan, N.A.C. *The Visitors — The History of International Rugby Teams in New Zealand* (Auckland: Moa Publications, 1990).

Dobbs, Brian. *Edwardians at Play* (London: Pelham Books, 1973).

Dunning, Eric, and Sheard, Kenneth. *Barbarians, Gentlemen and Players* (Oxford: Martin Robertson & Co., 1979).

Farrar-Hockley, Anthony. *The British Part in the Korean War, Vol 2, An Honourable Discharge* (London: HMSO, 1995).

Freyberg, Paul. *Bernard Freyberg VC — Soldier of Two Nations* (London: Hodder & Stoughton, 1991).

Godwin, Terry. *The Complete Who's Who of International Rugby* (Poole: Blandford Press, 1987).

Griffiths, John. *British Lions* (Swindon: The Crowood Press, 1990).

Hopkins, John. *Life with the Lions — The Inside Story of the 1977 New Zealand Tour* (London: Stanley Paul, 1977).

Jackson, Peter. *Lions of Wales* (Edinburgh: Mainstream Publishing, 1998).

McGeechan, Ian. *So Close to Glory* (London: Queen Anne Press, 1993).

McLean, Terry. *Kings of Rugby* (Wellington: A.H. & A.W. Reed, 1959).

   The Lion Tamers (Wellington: A.H. & A.W. Reed, 1966).

Palenski, Ron. *Our National Game — A Celebration of 100 Years of NZ Rugby* (Auckland: Moa Beckett, 1992).

   The Jersey (Auckland: Hodder Moa Beckett, 2001).

   Century in Black — 100 Years of All Black Test Rugby (Auckland: Hodder Moa Beckett, 2003).

Reason, John. *Lions Down Under — 1977 Tour of New Zealand* (London: Rugby Books, 1977).

Reyburn, Wallace. *The Lions* (London: Stanley Paul, 1967).

Scott, R.W.H., and McLean, T.P. *The Bob Scott Story* (Wellington: A.H. & A.W. Reed, 1956).

Thomas, Clem. *The History of the British Lions* (Edinburgh: Mainstream Publishing, 1996).

Thomas, J.B.G. *Lions Courageous* (London: Stanley Paul, 1960).

Walmsley, David. *Lions of Ireland* (Edinburgh: Mainstream Publishing, 2000).

Williams, D.J. *1950 — The Year of the Lions* (Hamilton: published by the author, 1988).

1904 Great Britain

1908 Anglo-Welsh

1930 Great Britain

1950 Lions

1959 Lions

1966 Lions

1971 Lions

1977 Lions

1983 Lions

1993 Lions

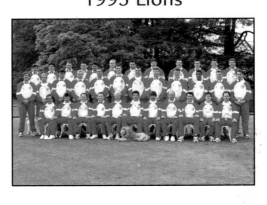